Critical acclaim for THE CATHOLIC CATECHISM

. . . a source book on the principal teachings of the Catholic Church. This goal has been accomplished with evident dedication and erudition. For students of the faith and their teachers, this book, *The Catholic Catechism,* will be a warmly welcome tool and, in the midst of confusion, a relief.

John Cardinal Wright

. . . a scholarly study which explores every facet of Catholic belief in a clear, readable style.

Library Journal

. . . a thoroughly modern piece of informative writing . . . should be welcomed as an indispensable guidebook . . . a reliable, learned, yet lucidly written exposition of Christian doctrine . . . I recommend this book as a very real and rewarding contribution in its field.

The Catholic Register

. . . a massive and impressive piece of scholarship which has integrated thought and worship, doctrine and ethics, the past (history) and the present (contemporary issues).

Christian Scholar's Review

. . . written with such clarity and felicity as to be studied without technical preparation but with immense profit.

Choice

. . . it is really an astonishing feat of scholarship.

Best Sellers

. . . the fullest, most adequate and most convenient treatment of Catholic belief anywhere on the market today.

The Catholic Review

. . . a substantial lighted candle itself for the Catholic faith and everyday living. Perhaps it will inspire those of other faiths to light similar candles.

Arkansas Democrat

. . . a most valuable contribution to the library of the average Catho-lic—and of the average non-Catholic Catholics profess and why.

THE QUESTION
AND ANSWER
CATHOLIC CATECHISM

THE QUESTION AND ANSWER CATHOLIC CATECHISM

JOHN A. HARDON, S.J.

IMAGE BOOKS
A DIVISION OF
DOUBLEDAY & COMPANY, INC.
GARDEN CITY, NEW YORK
1981

Excerpts from The Jerusalem Bible, copyright © 1966 by Darton, Longman & Todd, Ltd. and Doubleday & Company, Inc. Used by permission of the publisher.

Imprimi Potest: Michael J. Lavelle, S.J.
Provincial
Detroit Province
May 20, 1981
Nihil Obstat: William B. Smith, S.T.D.
Censor Librorum
Imprimatur:✠Joseph T. O'Keefe
Vicar General
Archdiocese of New York
July 7, 1981

The nihil obstat and imprimatur are official declarations that a book or pamphlet is free of doctrinal error. No implication is contained therein that those who have granted the nihil obstat and imprimatur agree with the contents, opinions, or statements expressed.

Library of Congress Cataloging in Publication Data

Hardon, John A.
    The question and answer Catholic catechism.

    1. Catholic Church—Catechisms and creeds—English.
I. Title.
BX1961.H37   238'.2
AACR2
ISBN: 0-385-13664-1
Library of Congress Catalog Card Number: 81–5547

CONTENTS

PART TWO

LIVING THE CHRISTIAN FAITH

ACKNOWLEDGMENTS

This catechism could not have been written without the generous help of many people. To all of them the author extends his sincere and prayerful thanks. The following deserve special mention: Sr. Linda Teders, O.S.F., of the Franciscan Sisters of the Sacred Heart, whose years of research first gave the impetus to write the manuscript; Robert Heller and Theresa D'Orsogna of the editorial offices of Doubleday. Readers of the manuscript who shared their professional knowledge included the Rev. Theodore J. Cunnion, S.J., the Rev. William R. Walsh, S.J., the Rev. William B. Smith, the Rev. Michael Wrenn, and the Rev. Vincent T. Mallon, M.M. Research, editing, and clerical services were provided by many persons, outstanding of whom were Geraldine E. Donovan, John F. Gonoud, Richard Gill, and Clare Fitzpatrick; also the Rev. Christopher M. Buckner, Sr. Mary Verona, D.S.M.P., Mary Bolan, Margaret Acer, Margaret Treacy, Eucharia Mulligan, Sr. Mary Sarah, S.N.D., and Sr. Mary Kevan, S.N.D. Special thanks are due to His Eminence Silvio Cardinal Oddi, Prefect of the Sacred Congregation for the Clergy, and Mother Teresa of Calcutta for their most welcome endorsements.

FOREWORD

Some present-day religious educators have expressed reservations concerning the efficacy of question and answer catechisms for teaching Christian doctrine. Father John A. Hardon is, happily, not one of these. On the contrary, after producing a superior work on Catholic doctrine in straight prose, he now offers a refreshing treatment of the same matter in question and answer form, thereby offering a genuine service to English-speaking Catholics.

Etymologically speaking, the word *catechism* does not signify a book of questions and answers. As a matter of fact, we might almost say that the word is internally contradictory since, in the original Greek, *catechesis* means oral instruction. But for centuries the word catechism has meant to Catholics a book of questions and answers about the basics of our faith. As any undergraduate in the history of pedagogy should easily be able to demonstrate, there is no reason to be ashamed of teaching through question and answer. From Mediterranean classical times even to the scientific age in the New World man's acquired knowledge has been passed on to future generations partly through the question and answer method. Today, specialists in internal medicine, engineering, and chemistry arm themselves with question and answer manuals to check themselves on recent developments in their respective fields. Far from lagging behind the pedagogical times, therefore, the Catholic Church is in the forefront of teaching technique when she espouses the use of question and answer as one of the more successful means of passing on the faith to generation upon generation.

Good catechetical style requires precision and brevity. Vague authors, therefore, eschew it, either because their thoughts are muddled or because they are wily enough not to put down what they really hold in black and white. Prolix authors avoid a question and answer approach because its success depends on succinct, incisive replies which are beyond them. Father Hardon, who is neither obscure in his theology nor wordy in its presentation, proves himself in this present book to be a master of catechetical pedagogy.

The Question and Answer Catholic Catechism could hardly be more timely. Today's Catholics, particularly the most faithful among them, need to know the latest developments in the Church's teaching and, above all, to be reassured that the faith has not changed. If the teachings of Jesus were to fluctuate from Church Council to Church Council, they would no longer be the teachings of Jesus, nor would the Church be any longer the Church of Christ. It is clear that Father Hardon has striven successfully to expound the authentic teaching of Holy Mother Church. Readers will find in the book an up-to-date, reliable presentation of the same dogmatic, moral, ascetical, and liturgical truths which the Catholic Church has always taught. Those yearning for heterodox novelty will not find it here.

Apart from doctrinal fidelity and theological precision, the scope of the book sets it apart from many of its genre. For example, there is a brief treatment of the Divine Office, which many laymen may consider a mysterious book. But even more important, *The Question and Answer Catholic Catechism* revives consideration of such notions as human act, sin, formed conscience, Sunday obligation, sacrifice, spiritual life, and some others which have been widely ignored in too many religious texts of recent years.

Captious critics have objected that the faith is not a series of answers to contrived questions but a way of life. The answer to this objection might well be another question: How can we live a Christian life until we first "know the truth" (John 8:32). It would be the uncommon man or woman who would attempt to commit to memory the answers to the hundreds of questions found in this work, nor obviously was this intended by the author. The purpose of the work is clearly to refresh the Catholic mind on the essentials of the deposit of faith. It is the work of the Church to teach the truth, for, as Pope John Paul II said to the American theologians gathered at Catholic University in Washington, D.C., on his visit in 1979, "the faithful have a right to the truth." The present work is rich in quotations from Sacred Scripture and in citations from the Magisterium. The reader is consequently assured that he is being offered not the personal opinions of one man, but the tradition of Catholicism.

My prayer is that of the Church, on this Thirteenth Sunday of the Year, that the divine light may shine within us and that "we may always live in the brightness of truth." May Father Hardon's catechism be for many a vehicle to that same truth of which the liturgy speaks.

Silvio Card. Oddi
Prefect of the Sacred Congregation
for the Clergy

June 28, 1981
Vatican City

FOR ALL WHO USE
THIS BOOK

L.D.M.

New York, June 26, 1981
Feast of the Sacred Heart of Jesus

   This catechism is a clear exposition of the teachings of the Church. It should be taught in schools and colleges, in religious formation programs, and in the family. Written in simple style, it is easy to understand, and it leaves no doubt in the mind as to what is required of us by the Church, as children of God and followers of Jesus Christ. To be fruitful, our study of catechism must be a prayer, for if we pray, the fruit of prayer is deepening of faith and we will believe, and if we believe we will love, and if we really love we will be able to go and proclaim the good news to the poor—through works of love—that are always works of peace.
   My prayer for you who use this book is that through its use you may grow in the knowledge of the faith taught by Christ through his Church and so became holy as your heavenly Father is holy.

God bless you,

M. Teresa, M.C.

PREFACE

In his apostolic exhortation, *Catechesi Tradendae,* on catechesis in our time, Pope John Paul II set down four qualities of a good catechism. These qualities, he said, are fundamental. A good catechism must be linked with the real life generation to which it is addressed, showing close acquaintance with the anxieties and questionings, struggles and hopes of the people. A good catechism tries to speak a language that is understood by the faithful. A good catechism gives the whole message of Christ and his Church, without neglecting or distorting anything and explaining this message in such a way as to highlight what is essential. And a good catechism really aims to give a better knowledge of the mysteries of Christ, directed at true conversion of heart and a life more in conformity with the will of God.

The Question and Answer Catholic Catechism honestly tries to fulfill these conditions and no effort was spared to achieve this purpose. It is meant to be used together with the author's *The Catholic Catechism*. The present volume is a concise synthesis of the Catholic faith directed to nourish the spiritual life of the reader. *The Catholic Catechism* develops this doctrine in more detail. Each volume complements the other.

In order to make sure it is addressed to real life situations, several years of research were spent becoming familiar with the basic problems and needs of our times. The language was adjusted to express what must be said in as simple terms as the mysteries of faith will allow. Nothing substantial has been omitted and everything necessary for salvation is treated. Above all, the author and his assistants always kept in view the spiritual good of those who will use this volume, to bring them closer to Jesus, the first Catechist, and to Mary, the Mother of the Church.

The question and answer method which the catechism follows goes back to the earliest days of Christianity. It is also supported by centuries of the Church's experience. Two benefits of this method are conciseness and easy memorization. The questions and answers are reduced to the least number of words with the greatest amount of content. The resulting value for memorizing the essentials of faith is common knowledge and, in fact, required by the popes and bishops of our time.

We are living in a Bible-conscious age, and the Church since the Second Vatican Council wants the faithful to know the scriptural roots of their faith. Hundreds of passages from the Old and New Testaments are woven into the answers as a treasury of biblical quotations. In scripture quotations, only the words omitted within a sentence are indicated by dots.

Not surprisingly, the Church wants catechetical instruction to be systematic. The doctrines of faith and morals should hold together; they should be logically connected in such a way that the whole body of Catholic belief appears for what it really is, a synthesis of revealed truth. St. Francis de Sales once wrote, "Union among different things makes order; order produces agreement; and a balanced proportion in a finished product, whose different parts agree, makes beauty." The Catholic religion is beautiful, and the beauty should appear in a catechism that, without being exhaustive, strives to be complete, while presenting the faith in a unified and orderly way, with necessary distinctions and showing how the truths we profess all agree and are related to one another in a balanced proportion that is pleasing to the eye of the soul that believes.

The order followed in *The Question and Answer Catholic Catechism* is basically that of all the Church's major catechisms since the fourth century. First is an explanation of the Apostles' Creed to lay the groundwork of the Catholic Faith.

Then follow the Commandments and Beatitudes, which build on the Creed, even as human conduct depends on the principles in which a person believes. In order to live the Christian life we must know what God expects of us. This knowledge of God's will comes to us through the voice of conscience enlightened by reason and revelation. Always implicit in the Church's teaching, but made explicit by the Second Vatican Council, is our duty as followers of Christ, to grow in holiness, "What God wants is for you all to be holy" (1 Thessalonians 4:3). Our holiness is manifest in the practice of virtue, is a result of the gifts and fruits of the Holy Spirit and leads to Christian perfection.

All the foregoing, however, is possible only by the grace of God. This grace is available through the sacraments and prayer. It is fortified by the sacramentals. Finally, since Christianity is a society of human beings united under Christ their Head, they must worship the Lord as a believing community and obtain from him in return the light and strength which they need. This is the liturgy, which is now celebrated on earth by the Church militant but is destined to continue in the Church triumphant for all eternity.

INTRODUCTION: THE PURPOSE OF LIFE

1. Why did God make us?

God made us to know him, love him, and serve him, and thereby reach heaven.

2. Why did God make other creatures?

God made other creatures to help us reach heaven.

3. How do creatures help us reach heaven?

Creatures help us reach heaven if we use them for the purpose of knowing, loving, and serving God.

4. Why does God want us to know him, love him, and serve him?

God wants us to know him because he is the eternal Truth; to love him because he is our most lovable Good; and to serve him because he is the sovereign Lord.

5. How are we to use creatures in this life?

We are to use creatures according to the will of God.

6. What does it mean to use creatures according to the will of God?

To use creatures according to the will of God means to possess, desire, and acquire things, and enjoy or endure them as God wants us to in our position and state of life.

7. What does it mean to avoid creatures if they hinder our eternal destiny?

To avoid creatures if they hinder our eternal destiny means not to possess things nor want them, insofar as they are contrary to God's will for us.

8. What is necessary if we are going to deal with the world wisely?

To deal wisely with the world, we must, with the help of God's grace, train ourselves to be free of undue attachment to persons, places, and things. We must learn to control our likes and dislikes, in order to free ourselves internally to praise, reverence, and serve God as we should.

9. Where do we mainly learn what is the will of God and how we are to do it?

We mainly learn God's will and how to fulfill it from the teaching of the Catholic Church.

10. Where does the Catholic Church teach us the will of God?

The Catholic Church teaches us the will of God in Christian doctrine.

11. What do we call a summary of Christian doctrine?

We call a summary of Christian doctrine the catechism.

12. What does the catechism especially teach us?

The catechism especially teaches us three things: 1) what we are to believe on the word of God as found in Scripture and Tradition; 2) what we are to do in order to love God by doing his will as expressed in the Commandments and Beatitudes; 3) what means of grace are available through the sacraments and prayer in order to serve God as we should.

PART ONE

CHRISTIAN BELIEF

I.
GOD SPEAKS AND MAN LISTENS

1. Divine Revelation

13. What is divine revelation?

Divine revelation is the manifestation which God has made to us of what we should know about him and his will in our regard, and how we are to worship him.

14. Why is this revelation called divine?

This revelation is called divine because it comes from God and leads us to the possession of God.

15. How has God revealed himself to us?

God has revealed himself to us in two ways, naturally and supernaturally.

16. What does natural revelation mean?

Natural revelation is the knowledge that we acquire about God by human reason through the wonderful works of his creation.

17. Why is it called natural?

It is called natural because we can rise to some knowledge of God by the light of our native reason through reflection on the objects and activities of nature. We can know that God exists by concluding from the effects in the universe to the existence of a First Cause who is himself not caused.

18. What is supernatural revelation?

Supernatural revelation is the knowledge that God discloses in a special way about himself and beyond what we can know of him by our reason.

19. Why is it called supernatural?

It is called supernatural because God directly inspires a holy person or sacred writer and thus gives him a share in his own divine authority to communicate the word of God to the rest of mankind.

20. Did God have to give us a supernatural revelation?

God did not have to give us a supernatural revelation. But in his love he wanted to help us know him better.

21. What is supernatural revelation commonly called?

Supernatural revelation is commonly called *revelation.*

22. How does revelation help us to know God better?

Revelation helps us to know God better in two ways. It enables everyone to arrive at the knowledge of the one true God with ease, firm certainty, and without contamination of error. Moreover, revelation makes known to us the divine mysteries.

23. How do we know from reason that God actually revealed himself?

We know from reason that God actually revealed himself by considering the miracles he has worked to confirm the fact of revelation. Indeed, he continues to perform miracles in order that our faith may be reasonable. Speaking of the miracles of the Savior, the evangelist says, "These are recorded so that you may believe that Jesus is the Christ, the Son of God, and that believing this you may have life through his name" (John 20:31).

24. How do miracles differ from other extraordinary actions?

Miracles differ from other extraordinary actions in three ways. They occur in answer to a holy person's desire or to prayer; they surpass the ordinary powers of visible nature; and they have the religious purpose of showing God's special presence.

25. How do miracles show that God is really with someone who claims to have received a revelation?

Miracles show that God is really with such a person because only God can work a miracle; so he would be confirming a lie if he worked a miracle in favor of a false prophet.

26. How was revelation completed with the apostolic age?

Revelation was completed with the apostolic age in that Christ is the fulfillment of all the prophecies before him, and his Incarnation is the perfect self-manifestation of God to the human race.

27. Has there been any addition to the revelation handed on by the apostles?

No, there has not been any addition to the public revelation handed on by the apostles. The revelation of what the world needs to be saved and sanctified was completed with the death of the last apostle.

28. Do we continue to receive supernatural revelation in modern times?

We do not receive any new supernatural revelation. All the divine truths necessary for salvation were revealed by the end of the apostolic age, about A.D. 100. However, the Church will continue to teach and explain these revealed truths until the end of time. The Christian waits in hope for the return of Christ, who said, "after I have gone and prepared you a place, I shall return to take you with me; so that where I am you may be too. You know the way to the place where I am going" (John 14:3–4).

29. What are private revelations?

Private revelations are supernatural manifestations of hidden truths that God makes to private individuals for their own spiritual benefit or that of others. Well known in the lives of the saints, private revelations differ from the public revelation in Scripture and Tradition in being helpful but not strictly necessary for our salvation.

30. How is revelation related to sacred doctrine?

What the Church teaches as sacred doctrine is always related to divine revelation, which the Church either presents or defines, concludes from or defends, explains or uses—for the spiritual welfare of the people of God.

31. What is sacred doctrine?

Sacred doctrine is the Church's authentic teaching of divine revelation.

32. How is sacred doctrine the Church's authentic teaching?

Sacred doctrine is the Church's authentic teaching insofar as the Church authoritatively proposes it to all the faithful for their belief and practice.

33. Is there a development of sacred doctrine?

Yes, there is development of sacred doctrine in the Church's ever greater understanding of what God has once and for all revealed to the human race.

34. Can this development ever contradict or cancel out what was formerly taught as sacred doctrine?

No, true development builds on and advances the Church's doctrine of faith and morals but never contradicts or cancels out any of the previous official teaching.

35. How, then, does development of doctrine take place?

Development of doctrine takes place in the minds of believers, under the guidance of the bishops in union with the bishop of Rome. This means that the revealed truths which are handed down from the apostles make progress in the Church, with the help of the Holy Spirit. The faithful grow in their understanding of divine revelation.

36. How does this growth in understanding come about?

This growth in understanding comes about in four ways, namely, through prayerful contemplation, through study and research by scholars faithful to the Church's teaching, from the intimate sense of spiritual realities obtained from lived experience, and from the preaching of those who have received, along with their right of succession in the episcopate, the sure charism of truth.

37. Among these sources of doctrinal development, which is the most important?

The most important source of true doctrinal development is the preaching of the bishops.

38. Why is the preaching of the bishops the most important source of doctrinal progress?

The preaching of bishops, under the bishop of Rome, is the most important source of doctrinal progress because the hierarchy is the divinely authorized guardian of revealed truth. Its teaching determines whether there is true development of doctrine and how the development is to be understood.

39. Is the Church, therefore, advancing in the possession of revealed truth?

Yes, as the centuries go by, the Church is always advancing toward the fullness of divine truth, until at the end of time the words of God are fulfilled in her. After the final resurrection, "The ban will be lifted. The throne of God and of the Lamb will be in its place in the city; his servants will worship him, they will see him face to face" (Revelation 22:3–4).

2. Divine Faith

40. What is the foundation of the Christian religion?

Divine faith is the foundation of the Christian religion.

41. How are revelation and faith related?

Revelation is related to faith in such a way that if we accept what God reveals, we believe. When God speaks, this is revelation; when we listen, this is faith. We are therefore to respond to God's revealed word by the humble acceptance of what he tells us is true. This response is at once human and divinely given. Insofar as we freely respond to God's revelation, our faith is human; insofar as it requires divine assistance, faith is a gift from God.

42. What does divine faith mean?

Divine faith is a voluntary assent of the mind in cooperation with grace by which we believe everything that God has revealed.

43. Is divine faith naturally possible?

No, divine faith is possible only because God gives us the grace to believe. Scripture tells us, "by grace you have been saved, through faith, not by anything of your own, but by a gift from God" (Ephesians 2:8). We are enabled to listen to the inspirations of the Holy Spirit, who enlightens the mind and moves the will and thus makes it possible for us to accept what God has revealed.

44. What must a Catholic believe with divine faith?

A Catholic must believe with divine faith the whole of revelation, which is contained in the written word of God and in Sacred Tradition. The apostle warns us: "Take care, brothers, that there is not in anyone of your community a wicked mind, so unbelieving as to turn away from the living God" (Hebrews 3:12).

45. Can a person be a Catholic if he believes most, but not all, the teachings of revelation?

A person cannot be a Catholic if he rejects even a single teaching that he knows has been revealed by God. As St. Paul wrote, "Anyone who teaches anything different, and does not keep to the sound teaching which is that of our Lord Jesus Christ, the doctrine which is in accordance with true religion, is simply ignorant and must be full of self-conceit—with a craze for questioning everything and arguing about words" (1 Timothy 6:3–4).

46. What will happen to those who lack "the faith necessary for salvation"?

Those will not be saved who lack the necessary faith because of their own sinful neglect or conduct. As Christ declared, "He who does not believe will be condemned" (Mark 16:16).

47. Why is divine faith called catholic?

Divine faith is called catholic or universal because a believer must accept everything God has revealed. He may not be selective about what he chooses to believe.

48. Is faith necessary for salvation?

Yes, faith is necessary for salvation because "it is impossible to please God without faith, since anyone who comes to him must believe that he exists and rewards those who try to find him" (Hebrews 11:6).

49. What is the motive for our faith?

The motive for our faith in what God has revealed is the authority of God himself.

50. How is faith a form of obedience to God?

Faith is a form of obedience to God because in faith man commits his whole self freely to God, offering the full submission of intellect and will, and then freely assenting to the truth communicated by God.

51. How do we know the meaning of what God has revealed?

We know the meaning of what God has revealed through the same teaching of the Church, with whom Christ promised to remain all days and to whom, through Peter and his successors, he gave the keys of knowledge to understand and explain the meaning of God's revealed truth. If Christ had not provided for interpreting divine revelation, he would have left his Church without protection against error and, contrary to his assurance, the gates of hell would prevail against her.

52. What does it mean to deepen our faith?

To deepen our faith means that we are able to understand better the meaning of what we believe, see the truths of faith more clearly and extensively, adhere to them more firmly, and put them into more effective practice in our Christian lives.

53. How can our faith be deepened?

Our faith can be deepened by prayer, study, and the practice of what we believe.

3. Mysteries of Christianity

54. Can we comprehend everything that God revealed?

We cannot comprehend all the truths of revelation because many of them are mysteries.

55. What is a mystery?

A mystery is a supernatural truth which is impossible for any creature even to conceive before revelation or to comprehend after it has been revealed.

56. Can we understand the mysteries of faith?

Yes, we can and should understand the mysteries of faith in various ways. Our mind can prove that it is reasonable to believe in the mysteries that God has revealed. Our reason can grasp something of the meaning of each mystery once it is revealed. We can defend the truth of God's mysteries before the bar of reason, to show they do not contradict what we know to be true from experience and natural revelation. And we can logically conclude from the mysteries of faith how they are to be put into practice in our daily lives.

57. How can we grow in our understanding of the mysteries of faith?

We can grow in our understanding of the mysteries of faith by comparing them with what we know through natural reason; for example, by looking at divine grace as a form of life, or the Church as a body, or the Eucharist as spiritual food, or mortal sin as the death of the soul. We can also grow in our understanding of the mysteries by comparing them with one another, and thus having each mystery shed light on the others; thus we can better understand the Incarnation by seeing it in the light of the Eucharist, and better appreciate the Holy Trinity by seeing it as the eternal source of the three Persons, and better grasp the meaning of sin by reflecting on Christ's Passion and Death. Finally, all the mysteries take on a deeper significance as we view them in the light of our own final destiny, since they are all intended to teach us what is the purpose of our existence, which is to reach God for whom we were created.

58. Why, then, have mysteries been revealed?

God has revealed mysteries to offer us the means of reaching our supernatural destiny, which is heaven. All the mysteries can be summed up in the Holy Trinity, from whom we came; the Incarnation, Church, and the sacraments by which we are saved; and the face to face vision of the Holy Trinity for which we were made.

4. *Sacred Scripture*

59. *Where do we find the truths revealed by God?*

We find the truths revealed by God in Sacred Scripture and Sacred Tradition.

60. *How does Sacred Scripture compare with Sacred Tradition?*

Both Sacred Scripture and Sacred Tradition are the inspired word of God, and both are forms of divine revelation. Sacred Scripture is divinely inspired writing, whereas Sacred Tradition is the unwritten word of inspired persons.

61. *What is another name for the Sacred Scriptures?*

Another name for the Sacred Scriptures is the Bible, which literally means the Writing or the Book. It is therefore the written word of God composed under the inspiration of the Holy Spirit. That is why we are told, "all Scripture is inspired by God" (2 Timothy 3:16).

62. *Why should the Bible be called the word of God?*

The Bible should be called the word of God because God so directs the mind, will, and other faculties of the sacred writer that he says only what God wants him to write and no more.

63. *Is God therefore the author of the Bible?*

Yes, God is the author of the Bible.

64. *Is God the only author of the Bible?*

No, God is not the only author of the Bible. The human writer is also responsible for the Bible.

65. *How is the human writer also responsible for the Bible?*

The human writer is also responsible for the Bible because God does not interfere with his freedom or other distinctively human and personal qualities.

66. Is the Bible therefore both a divine and human writing?

Yes, the Bible is divine insofar as it is inspired by God and human insofar as it is written by a human being.

67. What are some of the human features reflected in the Bible?

Some of the human features reflected in the Bible are the personality, experience, education, environment, distinctive purpose, and point of view of the biblical writer.

68. Does the Bible contain any errors?

No, the books of the Bible firmly, faithfully, and without error teach that truth which God, for the sake of our salvation, wished to confide to Sacred Scripture.

69. Were the biblical writers protected from saying anything untrue?

Yes, the Holy Spirit protected the biblical writers from writing any positive falsehood.

70. Is the whole Bible and every part of it inspired?

Yes, "all Scripture is inspired by God and can profitably be used for teaching, for refuting error, for guiding people's lives and teaching them to be holy. This is how the man who is dedicated to God becomes fully equipped and ready for any good work" (2 Timothy 3:16–17).

71. How is the Bible to be interpreted?

The Bible is to be interpreted in the spirit in which it was produced. As a divinely inspired document it must be treated with the reverence due to the word of God. As a humanly written document it may be studied as a literary composition. On both levels, however, it must be interpreted according to the mind and directives of the hierarchical Church.

72. How is the Bible divided?

The Bible is divided into the Old and New Testaments.

73. What is the Old Testament?

As revelation, the Old Testament is the covenant which God made with the Israelites. As inspired writing, it is that part of revelation which is set down in the Scriptures written before the time of Christ.

74. What was the covenant that God made with the Israelites?

The covenant of God with the Israelites was his promise to bless them as his chosen people if they remained faithful to his commands. He told them, "If you obey my voice and hold fast to my covenant, you of all the nations shall be my very own" (Exodus 19:5).

75. How many books are there in the Old Testament Scriptures?

There are forty-six books in the Old Testament Scriptures, as follows:

The Pentateuch—Genesis, Exodus, Leviticus, Numbers, Deuteronomy

Historical Books—Joshua, Judges, Ruth, Samuel (2), Kings (2), Chronicles (2), Ezra, Nehemiah, Tobit, Judith, Esther, Maccabees (2)

Wisdom Books—Job, Psalms, Proverbs, Ecclesiastes, Song of Songs, Wisdom, Ecclesiasticus

The Prophets—Isaiah, Jeremiah, Lamentations, Baruch, Ezekiel, Daniel, Hosea, Joel, Amos, Obadiah, Jonah, Micah, Nahum, Habakkuk, Zephaniah, Haggai, Zechariah, Malachi.

76. How does the number of books differ in the Catholic and Protestant Bible?

Most Protestant Bibles have seven fewer books than the Old Testament, namely Tobit, Judith, Wisdom, Ecclesiasticus, Baruch, I and II Maccabees. These books were removed from the Bible on the grounds that their biblical character had been disputed in early Christian times. But they are included in the Catholic Bible because the Church, under the popes, has always considered them divinely inspired.

77. What is the main theme of the Old Testament Scriptures?

Their main theme is the anticipation of the future Messiah. They prepare the people for the coming of Christ, the Anointed One, as the Redeemer of mankind, and for the kingdom of God that the Messiah was to establish.

78. How are the Old and New Testaments Scriptures related?

God, who is the author of the Bible, has so related the two Testaments that the New should be hidden in the Old and the Old should become manifest in the New.

79. What is the New Testament?

As revelation, the New Testament is the covenant that God has made with the whole human race. This covenant with mankind is Jesus Christ. "God loved the world so much that he gave his only Son, so everyone who believes in him may not be lost but may have eternal life" (John 3:16). It is, therefore, a sacred agreement by which God promises to bestow his graces in this life and heaven in the life to come on those who have faith in his Son, our Lord Jesus Christ. As inspired writing, the New Testament is that part of revelation which was composed during the Apostolic Age.

80. How many books are in the New Testament Scriptures?

The New Testament Scriptures contain twenty-seven books, as follows: the Gospels according to Matthew, Mark, Luke, and John; the Acts of the Apostles by Luke; St. Paul's letters to the Romans, Corinthians (2), Galatians, Ephesians, Philippians, Colossians, Thessalonians (2), Timothy (2), Titus, Philemon, and Hebrews; the letters of James, Peter (2), John (3), Jude; and the Book of Revelation or the Apocalypse by John.

81. Why are the books of the Bible said to be canonical?

The books of the Bible are canonical because, according to the Church's decision (canon), they are to be regarded as inspired. They were written, whole and entire, with all their parts, under the inspiration of the Holy Spirit.

82. What is the most eminent part of Sacred Scripture?

The most eminent part of Sacred Scripture is the Gospels because they are our principal source for the life and teaching of the Incarnate Word, our Savior.

83. Why should the Scriptures be read frequently?

The Scriptures should be read frequently because they are a special source of grace, light for the mind and strength for the will, to all who read them with faith and devotion. They are therefore food for the soul and a pure and lasting fount of the spiritual life. As expressed by the Second Vatican Council, "In the sacred books, the Father who is in heaven comes lovingly to meet his children, and talks with them" (Divine Revelation, 21).

5. Sacred Tradition

84. What is Sacred Tradition?

Sacred Tradition is the unwritten word of God that the prophets and apostles received through the inspiration of the Holy Spirit and, under his guidance, the Church has handed on to the Christian world. St. Paul told the faithful: "Stand firm, then, brothers, and keep the traditions that we taught you, whether by word of mouth or by letter" (2 Thessalonians 2:15).

85. How does Sacred Tradition differ from Sacred Scripture?

Sacred Tradition differs from Sacred Scripture in that it is a living reality. It is the living memory of divinely inspired persons and the record of their words and deeds. Sacred Scripture is rather a tangible and readable product contained in the inspired books. Both forms of inspiration, however, of persons and of writings, were completed with the death of the last apostle.

86. What was handed on from the prophets and apostles to the faithful?

What was handed on from the prophets and apostles to the faithful is everything that serves to make the people of God live their lives in holiness and increase their faith.

87. How has Sacred Tradition been handed on?

Sacred Tradition, which is divine revelation in oral form, has been handed on by the Church's doctrine, life, and worship.

88. What is the Church's role in Sacred Tradition?

The Church's role in Sacred Tradition is to preserve and pass on to every generation all that the Church herself is and all that she believes.

89. Why is Sacred Tradition of equal authority with the Bible?

The Bible and Sacred Tradition are of equal authority because they are equally the word of God; both derive from the inspired vision of the ancient prophets, and especially from the infinite wisdom of God incarnate who gave to the apostles what he came down on earth to teach, through them, to all of mankind.

90. Who is authorized to interpret Scripture and Tradition?

The Church's hierarchy, that is, the bishops under the pope, or the pope alone, is divinely authorized to decisively interpret Scripture and Tradition.

91. Can Sacred Tradition ever be in conflict with Sacred Scripture?

No, Sacred Tradition can never be in conflict with Sacred Scripture because the same Holy Spirit, working in the Church, is the source of both sources of revelation. Each source either adds to the other or explains the other, but they are never in contradiction.

II.
THE APOSTLES' CREED

First Article: "I believe in God the Father Almighty, Creator of heaven and earth"

1. Existence and Nature of God

92. Where do we find the chief truths of our faith?
We find the chief truths of our faith in the Apostles' Creed.

93. Why is it called the Apostles' Creed?
It is called the Apostles' Creed because its twelve articles or parts are a summary of the doctrines taught by the apostles, who were themselves instructed by the Savior.

94. What is the first article of the Apostles' Creed?
In the first article of the Apostles' Creed we say, "I believe in God the Father Almighty, Creator of heaven and earth."

95. What truths of our faith are included in this first article?
In the first article we profess to believe in the existence of God, the Holy Trinity, the creation of the world by God, the angels, and the creation and fall of man.

96. Who is God?
God is a pure and infinitely perfect divine spirit, Creator of all things, and supreme master of heaven and earth.

97. What is meant by pure spirit?

Pure spirit means that God is not made up of any matter whatsoever. He has no body or bodily parts.

98. What does infinitely perfect spirit mean?

Infinitely perfect spirit means that God has no limitation in his being or activity. He possesses the fullness of wisdom and love because there is nothing that he lacks. And he possesses fullness of power because there is nothing possible that he cannot do.

99. How do we know that God exists?

We know that God exists from divine revelation and by the light of natural reason.

100. How can we know from reason that God exists?

We can know from reason, or natural revelation, that God exists by concluding from the effects in the universe to the existence of a First Cause who is himself not caused.

101. Where does the Bible tell us about natural revelation?

The Bible tells us about natural revelation in the Old and New Testaments. Thus we are told that "naturally stupid are all men who have not known God and who, from the good things that are seen, have not been able to discover him-who-is" (Wisdom 13:1). And St. Paul writes that "ever since God created the world, his everlasting power and deity—however invisible—have been there for the mind to see in the things he has made" (Romans 1:20).

102. Where does the Bible tell us about supernatural revelation?

Throughout the Bible, in the Old and New Testaments, God revealed himself in a special way beyond the capacity of man's natural reason. St. Paul summarized all this supernatural revelation when he said that, "at various times in the past and in various different ways, God spoke to our ancestors through the prophets; but in our own time, the last days, he has spoken to us through his Son" (Hebrews 1:1–2).

103. What are the attributes of God?

The attributes of God are the perfections he has and that we attribute to him by comparison with similar qualities in creatures.

His internal attributes belong to God by his very nature. His relative attributes are in relationship to the world he created.

104. What are the principal internal attributes of God?

The principal internal attributes of God are his unchangeableness and eternity. He is unchangeable because he always possesses the fullness of being, "I, Yahweh, do not change" (Malachi 3:6). He is eternal because he has no beginning and no end, "Before the mountains were born, before the earth or the world came to birth, you were God from all eternity and for ever" (Psalms 90:2).

105. What are the main relative attributes of God?

The main attributes of God are his omnipotence, omniscience, omnipresence, justice, wisdom, and goodness. He is omnipotent or almighty because "nothing is impossible to God" (Luke 1:37). He is omniscient or all-knowing because "All things were known to him before they were created, and are still, now that they are finished" (Ecclesiasticus 23:29). He is omnipresent because God is everywhere, as he says, "Do I not fill heaven and earth?" (Jeremiah 23:24). He is all-just because he rewards those who do good and punishes those who do evil, for "he will repay each one as his works deserve" (Romans 2:6). He is all-wise because he directs all creatures to their appointed end, as we are told to "unload all your worries on to him, since he is looking after you" (1 Peter 5:7). And he is all-good because he now shares all of creation with us and is leading us to heaven to share in his own perfect happiness; that is why we pray, "Give thanks to Yahweh, for he is good, his love is everlasting" (Psalms 136:1).

106. How are the divine attributes of power, wisdom, and goodness particularly made manifest to us?

The divine attributes of power, wisdom, and goodness are made manifest to us in the works of creation, redemption, and sanctification. Thus we speak of the Father as power, of the Son as wisdom, and of the Holy Spirit as goodness. But whatever God does outside of the inner life of the Trinity is done by all three divine Persons, and by all three equally.

2. The Holy Trinity

107. What is the principal mystery of our faith?

The Blessed Trinity constitutes the very life of God and underlies all other mysteries of the faith, for example, the Incarnation, the Redemption, and the life of grace.

108. What is the mystery of the Blessed Trinity?

The mystery of the Blessed Trinity is the mystery of one God in three really distinct Persons.

109. What does "Trinity" mean?

This word means three Persons in one God.

110. Who are the three Persons in one God?

God the Father, God the Son, and God the Holy Spirit are the three divine Persons in one God.

111. How are the three Persons one and the same God?

The three Persons are one and the same God because they have one and the same nature and substance.

112. How do we know there are three Persons in God?

We know there are three Persons in God because Christ revealed this to us. His parting message to the apostles was to "make disciples of all the nations; baptize them in the name of the Father and of the Son and of the Holy Spirit" (Matthew 28:19).

113. Are the three Persons really distinct from one another?

Yes, the three Persons are really distinct from one another, for there is one person, or individual, who is the Father, another who is the Son, and another person who is the Holy Spirit. At the Last Supper, Jesus declared, "I came from the Father," to show that he and the Father are distinct; and he promised the Advocate, "whom I shall send to you from the Father, the Spirit of truth," to show that the Holy Spirit is distinct from the Father and the Son (John 16:28; 15:26).

114. How are the Persons in God distinct from one another?

The three Persons are distinct from one another in that the Father has no origin; the Son is begotten or comes from the Father alone; and the Holy Spirit proceeds or comes from the Father and the Son. Yet, though truly distinct, the three Persons have one and the same divine nature.

115. What are the operations that distinguish the divine Persons?

The operations that distinguish the divine Persons are called generation and spiration. From all eternity the Father begets the Son by an act of the divine mind (generation), somewhat as by our minds we are said to conceive thoughts and reproduce ourselves in spirit. From all eternity the Father and the Son issue forth the Holy Spirit (spiration), somewhat as two people in love express their affection by a mutual gift which they share.

116. What is meant by "missions" of the Blessed Trinity?

Mission means being sent. However, the Father being without origin is not sent, but the Father sends the Son, and the Father and the Son send the Holy Spirit (cf. John 8:42; 15:26).

117. What is meant by appropriation with regard to the Trinity?

By this we mean that a certain divine activity is applied to each of the three Persons. However, it must be remembered that whatever the Father, or the Son, or the Holy Spirit does outside the Trinity is done by all three Persons equally.

118. What divine activity in the world do we appropriate to God the Father?

The divine activity appropriated to God the Father is the creation of the universe. This is only proper since the Father is himself without origin and from him proceeds the Son, who with the Father is the origin of the Holy Spirit.

119. What divine activity in the world do we appropriate to God the Son?

The divine activity appropriated to God the Son is the work of redemption for the salvation of all men. This too is only proper since it was the second Person of the Trinity who became man and, as man, died on the Cross for our sins.

120. What divine activity in the world do we appropriate to God the Holy Spirit?

The divine activity appropriated to God the Holy Spirit is the sanctification of mankind through the communication of divine grace. This is suitable because the Holy Spirit proceeds from the mutual love of the Father and Son. And our sanctification is eminently the work of divine love.

121. How does the mystery of the Trinity teach us the meaning of selfless charity?

The mystery of the Trinity teaches us the meaning of selfless charity because there is a constant and perfect sharing of the divine Nature among the three Persons in God. The love of the Father for the Son and the Son for the Father is so perfect that within the very Godhead there comes forth the Holy Spirit as the perfect expression of love. The Trinity helps us to understand Christ's command to love one another by freely giving ourselves, as persons, in order to benefit other persons and thus help in the formation on earth of something like the triune heavenly community in God.

3. Creation and Divine Providence

122. What is creation?

Creation is the production by God of material and spiritual things in their whole substance, that is, "out of nothing." Moreover, we believe that God created the world "in time."

123. What does this mean?

By creation "out of nothing" we mean that God starts with no preexisting material and he parts with nothing of his own being in the act of creation. Creation "in time" means that the world was created along with time. Time began with creation, because time is a measure of change. The greatest change was from nothing to creation.

124. How do we know the world is not eternal?

We know the world is not eternal because this is revealed in the Bible. The opening words of the Scriptures declare that, "In the beginning God created the heavens and the earth" (Genesis 1:1). And Christ tells the heavenly Father, "You loved me before the foundation of the world" (John 17:24). The Church solemnly teaches that God, "From the very beginning of time has created both orders of creatures in the same way out of nothing, the spiritual or angelic world and the bodily or visible universe" (I Vatican Council, *Dei Filius,* 1).

125. Why did God create the world?

God created the world in order to manifest his perfection through the benefits which he bestows on creatures, not to increase his happiness nor acquire any perfection.

126. What does Sacred Scripture say about the creation of the world?

In the New Testament, God is said to have created the world. "Master, it is you who made heaven and earth and sea, and everything in them" (Acts 4:24). While Genesis merely implies creation out of nothing, the last of the historical volumes of the Old Testament clearly says, "Observe heaven and earth, consider all that is in them, and acknowledge that God made them out of what did not exist, and that mankind comes into being in the same way" (2 Maccabees 7:28).

127. Was God obliged to create the world?

God was not obliged to create the world. He was not constrained by anything within himself or by anything outside himself. His only motive for creation was to share something of his own perfection.

128. How is the world preserved by God?

God preserves the world by his almighty power which must be ever present to keep the world in existence. As we read in the Scriptures, "And how, had you not willed it, could a thing persist, how be conserved if not called forth by you?" (Wisdom 11:26).

129. How is the world governed by God?

The world is governed by God's providence. This means there is an eternal divine plan for the universe. God always knew how he would govern the world and willed to do so. Moreover, he is now putting this eternal world-plan into effect.

130. What is meant by the providence of God?

By his providence God watches over and directs all the things that he made for "every thing is uncovered and open to the eyes of the one to whom we must give account of ourselves (Hebrews 4:13). His wisdom "deploys her strength from one end of the earth to the other, ordering all things for good" (Wisdom 8:1).

131. What does divine providence imply?

Divine providence implies two things. God foresees even those things that are going to occur by the free action of creatures, and he directs all creatures to their proper end or destiny.

132. If God has planned everything, does man still act freely?

Yes, human freedom is a part of the divine plan. God wills the ultimate effects of all created actions and has provided that they be achieved, some by means of what we call necessary causes (like gravity) and others by means of truly free choices (like obedience).

133. Why pray if God already knows and determines what will happen before we pray?

We should pray even though God already knows and determines what will happen because he has foreseen our prayers from eternity and has included them in his plan for the universe, to give us what he knew we would ask for.

134. Why does God permit evil in the world if he is all good?

God permits evil in the world in order that he may bring good out of it.

135. How does God turn evil into good?

God turns evil into good by making it a source of merit. For example, the patience of the just presupposes persecution from the unjust; and the charity of those who have, presumes there are others in need.

136. What is God's plan for us and the rest of creation?

God's plan for us is that we should serve him as the Lord from whom we came and on whom we totally depend, and that we should love him as the destiny for which we were made. In the divine plan, the rest of creation is to help us please God by our loving service in this life as the means of reaching heaven in the life to come.

4. Angels, Good and Bad

137. *What is an angel?*

An angel is a spiritual creature naturally superior to man and often sent by God for certain duties on earth. The word angel means "one who is sent" or "messenger."

138. *How do we know that angels exist?*

We know that angels exist by the many references to them in Sacred Scripture (e.g., Psalms 148:2, 103:20–21; Genesis 48:16; Matthew 22:30; Luke 1:26; 2 Peter 2:4; Revelation 5:11) and from the teachings of the Church.

139. *Are angels more perfect than man?*

Angels are more perfect than man and more like God because they are pure spirits.

140. *Why are there good angels and bad angels?*

There are good and bad angels because some angels remained faithful to God when they were mysteriously tested by him, and some were unfaithful to God.

141. *What happened to the good angels?*

The good angels deserved to enter heaven and forever behold the Trinity.

142. *Which angels are named in Sacred Scripture?*

The angels named in Sacred Scripture are Michael (Revelation 12:7–9), Gabriel (Luke 1:11–20, 26–38), and Raphael (Tobit 12:6, 15).

143. *How are the good angels related to the world?*

The good angels have continual relations with the world of human beings. They are God's ministers in the government of mankind. They love us, and therefore protect us in soul and body. They pray for us and encourage us to do good. St. Paul tells us, "The truth is they are all spirits whose work is service, sent to help those who will be the heirs of salvation" (Hebrews 1:14).

144. What is a guardian angel?

A guardian angel is a special messenger whom God gives to everyone to guide us through life.

145. How do we know everyone has a guardian angel?

We know that everyone has a guardian angel because it is implied in Scripture and found in the Church's constant Tradition. According to St. Basil, "No one will deny that an angel is present to everyone of the faithful." When Peter appeared after being miraculously delivered from prison by God, the disciples who had gathered to pray were so astonished that they said, "It must be his angel" (Acts 12:15).

146. How do the guardian angels assist us by their care?

The guardian angels guide our minds and protect us from evil. As the psalmist says, "He will put you in his angels' charge, to guard you wherever you go" (Psalms 91:11).

147. How do the guardian angels protect us from evil?

Guardian angels protect us from evil by preserving us from temptation that would be too strong for us, by enlightening us on how to cope with the world, the flesh, and the devil; and by shielding us from physical evil that would bring us spiritual harm.

148. How do the guardian angels help us by their intercession?

The guardian angels never cease praying for us and present our own petitions before the throne of God.

149. How do the guardian angels guide our minds?

The guardian angels guide our minds through the heavenly inspirations they give us, telling what we should do to please God and how we are to carry it into effect.

150. What is our duty toward the guardian angels?

We are to venerate our guardian angels with great devotion, thank them for their constant care, ask them to help us, especially in time of temptation, and readily follow their inspirations. Already in the Old Testament the people were told by God, "I myself will send an angel before you to guard you as you go and to bring you to the place that I have prepared. Give him reverence and listen to all that he says. Offer him no defiance; he would not pardon such a fault, for my name is in him" (Exodus 23:20–21).

151. What happened to the bad angels?

The bad angels because of their disobedience were condemned to eternal punishment. St. Peter wrote, "When angels sinned, God did not spare them: he sent them down to the underworld and consigned them to the dark underground caves to be held there till the day of Judgment" (2 Peter 2:4).

152. What is the devil's work?

The devil's work is always malicious. His purpose is to seduce people because he wants to harm them spiritually and supernaturally, and, if possible, even eternally. He deliberately wants to lead people astray from their faithful service of the divine Majesty. "Be calm but vigilant," we are warned, "because your enemy the devil is prowling around like a roaring lion, looking for someone to eat. Stand up to him, strong in faith and in the knowledge that your brothers all over the world are suffering the same things" (1 Peter 5:8–9).

153. What is God's purpose in allowing the devil to tempt us?

God's purpose in allowing the devil to tempt us is to draw us closer to him; to try our loyalty by giving us the opportunity to show our faith and to trust in him; to test our virtue by giving us the chance to grow in grace because of the struggle that this costs; and to prove our fidelity by resisting the devil's temptations and thus more generously serving God.

5. Nature and Origin of Man

154. What is man?

Man is a creature composed of spirit and body.

155. What is meant by spirit?

By spirit is meant the immaterial soul. It is invisible only with the senses of the body. It can be seen with the eyes of the mind.

156. How does every human being have a twofold character?

Every human being has a bodily and a spiritual side to his nature. On the bodily side, we are of the same nature as the ground on which we walk and the air we breathe, but on the spiritual side, we share in the nature of the angels.

157. Why did God create man?

God created man to know, love, and serve his Creator and Lord in this life and in this way attain heaven and eternal happiness in the life to come.

158. What does Sacred Scripture teach us about the creation of man?

Sacred Scripture teaches us that God did not create man as a solitary being. From the beginning "male and female he created them" (Genesis 1:27). If man does not enter into community with other persons, he can neither live as he should nor develop the gifts he received from God.

159. How does man differ from mere animals?

Man is a rational animal. He has a material body, but, unlike mere animals, his body is animated by a rational soul. Man has the use of reason.

160. What is man's soul?

Man's soul is a spiritual, free, and immortal substance individually created by God and infused into the human body.

161. Why is the soul called a spiritual substance?

The soul is a spiritual substance because, although it is real, it has no weight, shape, or size and cannot, like a body, be divided into parts. Moreover, the soul can exist apart from the human body.

162. Why is the soul said to be free?

The soul is said to be free because it is endowed with understanding and free will. Therefore, it has the power of choosing to do good or to do evil.

163. How is the human soul immortal?

The soul is immortal because it will never die. It will live forever either enjoying everlasting happiness or suffering eternal damnation. As we read in the Scriptures, "But the souls of the virtuous are in the hands of God, no torment shall ever touch them. In the eyes of the unwise, they did appear to die . . . but they are in peace . . . their hope was rich with immortality" (Wisdom 3:1–4).

164. When is the soul created and infused into the body?

The human soul is directly created by God. It is not produced by the parents. They provide the beginnings of the human body. But God has to individually make the soul out of nothing, and unite it with the body prepared by the parents. This uniting of the soul with the body is called infusion. The creation of the soul and its infusion into the body take place at the moment of conception.

165. Why is it important to know that the soul is infused at the moment of conception?

This is important to know because it means that a human person exists from the moment of conception. Therefore any willful destruction of this newly conceived human being is a sin of murder.

166. Before Adam fell, what gifts did he and Eve possess?

Before Adam fell, he and Eve possessed supernatural and preternatural gifts.

167. What supernatural gifts did our first parents have before they sinned?

Before they sinned, our first parents had sanctifying grace, which meant they had supernatural life, the virtues of faith, hope, and charity, and a right to enter heaven. These are called supernatural gifts because no creature has a claim to them. They lead to the happiness that belongs by right to God alone.

168. What preternatural gifts did our first parents enjoy before they sinned?

Before they sinned, our first parents enjoyed bodily immortality and integrity. These are called preternatural gifts because they are special endowments that God can bestow on human beings, but they are not natural to man.

169. What was the gift of bodily immortality?

The gift of bodily immortality meant that our first parents were intended never to die, and this gift was to have been passed on to the whole human family.

170. What was the gift of integrity?

The gift of integrity meant that our first parents were free from concupiscence. They were not subject to the conflict between their desires and their reason.

171. How could our first parents sin if they were not subject to concupiscence?

Although not subject to concupiscence, our first parents could sin because they were not yet in the beatific vision. They still lived by faith, so that they had to believe (without fully understanding) God's command.

172. What must we hold regarding human evolution?

Regarding human evolution we must hold that it is only a theory and not an established fact. Moreover, even if man's body evolved from a lower species, man's soul was immediately created by God out of nothing. And finally if there was such an evolution of the body, God would have to exercise his special providence over the process, so that the first man could not literally be generated by brute beasts.

173. How did God make the first man, Adam?

As described in the Bible, "Yahweh God fashioned man of dust from the soil. Then he breathed into his nostrils a breath of life, and thus man became a living being" (Genesis 2:7).

174. How did the origin of man differ from that of other creatures?

When God created man he made him to his own image and likeness. This means that, like God, but unlike lower creatures, we have a mind with which to think and a will with which to love. Moreover, like God who is a trinity of Persons we are social beings who are to live and find our fulfillment in the society of other human beings.

175. Could those who lived before Christ be saved?

Yes, those who lived before Christ could be saved because of the foreseen merits of the Redeemer. The grace that Christ merited by his Passion and Death benefits all mankind, from our first parents after they sinned to the last human being until the end of time.

176. Does God give the grace of salvation to all human beings?

Yes, God gives sufficient grace for salvation to all human

beings. This means that even those who have not had the Gospel preached to them can reach heaven. They must be faithful to the inspirations of grace as manifested by reason and whatever form of revelation they have received.

177. Why did the Redeemer not come immediately after the fall of our first parents?

The Redeemer did not come immediately after the fall of our first parents in order to better prepare the human race for his coming. For centuries the prophets foretold the future Messiah in great detail. As a result many people eagerly awaited him. Fulfillment of the prophecies witnessed to the fact that Christ was indeed the Savior promised to mankind.

6. Original Sin

178. What is original sin?

Original sin is first of all the sin of Adam who, as the ancestor of the human race, offended God and thereby lost the right to heaven for himself and his posterity. Original sin is also the loss of sanctifying grace that we inherit from Adam when we enter the world. St. Paul teaches that "sin entered the world through one man, and through sin death" (Romans 5:12).

179. How do we know original sin really exists?

We know that original sin really exists from Sacred Scripture and from the teachings of the Church.

180. What prohibition did God place on Adam?

According to Scripture, God forbade Adam to eat of the tree of knowledge of good and evil: "For on the day you eat of it you shall most surely die" (Genesis 2:17).

181. Did Adam and Eve heed the divine prohibition?

Adam and Eve did not heed the divine prohibition. They followed the inspiration of the devil and disobeyed God.

182. What were the effects of their sin on Adam and Eve?

As a result of their sin, Adam and Eve lost all the gifts they had received over and above human nature. They especially lost the gift of sanctifying grace.

183. Did Adam's sin affect only himself?

No, as the Church teaches, Adam's sin was injurious not only to himself but also to his descendants, with the certain exception only of Jesus and Mary. Moreover, "it was not only death of the body which is punishment for sin" but also, "sin, the death of the soul, that passed from one man to all the human race" (II Council of Orange, approved by Pope Boniface II, A.D. 531).

184. What are the effects of original sin in us?

As a result of original sin, we are conceived without the possession of sanctifying grace.

185. Is original sin only the bad example that Adam passed on to his descendants?

Original sin is not only the bad example passed on by Adam. It is a real sin, though not in the ordinary sense of a transgression of God's law that we personally committed.

186. How is original sin in us a real sin?

Original sin in us is a real sin because it means the loss of the holiness we would have possessed if Adam had not sinned. It deprives us of a right to the beatific vision.

187. How is original sin passed on from the time of Adam?

Original sin is passed on by the father to his children, through human generation.

188. Does original sin totally corrupt our human nature?

Original sin does not totally corrupt our human nature. We are darkened in mind and weakened in will. But we are still capable of natural virtues and of freely cooperating with the grace of God.

189. Is the absence of sanctifying grace the only effect of original sin?

No, besides sanctifying grace, we also lost the gift of bodily immortality, which means we must suffer and die; and the gift of integrity, which explains why we have disorderly passions.

190. How does society further contribute to the sinfulness with which we enter the world?

Beyond original sin, society further contributes to our sinfulness by its previous history of sin and the bad example it gives to all who come into the world.

191. Has original sin remained without a remedy?

No, immediately after the fall, God promised to send a Redeemer so that man could recover sanctifying grace and cope with the effects of original sin.

192. How is original sin removed from our souls?

Original sin, as the absence of sanctifying grace, is ordinarily removed by the sacrament of baptism.

193. Do we also have a remedy for the sinfulness of human society?

Yes, we have a remedy for the sinfulness of human society through the teachings of the Church, the Sacrifice of the Mass and the sacraments, and the light and strength that come from prayer.

Second Article: "Jesus Christ his only Son, our Lord"

1. The Incarnation

194. What does the second article of the Apostles' Creed teach us?

This article teaches us that Jesus Christ is the Redeemer whom God promised to our first parents (cf. Genesis 3:15). He is the only begotten Son of God, and therefore the Lord of creation.

195. Who is Jesus Christ?

Jesus Christ is the second Person of the Blessed Trinity whom the Father sent into the world to become man of the Virgin Mary in order to save the world from sin. St. Peter made the confession of faith: "You are the Christ, the Son of the living God" (Matthew 16:16).

196. How did Christ prove his divinity?

Christ proved his divinity by the miracles he worked, especially rising from the dead after three days. He thus witnessed to the truth of his claims that he was one with the Father, that without him no one can be saved, and that he would come as Lord of creation to judge the human race at the end of the world.

197. What makes Christ different from other great religious teachers?

Christ was (and remains) different from other great religious teachers because, unlike them, he worked undeniable miracles, especially his own predicted resurrection from the dead; he lived a life of outstanding holiness; he preached a doctrine that rested not on mere human logic but on the divine authority that he personally claimed to possess; he not only enlightened the mind but also commanded the will of his followers to obey; inspired his disciples to follow him over the centuries even to martyrdom; and he founded a Church based on his Gospel, that has remained substantially unchanged for two thousand years, as the divinely established means of obtaining peace in this life and eternal happiness in the life to come.

198. What does the name "Jesus Christ" mean?

"Jesus" means Savior (Matthew 1:21), and the name "Christ" means Messiah or the Anointed One (Acts 10:38).

199. How did God prepare the Jewish people for the coming of Jesus?

God prepared the Jewish people, through their prophets, for the coming of Jesus by promising them a Redeemer; foretelling his virginal conception, personal qualities, and achievements; predicting the spiritual kingdom he would establish; describing his suffering, death, and resurrection; and keeping alive among the Jews the strong desire for a Savior whom they called the Messiah, or the One who is to come. As the prophet Isaiah told the Jews: "For there is a child born for us, a son given to us and dominion is laid on his shoulders; and this is the name they give him: Wonder Counselor, Mighty God, Eternal Father, Prince of Peace. Wide is his dominion in a peace that has no end, for the throne of David and for his royal power, which he establishes and makes secure in justice and integrity. From this time onwards and for ever, the jealous love of Yahweh Sabaoth will do this" (Isaiah 9:5–7).

200. Did God freely choose to become man?

Yes, God freely chose to become man because he wanted to show us how much he loves us and also to teach us how to love others after his example.

201. What is our highest motive for loving Jesus Christ?

Our highest motive for loving Jesus Christ is the Incarnation because it manifests the power, wisdom, goodness, and justice of God more strikingly than any other mystery. For this reason we are inspired to gratitude and, from gratitude, to selfless generosity.

202. How did the Word of God become man in the person of Jesus Christ?

The Word of God became man in the person of Jesus Christ through the Incarnation. This means that the second Person of the Trinity became united with our human nature, so that the man Jesus Christ is the eternal Son of God. As St. John tells us, "In the beginning was the Word: the Word was with God and the Word was God . . . The Word was made flesh, he lived among us, and we saw his glory, the glory that is his as the only Son of the Father, full of grace and truth" (John 1:1, 14).

203. How are the divine and human natures united in Christ?

The divine and human natures are united in Christ in such a way that he is one individual, at once true God and true man. This is the mystery of the Incarnation.

204. Why did God become man?

God became man to redeem us from sin and to give us a share in the happiness of eternal life through faith in his love. St. Paul says, "God loved us with so much love that he was generous with his mercy: when we were dead through our sins, he brought us to life with Christ" (Ephesians 2:4–5).

205. Could God have redeemed the world in some other way?

God could have redeemed the world in some other way. But

this would be less in keeping with his perfect justice and with the divine will to manifest his perfect love.

206. What do we profess in the mystery of the Incarnation?

In the mystery of the Incarnation, we profess with the infallible Church that there are in Christ two really distinct natures, one human like ours and one divine or of one substance with God the Father; yet united in such a way that Christ is one person, and unchanged so that each nature remains truly and unqualifyingly itself. He is God from all eternity, and became man in time.

207. What kind of union is this called?

This union is called the hypostatic union, which means personal union.

208. What do we mean by distinct natures?

By distinct natures we mean two perfect natures each distinct and perfect in itself.

209. If Christ has two perfect natures, how is he only one person?

Christ is only one person because his two perfect natures are united in one individual, which individual is divine.

210. What is Christ's human nature?

Christ's human nature is the same as our own, except for sin. He was born, lived, and died as other human beings. He had a human body and a human soul. He is true man.

211. What is Christ's divine Nature?

Christ's divine nature is the same as God the Father's. He is one in being with the Father and the Holy Spirit. He is true God.

2. True God and True Man

212. Did Jesus realize all his life that he was divine?

Jesus knew from the moment of his conception that he was divine. To suppose that his human soul only gradually came to know he was divine would be to deny that he was true God and true man from the first instant of the Incarnation in his mother's womb.

213. Did Christ ever make claims to be the Son of God?

Yes, throughout his public life, Christ claimed to be the natural Son of God. Thus he accepted Peter's saying to him: "You are the Christ, the Son of the living God" (Matthew 16:16). When the Jews pressed him, "If you are the Christ, tell us plainly," he told them, "The Father and I are one," at which they tried to stone him, and so he asked them, why. They answered, "You are only a man and you claim to be God" (John 10:24, 30, 33). And throughout the long discussion at the Last Supper (John 14, 15, 16, 17), Jesus speaks of God as his natural Father, of whom he said, "Everything the Father has is mine" (John 16:15).

214. How is Jesus Christ the King of the universe?

Jesus Christ is King of the universe by a twofold title: one in the order of natural creation, and another in the order of supernatural re-creation which is Redemption. Christ is therefore Lord of the world of nature and of grace.

215. When Christ was on earth, did he use only his human nature?

No, when Christ was on earth, he always used both his human and divine nature. In whatever he did, he acted as God and man.

216. Why did Jesus Christ assume a human nature?

Christ assumed a human nature in order to show us how much he loves the human family. By becoming human, he could suffer; and by suffering, he could die; and by dying, he redeemed; and by rising from the dead, he became the source of our grace.

217. Since Christ assumed a human nature was he subject to sin?

Even though Christ assumed a human nature he was not subject to sin because he is also God. Therefore he could not commit any personal sin, and he had no concupiscence, or unruly passions, which are the result of original sin.

218. How do we know that Jesus never sinned?

We know that Jesus never sinned because he was the Son of God in human form. Christ himself dared ask his enemies, "Can one of you convict me of sin?" (John 8:46). St. Peter says of the Savior that "he had not done anything wrong" (1 Peter 2:22), and St. Paul declares that "God made the sinless one into sin, so that in him we might become the goodness of God" (2 Corinthians 5:21).

219. What kind of knowledge did Christ have?

Christ had two kinds of knowledge: human and divine.

220. What kind of human knowledge did Christ have?

Christ had three kinds of human knowledge: the immediate vision of God, infused supernatural knowledge, and acquired or experimental knowledge.

221. What was Christ's immediate vision of God?

Christ's immediate vision of God was the beatific vision of seeing God face to face.

222. What was Christ's infused supernatural knowledge?

Christ's infused supernatural knowledge was the knowledge he had divinely conferred on him without previous human experience or reflection. It differed from the knowledge of vision in that things were known in their proper nature through ideas that were miraculously received from God.

223. What was the acquired or experimental knowledge of Christ?

The acquired or experimental knowledge of Christ was the knowledge he obtained from sense experience and through the reasoning power of his human intellect.

224. Was the human knowledge of Christ free from error?

Yes, the human knowledge of Christ was free from positive ignorance and from all error.

225. Was Christ ignorant of certain things that, as God, he should have known?

Christ, as God, knew all things, past, present, and future. And even as man, because his humanity was united to the Word of God, he had access to all knowledge; but since the nature he assumed was finite, his human knowledge was not infinite. Therefore, he could develop as man through the kind of experience he had as he grew from infancy, through childhood, and into adult age. But never was Christ ignorant of anything he could have known, as though he were not God-made-man from the first moment of the Incarnation; or ignorant of anything he should have known, as though his human nature was blinded, like ours, by original or personal sin.

Third Article: "Conceived by the Holy Spirit, born of the Virgin Mary"

The Blessed Virgin Mary: Her Privileges and Relation to Christ and His Church

226. What does the third article of the Apostles' Creed mainly teach us?

It teaches us that the second Person of the Holy Trinity became a human being through the operation of the Holy Spirit; that he was conceived in the womb of the Virgin Mary and born of her in Bethlehem. Mary is therefore the Immaculate Virgin Mother of God.

227. How was Jesus Christ conceived by the Holy Spirit?

Jesus Christ was conceived by the Holy Spirit in that he had no human father, but only a human mother. Yet he was truly conceived in the womb of Mary by the miraculous operation of the Holy Trinity.

228. Why do we attribute Christ's conception to the Holy Spirit?

We attribute Christ's conception to the Holy Spirit, even though the Incarnation was effected by all three Persons of the Trinity, because the third Person is the term of the eternal love between the Father and the Son. Since the Incarnation is the greatest manifestation of God's love in the world, it is rightly appropriated to the Holy Spirit, who expresses the love of God within the Holy Trinity.

229. Why did Christ choose to be conceived and born in humble circumstances?

Christ chose to be conceived and born in humble circumstances because he wished to teach us humility, attract us by his lowliness, merit our salvation by the sacrifice of earthly possessions, and keep ever before our minds the fact of the Incarnation, namely that God "emptied himself" to take on for love of us the condition of a slave.

230. Why did Jesus live a hidden life for thirty years?

Jesus lived a hidden life for thirty years at Nazareth and spent less than three years preaching to show that his mission on earth was divine and did not need a long time to be accomplished; to emphasize his truly human nature, which developed gradually from infancy, through childhood and youth into mature manhood; and to teach us the importance of solitude and union with God as the basis of all external labor, even the highest form of the apostolate.

231. Who is the blessed Virgin Mary?

The blessed Virgin Mary is a humble daughter of the family of David, whom God chose to be the Mother of his Son. The parents of Mary were St. Joachim and St. Anne, natives of Bethlehem who lived in Nazareth.

232. What were the main privileges of the blessed Virgin?

The main privileges of the blessed Virgin were the divine maternity, her perpetual virginity, Immaculate Conception, bodily Assumption into heaven, and her role as Mother of the Church.

233. Why is Mary truly the Mother of God?

Mary is truly the Mother of God because she contributed everything to Christ's human nature that all mothers give to the fruit of their womb; and because she conceived and bore the eternal Son of God who, according to the flesh, became the Son of Mary.

234. How did Mary become the Mother of the Redeemer?

Mary became the Mother of the Redeemer by the power of the Holy Spirit, as the angel told her, "The Holy Spirit will come upon you . . . and the power of the Most High will cover you with its shadow" (Luke 1:35). When she consented to be the Mother of Christ at the Annunciation, the second Person of the Trinity immediately took flesh in her womb. Consequently, when she conceived him and gave him birth, she also united herself to his sufferings, by which he redeemed the world.

235. Was Mary always a virgin?

Yes, Mary was always a virgin. She was a virgin when she conceived and gave birth to Christ, and she remained a virgin all her life, even after Jesus was born.

236. Who are the "brothers and sisters" of Jesus mentioned in the Gospels?

The "brothers and sisters" of Jesus mentioned in the Gospels are his near relations or close friends. Even today we speak of someone as our brother or sister, when a person is specially dear to us. Moreover, the kind of love we should have for others is said to be fraternal (brotherly) charity, although most of the people we love are not immediately related to us by blood.

237. If Mary was a virgin mother, what was the role of St. Joseph?

St. Joseph was the foster-father of Jesus, the legal husband of Mary, and the head of the Holy Family. He protected the good name of Mary and was used by Providence to safeguard the mystery of the Incarnation. "This is Joseph's son, surely?" the contemporaries of Jesus asked about him (Luke 4:22).

238. Why must we firmly believe in the Immaculate Conception?

We must firmly believe in the Immaculate Conception because it is a dogma of the faith. In the words of Pope Pius IX, "We declare, pronounce, and define: the doctrine that maintains that the most blessed Virgin Mary in the first instant of her conception, by a unique grace and privilege of the omnipotent God and in consideration of the merits of Christ Jesus the Savior of the human race, was preserved from all stain of original sin, is a doctrine revealed by God." This doctrine is implied in the title which the angel Gabriel gave to Mary when he addressed her: "Hail, full of grace, the Lord is with you" (Luke 1:28, *Vulgate translation*).

239. Why did Christ preserve Mary from sin?

Christ, as God, preserved Mary from sin because he wanted to do everything possible for her. He wanted to be conceived and born of a sinless Mother.

240. Why is exemption from original sin an extraordinary grace?

Exemption from original sin is an extraordinary grace because all other human beings, except Christ, are conceived with sin on their souls. "Death reigned over everyone as the consequence of one man's fall" (Romans 5:17), but not over Mary.

241. What follows from Mary's freedom from original sin?

Mary's freedom from original sin preserved her from all sinful passion or concupiscence and from every personal sin during the whole of her life.

242. Was Mary, then, impeccable?

Yes, Mary was impeccable. By a special privilege from God, she could not sin.

243. How could Mary acquire merit if she was incapable of sin?

Mary could acquire merit because she could exercise her freedom of choice. She could choose among a variety of good actions in exercising her great love of God.

244. What is meant by the Assumption of our Lady?

By the Assumption of our Lady is meant that after her life on earth, she was assumed body and soul into the glory of heaven.

245. On what grounds was Mary's Assumption defined by the Church?

Mary's Assumption was defined by the Church because she was the Mother of God; she was free from all sin; her body was preserved in spotless chastity; and she shared in her Son's redemptive work in the world.

246. Was Mary still living when she was assumed into heaven?

It is commonly believed that Mary died, but immediately after death her body and soul were reunited and taken up to heaven.

247. Why was Mary's body exempt from corruption in the grave?

Mary had been the living sanctuary of the Son of God and free from all sin; therefore her body was exempt from corruption in the grave.

248. Why did the Church wait so long (1854 and 1950) to proclaim the dogmas of the Immaculate Conception and the Assumption?

These two dogmas had always been true. But the Church grows in her clear realization of what is revealed truth, and this takes time. Moreover, these two Marian dogmas provide an effective means of leading the modern world to Jesus through his Mother.

249. Does sinful mankind need a mediator with the Eternal Father?

Yes, sinful mankind needs a mediator with the Eternal Father. Christ is the mediator.

250. What is a mediator?

A mediator is a person who holds a favorable position between parties at variance; and, therefore, comes between them as the equal friend of each.

251. Who is the only mediator between God and man?

Jesus Christ. "For there is only one God, and there is only one mediator between God and mankind, himself a man, Christ Jesus, who sacrificed himself as a ransom for them all" (1 Timothy 2:5–6).

252. How does Jesus Christ act as our mediator with God?

Jesus Christ acts as our mediator with God in three ways: by his hypostatic union, joining in one person the two natures that need to be mediated; divine, which he has in common with the Father; and human, which he shares with us; by the fact that his death atoned for man's sins; and because his humanity is now the universal channel of grace from God to mankind.

253. Why is Mary called our mediatrix?

Mary is called our mediatrix first because she cooperated in a unique way with Christ in his redemptive labors on earth. She is also mediatrix because she continues to intercede for us who are still working out our salvation on earth or suffering in purgatory.

254. Why does Mary deserve the title "Mother of Divine Grace"?

Mary deserves the title "Mother of Divine Grace" because Christ made her so exalted in holiness that on earth she merited a high place in heaven, and now in heaven is able to plead our cause with her Son more effectively than anyone else among the elect.

255. Does devotion to Mary detract from the dignity of Christ?

No, devotion to Mary does not in any way detract from or add anything to the dignity of Christ the one mediator. Sacred Scripture itself teaches that we should honor Mary, for in her song of praise, Mary said, "From this day forward all generations will call me blessed, for the Almighty has done great things for me" (Luke 1:48–49).

256. How is the blessed Virgin "Mother of the Church"?

Mary is Mother of the Church because she conceived and gave birth to Christ, who established the Church and is the Church's invisible Head. She is also Mother of the Church by the generous sacrifice of her Son on the Cross, at which time Christ made us children of Mary when he told John, "This is your mother" (John 19:27). Mary also mothered the early Church from Pentecost Sunday until her Assumption. And she continues to care and provide for the members of the Church as our Mother by her prayerful intercession in heaven at the throne of her Son.

257. What are the principal feasts honoring the blessed Virgin?

The principal feasts of the blessed Virgin are:

January 1: the Solemnity of Mary, Mother of God.
February 2: Purification of Mary (Presentation of the Lord)
February 11: Our Lady of Lourdes
March 25: Annunciation of Our Lady
May 31: Visitation of the Blessed Virgin
Saturday after the Second Sunday after Pentecost: Immaculate Heart of Mary
July 16: Our Lady of Mount Carmel
August 15: Assumption of the Blessed Virgin
August 22: Queenship of Mary
September 8: Birth of Mary
September 15: Our Lady of Sorrows
October 7: Our Lady of the Rosary
November 21: Presentation of Mary
December 8: Immaculate Conception
December 12: Our Lady of Guadalupe.

258. Should Mary, who is a mere creature, be given so much honor?

It is true that Mary is only a creature. But she is the Mother of God. She therefore deserves more veneration than anyone except Christ who, though man, is also God.

259. Are Catholics required to believe that the blessed Virgin really appeared at Lourdes and Fatima?

Once the Church officially approves certain shrines like Lourdes and Fatima, it would be rash for a Catholic to question the actual appearance at such places. Moreover, numerous spiritual favors and demonstrated miracles are a sign of God's approval of the people's devotion at these and similar shrines.

260. What is devotion to the Immaculate Heart of Mary?

Devotion to the Immaculate Heart of Mary is the special veneration given to our Lady as conceived without sin and Immaculate; and to our Lady as filled with the love of God and with a mother's love for mankind, which is symbolized by her Heart.

Fourth Article: "Suffered under Pontius Pilate, was crucified, died, and was buried"

The Passion, Death, and Burial of Jesus Christ

261. What does the fourth article of the Apostles' Creed teach us?

This article teaches us that Jesus Christ was condemned under Pontius Pilate to suffer and die on the Cross for our salvation and that his body was taken down from the Cross and was buried.

262. Why did Pontius Pilate condemn the Savior to be crucified?

Pilate condemned Christ to death although he knew the Savior was innocent, as all four evangelists testify. He finally gave in to the demands of the priests and Pharisees for Christ's death because he feared for his own position as Roman procurator of Judea. Self-interest and cowardice explain why Pilate consented to the crucifixion (cf. Mark 15:15).

263. How do we know that Christ really suffered and died?

We know that Christ really suffered and died from the evidence of history, as recorded in the New Testament and testified by the entire Christian tradition of the first century.

264. Why is it important to know that Christ actually died?

It is important to know that Christ actually died in order to establish the fact of his bodily resurrection.

265. What happened when Jesus died?

When Jesus died his body and soul were separated from each other, even as happens with other human beings in whom death is a separation of body and soul.

266. What happened after Christ died?

After Christ died his body and soul remained separated until the Resurrection. But his divinity remained hypostatically united with both the body and the soul.

267. What does it mean that Christ's divinity remained united with his separated body and soul after his death?

Since Christ's divinity remained united with the separated body and soul of Christ after his death, the dead body in the grave remained the body of the Son of God and his soul was also the human spirit of the second Person of the Trinity. Indeed, every drop of Christ's blood on Calvary was the blood of the incarnate Son of God.

268. Why did Christ wish to be buried?

Christ wished to be buried in order to more firmly prove that he really died so that his Resurrection would be more credible and his victory over death more glorious.

269. How did Christ suffer, as God or as man?

Although the one who suffered was God become man, Christ's actual suffering was in his human nature. God as God cannot suffer but that is why he became man. He was, as the Church teaches us, born to suffer (*natus pati*).

270. Did Christ have to undergo his Passion and Death?

No, Christ did not have to undergo his Passion and Death. He did so of his own free will. As Christ himself declared, "The Father loves me, because I lay down my life in order to take it up again. No one takes it from me; I lay it down of my own free will, and as it is in my power to lay it down, so it is in my power to take it up again" (John 10:17–18).

271. Why did Christ want to suffer and die?

Christ wanted to suffer and die first of all to satisfy the divine justice for our sins. As Isaiah had foretold, "Ours were the sufferings he bore, ours the sorrows he carried . . . Yet he was pierced through for our faults, crushed for our sins. On him lies a punishment that brings us peace, and through his wounds we are healed" (Isaiah 53:4–5). Secondly, Christ willed to suffer and die in order to evoke our grateful love. Seeing how much God loved us, even to death on the Cross, we are inspired to love him even to dying to ourselves in gratitude for his generosity. And finally, the sufferings of Christ teach us to embrace the Cross as the indispensable means of achieving holiness; nothing is more sanctifying than uniting one's own sufferings with those of the Savior in his blessed Passion and Death on Calvary.

272. What sins did Christ expiate?

Jesus Christ "is the sacrifice that takes our sins away, and not only ours, but the whole world's" (1 John 2:2). He therefore made satisfaction for original sin and all the other sins of the human race, from Adam to the end of the world.

273. Why could only Christ make full reparation for our sins?

Only Christ could make full reparation for our sins because the heavenly Father demanded complete satisfaction for the sins of mankind. Sin is an offense against the infinite majesty of God and therefore may require a satisfaction of infinite value, if God wills it. Since God willed it so, only Christ, who is the infinite Lord, could give this satisfaction by suffering as a human being and offering his sufferings to the Father with a human will.

274. Did Christ have to suffer the extreme pains of his Passion?

No, even the least suffering of the God-Man would have been sufficient to redeem the human race. But Christ wished to undergo the great pains he endured in order to teach us how much he loves us, how terrible is sin, and how patient we should be in carrying our Cross in imitation of him.

275. From what did Christ redeem us?

Christ redeemed us from the guilt of sin, and thus reconciled us with his heavenly Father; from the punishment we deserved for sin, in this life and in the life to come; and from the power of the evil spirit who, because of sin, became, as Christ said, "the prince of this world [that] is to be overthrown" (John 12:31).

276. What did Christ obtain for us by his Passion and Death?

By his Passion and Death, Christ obtained for us the right to heavenly glory, the graces we need to remain in God's friendship and grow in sanctity, and the power to actually become more pleasing to God by resisting temptation and struggling with our fallen human nature.

277. Did Christ suffer and die only for those who will be saved?

No, Christ suffered and died for all mankind without exception. As St. Paul tells us "there is only one mediator between God and mankind, himself a man, Christ Jesus, who sacrificed himself as a ransom for them all" (1 Timothy 2:5–6). Those who are not saved also receive sufficient grace for salvation through Christ's Redemption. If they are not saved, it is not because Christ did not die for them but because they refused to cooperate with the grace he merited for them on Calvary.

278. How do Catholics commemorate the Passion and Death of Christ?

Catholics commemorate the Passion and Death of Christ by their participation in the Sacrifice of the Mass, their observance of Fridays as obligatory days of penance in union with Christ's sufferings, their recitation of the sorrowful mysteries of the Rosary, and making the Way of the Cross.

Fifth Article: "He descended into hell, the third day he rose again from the dead"

Christ's Descent into Limbo and His Resurrection

279. What does the fifth article of the Apostles' Creed teach us?

The fifth article of the Apostles' Creed tells us what Christ did after his Death and before the Resurrection; and that he came back to human life three days after he was crucified.

280. What happened after Christ died?

When Jesus died, his body and soul were separated. His body remained in the grave, but his soul "descended into hell," as the Apostles' Creed declares.

281. What does it mean that Jesus "descended into hell"?

Christ's descent into hell means that after Christ's death, his soul visited the souls of the just who died up to that time and were detained in the limbo of the Fathers. They were awaiting admission to heaven as a result of the Savior's death on the Cross by which he redeemed the world. Taught by all the ancient creeds, the fact of Christ's descent into limbo is also implied in the statement of St. Peter, that Christ "died for the guilty, to lead us to God. In the body he was put to death, in the spirit he was raised to life, and, in the spirit, he went to preach to the spirits in prison" (1 Peter 3:18–19).

282. Why were the souls of the just detained in limbo?

They were detained in limbo because of sin. Heaven was first to be opened by Christ as the Redeemer.

283. Why did Christ descend into limbo?

Christ descended into limbo to manifest his power and authority over all creation, including the invisible world of the dead, as St. Paul tells us, "God raised him high and gave him the name which is above all other names so that all beings in the heavens, on earth and in the underworld, should bend the knee at the name of Jesus" (Philippians 2:9–10). Moreover, by his descent into limbo Christ manifested himself to the souls who were awaiting their deliverance, and together with him, their heavenly salvation.

284. What does it mean that on "the third day he rose again from the dead"?

By this we mean that on the third day after his death Christ, by his own power, reunited his soul to his body. He rose again from the grave as he had foretold. He said, "Destroy this sanctuary, and in three days I will raise it up." When the Jews replied, "It has taken forty-six years to build this sanctuary: are you going to raise it up in three days?" St. John explains, "He was speaking of the sanctuary that was his body, and when Jesus rose from the dead, his disciples remembered that he had said this, and they believed the scripture and the words he had said" (John 2:19–22).

285. Did Christ keep the marks of his Passion after the Resurrection?

Yes, he kept the marks of his wounds, in his hands, feet, and side. As he told the doubting Thomas, "Put your finger here; look, here are my hands. Give me your hand; put it into my side. Doubt no longer but believe" (John 20:27).

286. Does Christ still retain the wounds of his Passion, now that he is in heaven?

Yes, Christ still retains the marks of his Passion, even in heaven, for several reasons: as a witness of his victory over sin, and therefore the proof of our redemption; as evidence that he rose in the same body in which he had suffered; to teach us that we shall be glorified like him, provided, in this life, we have suffered with him; and to manifest for all eternity that, except for his Passion and Death, none of us would see the face of God.

287. Did Christ actually rise from the dead in body and not merely raise the hearts of his followers in spirit?

Christ actually rose from the dead in body because there were hundreds of witnesses to the fact; because this fact became the foundation of the faith of the early Christians, many of whom suffered martyrdom for their belief; and because no extraordinary fact of equal antiquity is better attested as provable history.

288. What should we learn from Christ's Resurrection?

Christ's Resurrection strengthens our faith in his divinity, because only God in human form could reunite his body and soul. It is the foundation of our hope in our own future resurrection from the dead. In the words of St. Peter, "Through him you now have faith in God, who raised him from the dead and gave him glory for that very reason—so that you would have faith and hope in God" (1 Peter 1:21). Finally, Christ's Resurrection inspires us to love him by dying to ourselves. In the words of St. Paul, "Since you have been brought back to true life with Christ, you must look for the things that are in heaven, where Christ is, sitting at God's right hand" (Colossians 3:1).

289. Why did Christ remain on earth in visible form for forty days after his Resurrection?

Christ remained visibly on earth for forty days after his Resurrection to witness to the fact that he really arose from the dead, to strengthen the faith of the disciples, to complete his teaching and training of the apostles, to give the apostles the power of forgiving sins through the sacrament of penance, to confer on Peter the primacy as visible head of the Church, and to inspire Christians for all times with the desire to follow in his footsteps through suffering in order to be one day united with him in glory.

Sixth Article: "He ascended into heaven, and sits at the right hand of God the Father Almighty"

The Ascension of Christ and His Glorified Existence

290. What do we mean when we say Christ ascended into heaven?

Christ ascended into heaven in the sense that, forty days after the Resurrection, he left the earth in visible form to return to his heavenly Father in body and soul. Yet he remains on earth invisibly present as God and man, in the Blessed Sacrament of the altar. At the Ascension, the angels repeated Christ's promise that he would return in glory on the Last Day (cf. Acts 1:9–11).

291. Did Christ ascend alone into heaven?

No, at his Ascension he took with him to heaven all the souls of the just whom he had delivered from the limbo of the Fathers. In St. Paul's words, "When he ascended to the height, he captured prisoners, he gave gifts to men" (Ephesians 4:8).

292. Why did Christ ascend into heaven?

He ascended into heaven to possess the glory he had gained as conqueror of sin and death (cf. Philippians 2:8–11); to be our mediator and advocate with his heavenly Father (cf. Hebrews 9:24); to send the Holy Spirit whom he had promised (cf. John 16:7); to open the gates of heaven and prepare a place for us (cf. John 14:2).

293. Christ is now seated at the right hand of the Father. What does this mean?

Christ is now seated at the right hand of the Father because he entered heaven by right of nature as God and by merit as the redeemer; he shares in the power of the Father to judge the living and the dead; and as Christ the king, he is the undisputed ruler of the universe.

294. If Christ is in heaven, is he not then everywhere?

Christ is everywhere as God, but he is not everywhere as the God-Man. He is present as the God-Man only in heaven at the right hand of his Father, and on earth in the Holy Eucharist.

295. How is Christ present among us by his Real Presence?

By his Real Presence, Christ is present not only by what he does, but by his actual existence in our midst. In the Eucharist he is present as the whole Christ, true God and true man, with his divinity and humanity, body and soul, human thoughts and emotions, with flesh and blood, and all the qualities of a living human being.

296. Is Christ present only in a symbolic or a spiritual sense in the Eucharist?

Absolutely not. Christ is just as truly present in the Eucharist on earth as he is present at the right hand of the Father in heaven. The only difference is that on earth in the Eucharist we cannot see him with bodily eyes, but we believe with divine faith that he is really here.

297. Is Christ also present in our midst in other ways?

Yes, besides the Real Presence, Christ is also in our midst by his continued activity in the Church.

298. How is Christ present among us by his activity in the Church?

Christ is present by his activity in the Church when she prays and performs her works of mercy. He is present in the Church by the graces he confers on the faithful as they struggle in their pilgrimage through life. He is present by the light he gives the Church's teachers, as successors of Peter and the apostles. He is present as she administers the sacraments.

Seventh Article: "From thence he shall come to judge the living and the dead"

1. The General Judgment

299. What does the seventh article of the Apostles' Creed teach us?

It teaches us that Jesus Christ will come at the end of time to judge the human race. It is called the Second Coming and was foretold by the angels on the day of his Ascension. They told the disciples, "Jesus who has been taken up from you into heaven, this same Jesus will come back in the same way as you have seen him go there" (Acts 1:11).

300. How many kinds of judgment are there?

There are two kinds of judgment: a particular judgment at the end of our own life, and a general judgment at the end of the world.

301. What happens to us immediately after death?

Immediately after death we shall be judged about our service of God and our moral conduct during life. This is called the particular judgment, and is promptly carried into effect. We are told in Scripture that "men only die once, and after that comes judgment" (Hebrews 9:27).

302. On what is a person judged?

A person is judged on the moral good and evil that he has done. "Each will duly be paid according to his share in the work" (1 Corinthians 3:8).

303. What is the general judgment at the end of the world?

The general judgment is a social judgment. We shall be judged as members of the human race, to reveal to the world God's justice in those he condemns and his mercy in those who are saved. A deeper reason for the general judgment is to make manifest the chain of consequences of men's actions, even long after the actions were done, up to the end of time. Of the general judgment, Jesus told us, "The hour is coming when the dead will leave their graves at the sound of his voice: those who did good will rise again to life; and those who did evil, to condemnation" (John 5:28–29).

304. Will the sentence pronounced at the general judgment differ from that of the particular judgment?

The general judgment will not differ from the particular judgment except to give it solemn confirmation. However, since the general judgment will take place after the resurrection, it will affect the whole man, body and soul. Man's final destiny, therefore, includes also the body which is to share in his reward or punishment.

305. What will the Lord say to the just at the last judgment?

To the just our Lord will say, "Come, you whom my Father has blessed, take for your heritage the kingdom prepared for you since the foundation of the world" (Matthew 25:34).

306. What are the two kinds of reward given to the just?

The two kinds of reward given to the just are possession of God and enjoyment of creatures.

2. Eternal Punishment

307. What will our Lord say to the wicked at the last judgment?

To the wicked our Lord will say, "Go away from me, with your curse upon you, to the eternal fire prepared for the devil and his angels" (Matthew 25:41).

308. What are the two kinds of pain threatened to the wicked?

The two kinds of pain threatened to the wicked are the loss of the beatific vision and the experience of pain from creatures.

309. What is hell?

Hell is a place of endless punishment to which the wicked are condemned forever with the evil spirits.

310. What is the main suffering of hell?

The main suffering of hell is the pain of losing the vision of God for whose possession man was created. As Christ foretold, "Then there will be weeping and grinding of teeth, when you see Abraham and Isaac and Jacob and all the prophets in the kingdom of God, and yourselves turned outside" (Luke 13:28).

311. What is a further suffering in hell?

A further suffering in hell is the pain of sense. This is caused by a creature outside the person and is described in divine revelation as fire. It is a fire that causes pain to body and soul without consuming the one in torment. Speaking of hell, Jesus said, "The chaff he will burn in a fire that will never go out" (Matthew 3:12).

312. Who is in hell?

Besides the evil spirits, those are in hell who die in the state of mortal sin. They are the unrepentant sinners.

313. Are the sufferings in hell eternal?

Yes, the sufferings in hell are as eternal as the happiness of heaven. When Christ predicted the final judgment, he declared that both heaven and hell will last forever. He used the same word "eternal" to describe both, saying of the lost, "They will go away to eternal punishment," then of the saved, "and the virtuous to eternal life" (Matthew 25:46). And St. Paul teaches, speaking of the wicked, "It will be their punishment to be lost eternally, excluded from the presence of the Lord" (2 Thessalonians 1:9).

314. Are the pains of hell the same for everyone?

The pains of hell are not the same for everyone. Justice demands that they be imposed according to the nature and number of the sins of each of the condemned.

315. Why does an all-good God condemn his creatures to hell?

God, who is all-good, allows his creatures to condemn themselves to hell because he does not interfere with their freedom.

They voluntarily choose to reject him and, in his justice, he permits them to remain separated from the God they rejected.

3. Purgatory

316. What is purgatory?

Purgatory is a state or condition in which the souls of the just, who die with the stains of sin, are cleansed before they are admitted to heaven. This cleansing is necessary, for "nothing unclean may come into it . . ." (Revelation 21:27).

317. What is meant by "stain of sin"?

Stain of sin means the temporal punishment still due to venial or forgiven mortal sins. If the punishment has not been satisfied before death, a person must suffer in purgatory to repay this debt which is owed to the divine Majesty.

318. Who are the souls of the just?

The souls of the just are those that leave the body in the state of grace and are therefore destined by right to enter heavenly glory.

319. Are the souls in purgatory certain they are saved?

Yes, the souls in purgatory are certain they are saved. It is for this reason that their suffering is only temporary.

320. What kind of suffering do the souls in purgatory endure?

The souls in purgatory endure two kinds of suffering: the pain of loss which is the temporary loss of the vision of God and the endurance of physical pain. The sufferings of purgatory are more intense than any suffering on earth.

321. Do the souls in purgatory experience joy?

Yes, the souls in purgatory experience intense spiritual joy because they are absolutely sure of their salvation. They have faith, hope, and great charity. They know themselves to be in divine friendship, confirmed in grace and no longer able to offend their heavenly Father.

322. Can the souls in purgatory make satisfaction for their sins?

No, the souls in purgatory cannot make satisfaction for their sins because satisfaction as merit is possible only during one's lifetime on earth. There is no true merit after death.

323. Who may help the souls in purgatory?

All who belong to the communion of saints can help the souls in purgatory, that is, the faithful on earth, and the angels and saints in heaven. God's mercy continues for those in purgatory.

324. How can the faithful on earth help the souls in purgatory?

The faithful on earth can help the souls in purgatory by their suffrages, that is, through the Sacrifice of the Mass, prayers, alms-giving, and every kind of good work.

325. How do the angels and saints help the souls in purgatory?

The angels and saints help the souls in purgatory not by way of merit or satisfaction but by their prayers and intercession with God.

326. Are the faithful obliged to help the souls in purgatory?

Yes, the faithful are obliged to help the souls in purgatory. It is at once a duty of justice and of charity. It is also a duty of personal interest since one day we may expect others to help us in the same way.

327. How do we know there is a purgatory?

In the Old Testament we are told that the Israelites prayed for the dead "that they might be released from their sin" (2 Maccabees 12:45). In the New Testament, Christ spoke of the sin of despair as not forgiven "either in this world or in the next" (Matthew 12:32), implying that certain faults are pardoned in the life to come. The Church's Tradition, expressed in her doctrine, explicitly teaches that there is a purgatory, that purgatory is temporary, and that the poor souls can be helped by the prayers and good works of the faithful, especially offering the Sacrifice of the Mass.

328. Can we invoke the souls in purgatory?

Yes, we can invoke the souls in purgatory and are encouraged to ask them with the confidence of being heard. They understand our needs and are grateful for the prayers and sacrifices we offer on their behalf.

329. Can the souls in purgatory pray and obtain blessings for those on earth?

It is certain that the souls in purgatory can pray and obtain blessings for those on earth, as they are united with the Pilgrim Church in the communion of saints.

Eighth Article: "I believe in the Holy Spirit"

The Holy Spirit in the Trinity and His Mission in the World

330. What does the eighth article of the Apostles' Creed teach us?

This article teaches us that there is a Holy Spirit who was sent by Christ to sanctify the human race.

331. Who is the Holy Spirit?

The Holy Spirit is the third Person of the Blessed Trinity, true God with the Father and the Son. He proceeds in an eternal procession from the Father and the Son.

332. Is the Holy Spirit equal to the Father and the Son?

Yes, the Holy Spirit is equal, as God, to the Father and the Son. Together with the Father and the Son, he is eternal and almighty, Creator of heaven and earth and, like the Father and the Son, he is infinite in wisdom and power and majesty. In the New Testament, the name "Holy Spirit" and "God" are used alternately (cf. Acts 5:3–4; cf. 1 Corinthians 3:16). In the formula of baptism given by Christ, the Holy Spirit is made equal to the Father and the Son who are truly God (cf. Matthew 28:19).

333. When did Christ promise to send the Holy Spirit?

He promised to send the Holy Spirit many times during his visible stay on earth but especially at the Last Supper and just before his Ascension. At the Last Supper he declared, "When the Advocate comes, whom I shall send to you from the Father, the

Spirit of truth who issues from the Father, he will be my witness" (John 15:26). Shortly before his Ascension, Christ told the disciples, and through them told us, "You will receive power when the Holy Spirit comes on you, and then you will be my witnesses not only in Jerusalem but throughout Judaea and Samaria, and indeed to the ends of the earth" (Acts 1:8).

334. What, then, is the role of the Holy Spirit in our lives?

The role of the Holy Spirit in our lives is to sanctify us, as the very name "Holy" implies.

335. How does the Holy Spirit sanctify us?

The Holy Spirit sanctifies us by his presence in the souls of the just. This is the uncreated Grace of God. He also sanctifies us by enlightening our minds to know God by faith, and thus we are united with the mind of God. He finally sanctifies us by enabling us to do the will of God, and thus we are united with the Heart of God. This sharing in God's Being, Wisdom, and Love is our sanctification.

336. What happened on Pentecost Sunday?

On Pentecost Sunday the Holy Spirit came down on the apostles.

337. How did the Holy Spirit come down upon the apostles?

The Holy Spirit came upon the apostles in the form of fiery tongues. This showed they were receiving the light necessary to accept all that Jesus had told them during his visible stay on earth, and the warmth of divine love needed to live up to Christ's expectations of his followers. Moreover, they were inspired with zeal to share this faith and charity with others, as Christ had commanded them to do (cf. Acts 2:3–4).

338. How is the Holy Spirit related to the Church?

The Holy Spirit is related to the Church as her source of life. Those who are baptized and believe in Christ are the Church's members and therefore her visible body; the Holy Spirit, who is the Spirit of Christ, is the Church's vital principle, that is, he gives the Church her very life and, therefore, her invisible soul. Speaking of the Holy Spirit, Christ told the disciples, "He will glorify me, since all he tells you will be taken from what is mine.

Everything the Father has is mine; that is why I said: All he tells you will be taken from what is mine" (John 16:14–15).

339. How should we practice devotion to the Holy Spirit?

We should practice devotion to the Holy Spirit by our conscious awareness of his presence in our souls through sanctifying grace; invoke his aid by asking him to enlighten our minds and strengthen our wills; by fidelity to the illuminations of his grace in recognizing the will of God and our loyalty to his inspirations by responding immediately to what he wants us to do.

340. Why should we practice devotion to the Holy Spirit?

We should practice devotion to the Holy Spirit because he is God. He is therefore equally worthy of adoration as are the Father and the Son. But to the Holy Spirit are specially attributed all blessings of the supernatural life, beginning with the Incarnation and continuing through the graces he gives us on the way to heaven. He is therefore the expression of God's love, whom we should love with all our heart in return.

Ninth Article: "The Holy Catholic Church; the communion of saints"

1. Mystical Body of Christ

341. What does the ninth article of the Apostles' Creed teach us?

The ninth article of the Apostles' Creed teaches us that there exists a Catholic Church which may also be called the communion of saints.

342. What is the Catholic Church?

The Catholic Church is a society of all who have been baptized, profess the faith of Christ, and are governed by their bishops under one visible head, the bishop of Rome.

343. What do we mean by the Church?

By the Church we mean all those who, in faith, look upon

Jesus Christ as the Author of Salvation and the goal of human destiny. By the Church we can also mean the particular church of one city or locality. Moreover, the word "church" is used to refer to the building or sacred edifice where the people gather to worship God.

344. Who founded the Catholic Church?

Jesus Christ himself founded the Catholic Church.

345. When did the Church come into being?

The Church first came into being when Christ expired on the Cross. He prepared the founding of the Church during his public ministry, and he established the Church as a visible society when he sent his Spirit on the apostles on Pentecost Sunday.

346. How did Christ actually bring the Church into existence?

Christ actually brought the Church into existence by his death on Calvary, by which he won the graces that, through the Church, would be communicated to all mankind.

347. How did Christ proclaim the Church?

Christ proclaimed the Church by pouring out on his apostles the Spirit promised by the Father. Hence the Church, endowed with the gifts of charity, humility, and self-denial, receives the mission of proclaiming and establishing among all peoples the kingdom of Christ and of God. The Church on earth is the seed and the beginning of the kingdom of heaven.

348. What is the Mystical Body of Christ?

The Mystical Body of Christ is the whole Christ, head and members, now existing as the Church militant on earth, the Church suffering in purgatory, and the Church triumphant in heaven.

349. How is the Mystical Body a mystery?

The Mystical Body is a mystery because we cannot comprehend it by reason but believe in its existence and activity only by faith. It is also a mystery because it is the great sacrament, visibly instituted by Christ, through which he confers the invisible blessings of his grace on all of mankind.

350. How is the Mystical Body a body?

The Mystical Body is a body because it is sensibly perceptible in its visible head, the vicar of Christ; in its members, by their external profession of one faith; in its Mass and the sacraments, by which grace is conferred; and in its doctrines and precepts, which are manifest to the faithful by the teaching of the hierarchy.

351. What is the role of Christ in the Mystical Body?

Christ now fulfills the role of the invisible head of the Mystical Body and fills the whole of it with the riches of his glory.

352. What is the Church militant?

The Church militant is the Catholic Church on earth. She is called militant because her members must engage in struggle with the world, the flesh, and the devil in order to win their heavenly reward.

353. What is the Church suffering?

The Church suffering is the society of the souls in purgatory who have merited heaven but must still expiate the temporal punishment due to their sins before they enter into glory.

354. What is the Church triumphant?

The Church triumphant is the society of the saints in heaven who have successfully overcome temptations and trials during their mortal lives. She is called triumphant because, like Christ, her members have won the victory over sin.

2. Marks of the True Church

355. How can the Catholic Church be recognized as the true Church?

The Catholic Church can be recognized as the true Church by certain distinctive marks. We believe in the one, holy, Catholic, and apostolic Church.

356. What is meant by saying the Church is one?

When we say that the Church is one we mean that there are two forms of unity in the Church: the Unity of Faith and the Unity of Communion.

357. What is meant by Unity of Faith?

By the Unity of Faith we mean that those who belong to the Church believe the same faith proposed to them by the Church.

358. What is meant by Unity of Communion?

By the Unity of Communion we mean that the faithful are submissive to the authority of the bishops under the Roman pontiff. It also describes the mutual bond among the members themselves because they are joined together socially in sharing the same sacraments and forms of worship as channels of divine grace.

359. How many Churches are there?

There is only one Church established by Christ: not only one, but uniquely one. We believe, "There is one Body, one Spirit, just as you were all called into one and the same hope when you were called. There is one Lord, one faith, one baptism" (Ephesians 4:4–5).

360. What about the many "Churches" in Christianity today?

The Catholic Church believes she is joined in many ways to the baptized in other "Churches" who are honored by the name of Christian. These other Christian bodies do not possess the marks of the one true Church in their fullness. They have these qualities of the true Church in greater or less degree. Their members therefore enjoy more or less of the blessings which are available in their fulness only in the one true Church, founded by Christ, whose visible head on earth is the Roman pontiff.

361. Where is the Church of Christ?

The Church of Christ can be found in its fullness in the Catholic Church, which is governed by the successor of St. Peter and by the bishops in communion with him.

362. How is the fullness of the Church of Christ found in the Catholic Church?

The fullness of the Church of Christ is found in the Catholic Church because she possesses the whole of Christ's heritage. The revelation he gave, the sacraments he instituted, and the authority he established on earth, all fully reside in the Catholic Church, of which the bishop of Rome is the visible head.

363. Who is the Roman pontiff?

The Roman pontiff is the vicar of Christ, the successor of St. Peter and the visible head of the Church.

364. Under Christ, does the pope have supreme authority over the whole Church on earth?

Yes, under Christ, the pope has supreme authority over the whole Church on earth. He is the pastor of all the faithful to ensure the common good of the universal Church, and the good of the individual churches. He has supreme power over all the faithful and all the churches in everything pertaining to faith, morals, and divine worship. Christ promised St. Peter, "I will give you the keys of the kingdom of heaven" (Matthew 16:19). This promise was made, through Peter, to all his successors as bishops of Rome.

365. How is the Church holy?

The Church is holy by reason of her Founder and by the means she provides for the sanctification of the faithful.

366. Are the means the Church provides to become holy open to all?

Yes, the means that the Church provides for the faithful to become holy are open to all, regardless of their rank or status; in fact, they are available to all mankind.

367. What is heresy?

Heresy is the willful doubt or denial of any truth which God has revealed, such as the physical presence of Christ in the Holy Eucharist, or the authority of the pope as successor of St. Peter.

368. What is schism?

Schism is the sinful refusal to submit to the Roman pontiff or to associate with the faithful who are subject to him.

369. What is apostasy?

Apostasy is the total rejection of the Christian faith, as when a former Catholic denies everything which the Church teaches has been revealed by God.

370. Are those guilty of heresy, schism, or apostasy totally severed from the Church?

No, those guilty of heresy, schism, or apostasy are not severed from the bond of their baptismal character. But they are separated from the visible part of the Church, which includes the right to receive the sacraments, until they repent.

371. Do other grave sins separate persons from the body of the Church?

No, other grave sins do not separate persons from the body of the Church, but the sinful condition deprives them of the life of grace in the soul, and if they should die in this state, they will not be saved. They remain members of the Church, although sinful members, because of their baptismal character.

372. Why is the Church called Catholic?

The Church is called Catholic because she is universal.

373. In what sense is the Church universal?

The Church is universal because Christ wants everyone to belong. Rich and poor, the learned and unlearned are welcome. No people or culture are to be excluded from what the Savior instituted to be the universal sacrament of salvation. Christ commanded his followers to "Go, therefore, make disciples of all the nations" (Matthew 28:19).

374. What is the missionary nature of the Church?

The Church's missionary nature is her quality of propagating the Gospel to every land and people. It is the Church's catholicity in action.

375. Why is the Catholic Church apostolic?

The Church is apostolic because her origin goes back to Christ's choice and ordination of the apostles; her doctrine has remained faithful to the teaching of the apostles; the pope and bishops derive their authority in direct succession from Peter and the other apostles. It is especially this apostolic succession in unbroken line over the centuries that witnesses to the oneness of the Catholic Church today with the Church originally founded by Christ on the apostles. "You are part of a building that has the apostles and prophets for its foundations, and Christ Jesus himself for its main cornerstone" (Ephesians 2:20).

376. Who were the apostles?

The apostles were the twelve men whom Christ called (vocation) in order to send them (mission) to proclaim his Gospel to the whole world. He said to them: "Go out to the whole world; proclaim the Good News to all creation" (Mark 16:15).

377. What does the word "apostle" mean?

The word "apostle" means one who is sent. An apostle is an envoy or messenger of God.

378. Name the original twelve apostles.

The original twelve apostles were Simon Peter, Andrew (brother of Simon Peter), James the Greater (son of Zebedee), John the Evangelist, Philip of Bethsaida, James the Less (son of Alphaeus), Thomas (the twin), Matthew the Evangelist (formerly Levi), Judas Iscariot (who betrayed Christ), Bartholomew (Nathaniel), Thaddaeus (Jude), and Simon the Canaanean. After Christ's Ascension, Matthias was chosen to replace Judas Iscariot.

379. Why did Christ want the apostles to exercise their office only under the authority of St. Peter?

In this way Christ wished to maintain the unity of his Church and union with himself. He wanted his members to be united under his visible representative on earth.

380. But is not Christ himself the head of the Church?

Christ is indeed the eternal and divine invisible head of the Church. But the successor of Peter is the visible head, under Christ and empowered by his grace to govern the Church on earth as a visible society.

381. Does the Catholic Church therefore have two heads?

The Church does not have two heads, as though one were independent of the other. Since the Church militant is composed of visible members, who must use visible means of salvation, they need a visible head to teach them what to believe, how to worship, and how to observe the commandments which Christ told the apostles they were to proclaim to all nations. Christ in his wisdom provided a visible bond of unity for the Church with whom he promised to remain until the end of time.

382. How do we know that Christ wanted Peter to be the supreme head of the Church on earth?

Everything the Savior said and did confirms this fact. Christ promised Peter he would make him the rock on which he would build the Church (cf. Matthew 16:18). After the Resurrection, Christ told Peter to feed his lambs and his sheep, thus carrying into effect the promise he had earlier made (cf. John 21:15–17). Christ foretold that he would strengthen the faith of Peter so that Peter in turn might strengthen the faith of his brethren among the apostles (cf. Luke 22:32). Then after Christ's Ascension, Peter exercised the office of visible head of the Church, from Pentecost Sunday when he preached the first sermon, later worked the first miracle, and directed the work of evangelization as shown in the two letters of Peter that have come down to us from apostolic times.

383. Was the papal supremacy of the Church on earth to cease after the death of St. Peter?

No, the papal supremacy of the Church on earth was to continue after the death of St. Peter in his successors until the end of the world. Otherwise the Church which Christ founded would have become something else. Moreover, we know from history that the bishops of Rome have come, from the first centuries, to be recognized by all believing Catholics as successors of Peter and vicars of Christ, with Christ's delegated authority to govern the people of God.

384. How did the apostles hand on their powers to others?

The apostles handed on their powers to others by the laying on of hands.

385. Why did they hand on their apostolic powers to others?

The apostles handed on their powers to others because Christ wanted his Church to continue always under the guidance of the bishops as successors of the apostles, under the bishop of Rome, the successor of St. Peter.

386. Who are the successors of the apostles?

The successors of the apostles are the bishops who are validly consecrated and are in communion with the visible head of the

Church, the bishop of Rome. They are the bishops of the Roman Catholic Church.

387. What is a bishop?

A bishop is a successor of the apostles, who has received the fullness of Christ's priesthood. His most distinctive power is to ordain priests and other bishops.

388. Are all successors of the apostles in communion with the bishop of Rome?

All true successors of the apostles are in communion with the bishop of Rome. Separated from him they can be validly consecrated bishops, but they do not share in the unique powers of the apostolic succession, that is, they do not have the light promised by Christ to teach the faithful, nor the right to command obedience of Christ's members unless they are united with the pope as successor of St. Peter.

389. Is the pope alone to govern the Catholic Church?

Along with the pope the bishops are also divinely appointed to govern the Church of God. But they can do so legitimately and effectively only with and under the pope as the visible head of the Church.

390. How does the authority of the pope differ from that of the bishops?

The authority of the pope is universal, whereas the authority of bishops is local. Just as the pope is pastor and head of the whole Church, so bishops who are ordinaries are pastors and heads of their respective dioceses. But while the pope possesses authority over all the faithful, bishops exercise theirs only within the limits of their respective dioceses.

391. How do bishops govern in the Catholic Church?

Bishops govern in the Catholic Church in two ways: they govern the dioceses assigned to them by the pope and have authority from God to do so. They also share in the government of the universal Church ordinarily by the advice and assistance they give the pope and their fellow bishops and extraordinarily when they meet as a group in national conferences, international synods, or ecumenical councils. But in every case their deliberations and

even decisions must be ratified by the pope, at least implicitly, to be binding on the consciences of the faithful.

392. What is this sharing in the government of the universal Church called?

This sharing by the bishops in the government of the universal Church is a form of collegiality.

393. What is collegiality?

Collegiality is the collective existence of the bishops as an episcopal community, succeeding the community of the apostles gathered together by Christ. Collegiality is also the cooperative activity of the bishops working together for the common good of the Catholic Church. Both as a community of bishops and as a cooperative among bishops, collegiality depends absolutely for its existence and divine assistance on papal primacy. Without the pope as their primate, there is no episcopal collegiality.

394. What is an ecumenical council?

An ecumenical council is a general assembly of all the bishops of the Church, gathered together under the authority of the pope to deliberate and decide on matters of faith, worship, and morals for the Catholic Church.

395. What is a conference of bishops?

A conference of bishops is an association of the bishops of a country or region, decreed by the Second Vatican Council, to cooperate for the spiritual welfare of the faithful in their collective territory. The ecclesiastical decisions of a conference of bishops are subject to the authority and approval of the bishop of Rome.

396. What is a synod of bishops?

A synod of bishops is the periodic meeting of chosen representatives from the national conferences of bishops in the Church. The synod meets in Rome under the guidance and authority of the pope. It is a consultative body to advise its own membership and the pope on whatever pertains to faith and morals in the Catholic Church.

397. Do bishops differ in their possession of authority?

Yes, bishops differ in their Church authority, depending on whether they are in charge of a diocese. If they have charge of a

diocese, they are called ordinaries; otherwise they are titular bishops.

398. What is the authority of the ordinary of a diocese?

The bishop who is ordinary of a diocese has the authority to teach and govern the people under his jurisdiction.

399. What is a diocese?

A diocese is a portion of the people of God which is entrusted to a bishop to be cared for with the assistance of his priests. Loyal to their bishop and united with him under the Gospel and through the Eucharist, the people of a diocese form a particular church. It is here that the one, holy, catholic, and apostolic Church of Christ is really present and active.

400. What is the authority of a titular bishop?

The authority of a titular bishop depends on his office in the Church. If he is an auxiliary bishop, this authority is likewise determined either by the pope, or by the bishop or bishops under whose jurisdiction he serves the needs of the faithful. He is called titular bishop only because to his name is attached the name of a diocese, now extinct, that is said to be a titular see.

3. Sacrament of Salvation

401. Why did Christ establish the Church?

Christ established the Church as a universal sacrament of salvation.

402. How is the Church the universal sacrament of salvation?

The Church is the universal sacrament of salvation as the divinely instituted means of conferring grace on all the members of the human family.

403. How does the Church communicate divine grace to mankind?

The Church communicates grace to mankind by her teaching of revealed truth, her celebration of Mass and administration of the sacraments, her prayers and the practice of virtue by her

members, and her guidance and government of the faithful according to the will of God.

404. Who are the principal collaborators of the bishops?

The principal collaborators of the bishops are the priests in charge of parishes, according to the circumstances or nature of various localities.

405. What is a parish?

A parish is an established group of people under a pastor, who takes the place of the bishop. The parish represents the visible Church constituted throughout the world.

406. What is a pastor?

A pastor or parish priest is a fellow worker of the bishop, under whose authority he is entrusted with the care of the faithful who belong to his parochial territory.

407. Are only diocesan priests subject to the authority of the bishop?

No, priests belonging to religious orders or congregations are also subject to the authority of the local bishop in whatever pertains to the spiritual welfare of the diocese.

408. What relationship should exist between bishops and priests?

All priests, whether diocesan or religious, share with the bishop in the one priesthood of Christ and are therefore appointed as the prudent co-workers of the episcopal order.

409. How are priests to exercise their priestly office?

Priests are to exercise their priestly ministry in hierarchical union with the whole body of the Church. Pastoral charity urges them to act within this communion and by obedience to dedicate their lives in the service of God and their fellow Christians. They are to accept and carry out in the spirit of faith the commands and directives of the pope, their bishop, and other superiors. They are gladly to spend themselves in whatever office is entrusted to them. St. Peter wrote, "Be the shepherds of the flock of God that is entrusted to you: watch over it, not simply as a duty but gladly, because God wants it; not for sordid money, but because you are eager to do it. Never be a dictator over any group

that is put in your charge, but be an example that the whole flock can follow" (1 Peter 5:2–3).

410. What is the ecumenical movement?

The ecumenical movement is the effort toward reunion among the separated Churches of Christendom. Christ prayed for his followers, "May they all be one. Father, may they be one in us, as you are in me and I am in you" (John 17:21).

411. What is spiritual ecumenism?

Spiritual ecumenism is the practice of prayer and holiness of life, to merit divine grace for all Christians to once again be united as one flock under one shepherd.

412. Is the Church necessary for salvation?

Yes, the Church is necessary for salvation. Christ himself declared that no one can be saved except through faith and baptism. He thereby affirmed the necessity of the Church, to which he entrusted the fullness of revelation and into which a person enters, as through a door, in the sacrament of baptism. Christ's words on this are clear, "He who believes and is baptized will be saved; he who does not believe will be condemned" (Mark 16:16).

413. For whom is there no salvation outside the Church?

There is no salvation for those who, though incorporated in the Church by baptism, fail to persevere in sanctifying grace and die in the state of mortal sin. Those also are not saved who realize what they are doing but refuse to be baptized and accept the Church's means of salvation.

414. Who are actually incorporated into the Church?

Those who have been baptized by water in the name of the Holy Trinity are actually incorporated into the Church.

415. Do baptized non-Catholics belong to the Catholic Church?

Yes, everyone who is baptized by water and in the name of the Trinity is a member of the Catholic Church. But only those enjoy full membership who profess the same Catholic faith, receive the same sacraments, and profess allegiance to the same bishops, as successors of the apostles, under the sovereign pontiff, the bishop of Rome.

416. What is the Catholic attitude toward Christians separated from Rome?

The Catholic attitude toward Christians separated from Rome is to bring them to a complete sharing in the mystery of Christ.

417. What is the Catholic attitude toward non-Christians?

The Catholic attitude toward non-Christians is to bring them the true faith, the blessings of baptism and the other sacraments, and to incorporate them in the Mystical Body of Christ.

418. How can non-Christians be saved?

Non-Christians can be saved through the Church according to their faith in whatever historical revelation they come to know and by their cooperation with the internal graces of the Holy Spirit which they receive.

4. Teaching Authority and Infallibility

419. What is the Church's magisterium?

The Church's magisterium is her universal teaching authority, her possession of light from God and therefore the divine right to teach all the faithful the truths of salvation.

420. How is the Church's magisterium exercised?

The Church's magisterium is exercised in an ordinary or extraordinary way.

421. What is the Church's ordinary magisterium?

The Church's ordinary magisterium is her day-by-day and worldwide teaching of faith and morals.

422. What is the Church's extraordinary magisterium?

The Church's extraordinary magisterium is the special exercise of her teaching authority through an ecumenical council or through occasional solemn declarations of the holy father.

423. Is the Church's magisterium infallible?

Yes, the Church's magisterium, which is vested exclusively in the successors of Peter and the other apostles, is infallible.

424. Who, then, has the gift of infallibility in teaching?

The pope and the community of bishops under the pope possess the gift of infallibility in teaching.

425. What is infallibility?

Infallibility is immunity from error, excluding not only its existence but even its possibility.

426. When is the pope infallible?

The pope is infallible when he acts as the father and ruler of all the faithful. He enjoys the unique grace which protects him from error when he actually and specifically exercises the office of teacher of the universal Church and supreme judge in matters of faith and morals. What Christ promised to Peter, he gives to all of Peter's successors, "I will give you the keys of the kingdom of heaven: whatever you bind on earth shall be considered bound in heaven" (Matthew 16:19).

427. How does infallibility differ from impeccability?

Infallibility differs from impeccability in that infallibility is the impossibility either of deceiving or being deceived in teaching others; impeccability is the impossibility of offending God by committing sin. The pope is infallible but not impeccable.

428. Who is absolutely infallible?

Only God is absolutely infallible. But he deigned to bestow on the Church a shared infallibility.

429. How is the pope infallible?

The pope is infallible in virtue of the special promise of Christ always to protect his Church from error. Although assisted by this grace, he is bound by his office to take suitable means for ascertaining the truth before proclaiming it.

430. What is the scope of papal infallibility?

Papal infallibility is to preserve the flock of Christ from the poison of error. It covers two forms of teaching, i.e., of faith and morals. It may be a doctrine that is simply to be accepted by the mind as true, or a doctrine that is also to be acted upon by the will as good. It may be something revealed by God, like the mystery of the Immaculate Conception; or something knowable by reason, like the sinfulness of abortion or contraception.

431. Are individual bishops infallible?

Bishops individually or a group of bishops do not enjoy the privilege of personal infallibility. But there are circumstances when they proclaim infallibly the doctrine of Christ.

432. When are bishops infallible?

Bishops are infallible when, united with the pope, as authorized teachers on faith and morals they agree on one position to be held as definitive.

433. How do we know the Church is infallible?

We know the Church is infallible because Christ promised to remain with her, even to the end of time (Matthew 28:20). If the Church could make a mistake in matters of faith or morals and oblige her members to obey what was untrue, Christ's promise would have failed.

434. How does the Church share in the divine infallibility?

The Church shares in the divine infallibility, but within three restricted limitations: in matters of faith and morals; when the whole people of God unhesitatingly hold a point of doctrine pertaining to these matters; and always dependent on the wise providence and anointing of the grace of the Holy Spirit, who leads the Church into all truth until the glorious coming of her Lord. Christ promised, "When the Spirit of truth comes he will lead you to the complete truth" (John 16:13). We may call this the Church's possession of infallible truth, as distinct from the pope's and bishops' declaration of infallible truth.

435. Must the pope consult the "whole people of God" before making a doctrinal proclamation?

No, the pope does not have to consult either the whole or any part of the people of God before making a doctrinal proclamation. He may do so if he wishes. But if he does not consult and then teaches the universal Church as vicar of Christ, his doctrine is nevertheless certainly true and binding in conscience on all the faithful.

436. How are the faithful infallible in their community of belief?

The faithful are infallible in their community of belief in that the whole body of the faithful who have an anointing that comes from the Holy Spirit cannot err in matters of belief. This is a property which belongs not to any one of the faithful but to the people as a whole. They make this manifest by a supernatural discernment of faith when, from bishops to the most obscure layman, they show their universal agreement in matters of faith and morals.

5. Communion of Saints

437. What is the communion of saints?

The unity and cooperation of the members of the Church on earth with those in heaven and in purgatory is the communion of saints. They are united in forming one Mystical Body. And they cooperate by sharing their merits and prayers with one another, for the greater glory of God and the upbuilding of Christ's Body which is his Church.

438. How are the members in the communion of saints united?

The members of the communion of saints are united in having one head who is Jesus Christ and in sharing one Holy Spirit who is the soul of the Mystical Body. In the words of St. Paul, "Just as each of our bodies has several parts and each part has a separate function, so all of us, in union with Christ, form one body, and as parts of it we belong to each other" (Romans 12:4–5).

439. Why are the members of the Mystical Body said to be saints?

The members of the Mystical Body are said to be saints because, in the words of St. Paul, "What God wants is for you all to be holy" (1 Thessalonians 4:3). We are already sanctified in baptism and, by God's grace, are to grow in sanctity. Those in purgatory are in God's friendship, and the souls in heaven have reached their destiny.

440. Are all members of the communion of saints equally holy?

No, not all members of the communion of saints are equally holy. Some are specially honored as saints in the Catholic Church.

441. Whom does the Church honor as saints?

Saints are persons who, in their life on earth, practiced extraordinary virtue that we are bidden to imitate. They now enjoy the beatific vision in heaven and are powerful intercessors for us before the throne of God.

442. What is beatification?

Beatification is the Church's declaration that a person who practiced heroic virtue may be venerated locally or by a limited number of people.

443. What is canonization?

Canonization is the solemn declaration by the pope that the faithful should universally invoke a person as a saint. The practice of canonization goes back to the late twelfth century. Before then, the Church approved the invocation of certain people as saints but without the now extensive process of canonization.

444. What does it mean that a person is declared venerable or a servant of God?

A venerable or servant of God is one whom the Church officially declares to have practiced heroic virtue. This is the first step in the process of canonization, and involves extensive investigation through witnesses and a complete examination of the person's writings.

445. Who are the biblical saints?

Biblical saints are the heroic men and women in the Bible who died before the end of the Apostolic Age, for example, our Lady, St. Joseph, and the apostles.

446. Who are the traditional saints?

Traditional saints are the martyrs, confessors, virgins, religious, and others who lived and died after the Apostolic Age but whom the Church has not officially canonized. Thus Ignatius of Antioch, Justin the Martyr, Agnes, Cecilia, Augustine, Benedict, Patrick, Leo I, Gregory I, and many others, venerated as saints although they have never been formally raised to the honors of the altar.

447. Who are the ecclesiastical saints?

Ecclesiastical saints are those whom the Church has canonized through what is called a process of canonization.

6. Church and State

448. What should be the relationship of Church and State?

The Church and State differ in origin in that the Church was founded by a free act of God, while the State has its origin from man's natural needs and tendencies. They differ in purpose in that the Church aims to lead all men to eternal salvation, while the State exists to procure the temporal prosperity of its citizens. The Church's authority is above the State's as faith is above reason, and man's spiritual needs are above those of space and time. The relationship between the two should be one of harmony, for each is to recognize the rights of the other for the personal and social welfare of mankind.

449. May the State totally separate itself from the Church?

No, the State may not totally separate itself from the Church because the State cannot be opposed to the laws of God or the rule of Christ.

450. What are the duties of citizenship in the New Testament?

According to the New Testament, citizens are to accept the established forms of government and submit to those in authority since all *legitimate* government comes from God.

451. Must a Christian always obey the State?

No, a Christian may not obey the State in any civil law that his conscience, enlightened by faith, tells him is contrary to the law of God. Thus, abortion, contraception, and remarriage after a mere civil divorce, although legalized by the State, are contrary to the divine law and not binding in conscience.

452. What kinds of freedom does the Church claim?

On the social level, the Church claims her right to exist and to operate according to the will of her Founder. She therefore claims the right to corporate existence as a visible society established by

Christ, and to the exercise of her ministry among the faithful and from the faithful to the rest of mankind. On the personal level, the Church claims for her members as individuals the right to be Catholics, to profess their faith, and to exercise their religious duties without hindrance or opposition from civil authorities.

453. Does everyone have a right to religious freedom?

Yes, everyone has the right to religious freedom. This means that no one may be coerced in any way to act against his religious convictions, nor be prevented from acting on these convictions, whether alone or in association with others.

454. What is the basis for religious freedom?

The very nature of an individual as a person with duties to God is the basis for religious freedom. Consequently, the right to this freedom continues even in those who do not live up to their obligation of seeking the truth or living up to what they know is God's will.

455. Are there any limitations to the exercise of religious freedom?

There can be no limitations to the exercise of religious freedom as long as the just requirements of public order are observed.

456. Who are the primary educators of children?

Parents are the primary educators of children. Since they gave life to their children, they are, therefore, seriously bound to educate their offspring in all matters, but especially in religious belief and moral conduct.

457. What are the Church's rights in education?

The Church's rights in education are above the State, since the Church was established by Christ to teach all nations the way of salvation.

458. What are the State's rights in education?

The rights of the State in education are not above the rights of the parents or the Church. Rather, the State has the duty to ensure that all its citizens are adequately trained in such knowledge and skills as they need for the proper exercise of their civil rights and duties.

Tenth Article: "The forgiveness of sin"

The Mercy of God in the World Today

459. What does the tenth article of the Apostles' Creed teach us?

This article teaches us that God is merciful and therefore forgives sinners who are truly repentant. It further teaches us that God became man to save us from our sins.

460. What sins can be forgiven?

God forgives all sins without exception, provided we are truly repentant.

461. What does the Catholic Church believe about the forgiveness of sins?

She believes it is God's will that no one is forgiven except through the merits of Jesus Christ, and that these merits are uniquely channeled through the Church he founded. Consequently, even as the Church is the universal sacrament of salvation, she is also the universal sacrament of reconciliation.

462. How does the Church communicate the merits of Christ's mercy to sinners?

The Church communicates Christ's mercy to sinners through the Mass and the sacraments, and all the prayers and good works of the faithful.

463. What is the Church's role in the reconciliation of sinners to God?

The Church reconciles sinners to God mainly by her exercise of God's mercy, through the sacraments which he instituted.

Eleventh Article: "The resurrection of the body"

Death and Final Resurrection

464. What does the eleventh article of the Apostles' Creed teach us?

This article directly teaches us that our bodies are destined to rise from the grave on the Last Day, but it also teaches that we shall all die and after death will be judged on our eternal destiny.

465. Why must every human being die?

We must all die because we have all sinned in Adam. St. Paul tells us, "Sin entered the world through one man, and through sin death" (Romans 5:12).

466. What is death?

Death is the separation of body and soul for a period of time.

467. What is the meaning of death?

The meaning of death is that we do not really die but merely change our earthly dwelling for a heavenly one. "There is no eternal city for us in this life but we look for one in the life to come" (Hebrews 13:14).

468. Why should we not fear death?

We should not fear death because it ends our earthly exile and admits our souls into that eternal home which Christ has gone ahead to prepare for us. As Christ told Martha, who was grieving over the death of her brother Lazarus, "Whoever lives and believes in me will never die. Do you believe this?" (John 11:26).

469. Why is our present life called a "time of probation"?

Our present life is called a "time of probation" because we are now being tried in our loyalty to God. If we use our freedom to serve God faithfully in this life, we shall be rewarded in the life to come. Christ warned us always to be ready, "You too must stand ready, because the Son of Man is coming at an hour you do not expect" (Luke 12:40).

470. Why has God hidden from us the time of our death?

In this way God wants us to be better prepared for his coming. It also inspires us with a healthy fear to serve God more faithfully. Moreover, not knowing when we shall die enables us to resign ourselves to God's will many times before he finally calls us into eternity.

471. What happens immediately after death?

Immediately after death we shall be judged on our final destiny. This is called the individual or particular judgment.

472. How long will the body remain in the earth?

The body will remain in the earth until the day of final or general judgment. Speaking of himself, Christ foretold that "the hour is coming when the dead will leave their graves at the sound of his voice: those who did good will rise again to life; and those who did evil, to condemnation" (John 5:28–29).

473. How can dead bodies rise to life again?

God who is almighty can as easily raise our dead bodies back to life as he once made them out of nothing. This is the great lesson of Christ's Resurrection from the dead. It is also the reason why, before he raised Lazarus from the grave, he declared, "I am the resurrection. If anyone believes in me, even though he dies, he will live" (John 11:25).

474. Why will our bodies rise from the dead?

They will rise from the dead in order to share with our souls in the eternal reward we merited during our stay on earth. Our final resurrection will also complete the victory of Christ over death which he began on Easter Sunday. With him we shall be able to say, "Death is swallowed up in victory. Death, where is your victory? Death, where is your sting?" (1 Corinthians 15:54–55).

475. What are the qualities of the risen body?

The qualities of the risen body are: impassibility, or immunity from death and pain; subtility, or freedom from restraint by matter; agility, or obedience to spirit with relation to movement and space; and clarity, or extraordinary beauty of the soul manifested in the body.

476. Are these qualities similar to those enjoyed by the risen Christ?

Yes, the qualities of the risen body are similar to those enjoyed by Christ after his resurrection. He can no longer suffer or die; he entered the upper room in Jerusalem through closed doors; he ascended into heaven in body at the command of his will; and he is the most beautiful object of bodily vision, now beheld by the angels and saints.

477. Are we still the same persons after the resurrection?

Yes, although we are greatly changed for the better in our glorified state, we shall remain essentially the same after the resurrection. We retain our own personal identity.

Twelfth Article: "And life everlasting. Amen."

Heaven and the Four Last Things

478. What does the twelfth article of the Apostles' Creed teach us?

This article teaches us that although we are born in time we are meant to live for all eternity.

479. Is every human being destined to live eternally?

Yes, every human being is destined to live always, either in the possession or the loss of God forever.

480. Which part of our being is naturally immortal?

Our souls are naturally immortal. Because they are spiritual beings they cannot naturally die. They could only be annihilated by God, if he wished to reduce them to the nothingness from which they came. But faith assures us that God will not do this. Our bodies, on the other hand, are naturally mortal. They will die by being separated from our souls, to be reunited with these bodies on the Last Day.

481. Is life everlasting for everyone?

Yes, life everlasting is for everyone. All human beings will live on forever, in their souls, which cannot die, and in their bodies which will rise on the Day of Judgment.

482. Will the good and the wicked have the same life everlasting?

No, the good will enter, as Christ promised, into eternal happiness, and the wicked into everlasting pain.

483. What is heaven?

Heaven is the place and condition of perfect supernatural happiness. This happiness consists mainly in the beatific vision of God and secondly in the knowledge, love, and enjoyment of creatures.

484. What is the beatific vision?

The beatific vision is a direct seeing of the Holy Trinity, with no creature standing between the soul and God. It is beatific because it will produce intense happiness, such as only God has a right to enjoy but that he shares with those who enter heaven because they had served him faithfully on earth. According to St. Paul, "We teach what scripture calls: the things that no eye has seen and no ear has heard, things beyond the mind of man, all that God has prepared for those who love him" (1 Corinthians 2:9).

485. Is there communication among the persons in heaven?

Yes, the angels and saints communicate with one another in heaven. Ties of blood and friendship begun on earth will somehow continue into eternity. We shall enjoy the company of Christ in his humanity, the blessed Virgin, and angels and saints in glory.

486. Who are in heaven?

Besides the angels, those now in heaven are the souls who entered eternity in the state of grace. They were either entirely free from temporal punishment due to sin when they died or, after death, were cleansed of this debt in purgatory.

487. What are the four last things awaiting every human being?

The four last things awaiting every human being are death, judgment, heaven, and hell.

488. Why are they called the four last things?

They are thus called because they are the last things in our lives at the end of time and the beginning of eternity. In the Church's official language they are called the first things (*novissima*) because they identify the beginning of life everlasting for every human being.

489. Why is it important often to think of the four last things?

It is important often to think of the four last things in order to keep us faithful in the service of God. As the Holy Spirit tells us, "In everything you do, remember your end, and you will never sin" (Ecclesiasticus 7:40).

490. Will the happiness of heaven differ after the Last Day?

The happiness of heaven will differ after the Last Day because then we shall have our glorified bodies. This means that we shall enjoy not only God and the angels but also bodily creatures, and not only in spirit but also with our bodily senses and emotions. As described by St. John in his vision of the heavenly kingdom, "I saw the holy city . . . The world of the past has gone" (Revelation 21:2–4).

491. How do we conclude the Apostles' Creed?

We conclude the Apostles' Creed with the word "Amen." This is an expression of religious acceptance of all that has preceded. It means that we firmly believe in all the articles of the Creed.

PART TWO

LIVING THE CHRISTIAN FAITH

I.
NORMS OF MORALITY

1. Human Responsibility

492. Is faith in what God revealed sufficient for salvation?

No, we must also keep his Commandments. As Christ himself told us, "If you wish to enter into life, keep the commandments" (Matthew 19:17).

493. How do we keep the Commandments of God?

We keep the Commandments of God by living a good moral life.

494. How do we live a good moral life?

We live a good moral life by doing the will of God.

495. How does God manifest his will to us?

God manifests his will to us by the natural law, which we know from reason, and by his revelation which we know on faith.

496. What do we call those actions by which we respond to the known will of God?

They are called human acts.

497. What are human acts?

Human acts are those we perform knowingly, willingly, and not through physical necessity, inadvertence, or mere natural instinct.

498. What are the acts we perform without reflection?

The acts we perform without reflection are called acts of man. Such acts are involuntary likes and dislikes, first impulses of feeling or passion, acts done during sleep or delirium or under the influence of drugs, drink, or bodily changes.

499. How is the moral quality of our human acts determined?

The moral quality of our human acts is determined from three sources: the object, the end or purpose, and the circumstances.

500. What is meant by the object of a human act?

The object of a human act is what we do. It is that with which an action is essentially concerned; thus an act of prayer is morally good; an act of blasphemy is morally bad.

501. What is the end or purpose of a human act?

The end or purpose of a human act is why we do it. This is the motive for which something is done. If the motive is sinful, the action is sinful.

502. What do we mean by the circumstances of a human act?

The circumstances of a human act are the conditions under which it is performed. They are the situations which may change the whole moral tone of human conduct. Who does something, in whose presence, when, where, and the way it is done—all these are called the circumstances and they deeply affect the morality of our conduct. For example, the misconduct of a public official gives greater scandal than that of a private individual, to speak unkindly of a person before a group of people is worse than before one person, and to practice charity toward an enemy is normally more virtuous than toward a friend.

503. What is a moral act?

A moral act is a human act. It is an action that is done freely and deliberately, and is therefore imputable to the person who does it.

504. What kind of moral acts are there?

Moral acts are either good or bad. An action is morally good when the object, circumstances, and purpose of what is done are all good. An act is morally bad when either the object, circumstances, or purpose of an act is bad.

505. What is a morally good action?

A morally good action is one that leads us to heaven, and a

morally bad action is one that leads us away from our eternal destiny.

506. Is not every act morally good, provided our intention or purpose is a good one?

No, to be morally good, not only the purpose but the action itself and its circumstances must also be good.

507. What are some human acts that are always morally bad?

Some human acts that are always morally bad are blasphemy, murder, and adultery.

508. What acts are morally indifferent?

Acts like walking, speaking, driving, or reading are morally indifferent because they may be directed to good or evil ends and become virtuous or sinful according to the purpose intended.

509. What is responsibility?

Responsibility is the duty that people assume for the actions they perform. They deserve to be praised or blamed, and rewarded or punished, depending on whether their conduct is morally good or morally bad.

510. What are the conditions for moral responsibility?

The conditions for moral responsibility are knowledge and freedom.

511. What is human freedom?

Human freedom is the ability to choose what we want even when there is no external constraint and the opposite is more appealing. This power of choice is the foundation of the moral order.

512. What are the factors that diminish responsibility?

The factors that diminish responsibility are ignorance, emotion or passion, fear, past habits, and external force or violence.

513. What is ignorance?

Ignorance is the absence of knowledge that should be present, especially about moral matters that ought to be known. If we are sinfully responsible for not knowing something, this is vincible ignorance; otherwise it is called invincible. Ignorance of God's law excuses a person only if there was no negligence about finding out what God has commanded and wants to be done, or what he forbids and wants us to avoid.

514. What are emotions?

Emotions are strong bodily reactions to stimuli. They interfere with clear thinking and free choice. When the feelings are aroused before there is chance for deliberation they lessen a person's guilt for what is done under emotional strain. But when the feelings are consciously fostered, as when someone nurses a grudge over an injury, this does not lessen but increases one's moral responsibility. A certain amount of control is necessary. "An open town, and without defenses: such is the man lacking self-control" (Proverbs 25:28).

515. What is fear?

Fear is a strong, instinctive response to a present or future danger. It has an enormous influence on human conduct.

516. What are the effects of fear?

Fear is seldom so great as to deprive a person of all responsibility for actions performed. Therefore, bad actions done through fear are normally culpable and good actions are normally meritorious. Liberty is diminished or sometimes even erased when, except for the fear, the action would not have been performed.

2. Divine and Human Law

517. What is law?

Law is a practical decision by which one who has authority over a people informs and commands them to do or avoid something for the common good of the society, and takes effective means to see that his command is obeyed.

518. What is the difference between precept and law?

Laws are permanent binding norms for a whole people. Precepts are specific commands given directly, not to a community, but to an individual.

519. Where do laws and precepts come from?

All valid laws and precepts finally come from God.

520. What is divine law?

Divine law comes directly from God. By this law he directs all creatures in all their activities. Divine law may be called eternal, natural, or revealed, depending on its particular form.

521. Who is subject to the divine law?

All who have the use of reason are subject to the divine law.

522. Are all laws derived from the divine law?

Yes, all laws are derived from the divine law, hence, another name for divine law is the eternal law.

523. What is meant by eternal law?

Eternal law is the divine reason which governs the whole universe. It is called eternal because it is conceived in the mind of God not in time but from all eternity. It is called law because it governs the activity of all creatures, whether rational or nonrational. It embraces both the physical and moral laws. The moral laws bind human wills to conform to the divine will. The eternal law manifests itself in both the natural law and the revealed law.

524. How does the eternal law manifest itself?

The eternal law manifests itself differently in nonrational and rational creatures. In nonrational creatures it becomes the physical law that is always and necessarily obeyed. In rational creatures, it becomes the moral law that human beings, because they are free, can either obey or disobey.

525. How do we come to know the moral law?

When we come to know the moral law naturally, this is the natural law; when we know it supernaturally, this is revealed law.

526. What is the natural law?

The natural law is the law by which man comes to know the eternal law from created nature through the light of his native reason.

527. Where does the natural law manifest itself?

Natural law manifests itself to each person's conscience in the world of natural creation. It is knowable by the light of man's reason. Thus we know that lying is wrong because it tends to break down the mutual confidence between human beings, and that obedience to just authority is good because otherwise society would be impossible. "For instance, pagans who never heard of the Law but are led by reason to do what the Law commands, may not actually 'possess' the Law, but they can be said to 'be' the Law. They can point to the substance of the Law engraved on their hearts—they can call a witness, that is, their own conscience" (Romans 2:14–15).

528. What are the marks of the natural law?

Natural law is universal because it applies to all human beings. Thus we are all obliged to be honest and chaste. It is immutable because it is not subject to basic change. So we cannot say that adultery might have been wrong in former days but is now permissible; or the murder of unborn children is allowed where legalized by the State. It is absolute because it must be observed at all costs; so that I may not lie, no matter how embarrassing I may find it to tell the truth.

529. What is revealed law?

Revealed law is that by which man comes to know the eternal law through divine revelation. Revealed law spans the whole of God's special communication of his will, through the prophets in time past, and in our own time through his Son Jesus Christ. Among other revealed laws are the precept of baptism, the obligation to receive the sacraments of penance and the Eucharist, Christ's command to love our enemies, and his teaching about the indissolubility of Christian marriage.

530. What is human law?

Human law is the divine law expressed by human legislators.

531. How binding is human law?

Human law is binding insofar as it agrees with the eternal law of God. Thus all unjust laws passed by the State, like abortion or the prohibition to teach Christianity, are not binding.

532. What is ecclesiastical law?

Ecclesiastical law is an ordinance issued by legitimate authority in the Catholic Church. The legislators for the entire Church are the pope through the Roman Curia or an ecumenical council together with the pope. Bishops may also legislate for their respective dioceses.

533. What are civil laws?

Civil laws are those passed by the government in a political society. Civil laws that are just are morally binding in conscience as the Church's tradition since biblical times testifies. As St. Peter told the early Christians, "For the sake of the Lord, accept the authority of every social institution: the emperor, as the supreme authority, and the governors as commissioned by him to punish criminals and praise good citizenship. God wants you to be good citizens" (1 Peter 2:13–15).

534. What are penal laws?

Penal laws are those to which a penalty for a transgression is attached.

535. Is a person obliged to pay the penalty for a transgression?

Yes, a person is obliged to pay the penalty for the transgression of a just law. However, he is not obliged in conscience to pay the penalty unless he is first convicted of the transgression. Circumstances, however, may urge paying the penalty before actual conviction.

3. The Decalogue

536. What is the decalogue?

The decalogue is the Ten Commandments. It declares the ten principal duties we have toward God and one another.

537. What are the Ten Commandments?

The Ten Commandments are as follows:

1. I am Yahweh your God. You shall have no gods except me.
2. You shall not take the name of the Lord your God in vain.
3. Remember to keep holy the Lord's day.
4. Honor your father and your mother.
5. You shall not kill.
6. You shall not commit adultery.
7. You shall not steal.
8. You shall not bear false witness against your neighbor.
9. You shall not covet your neighbor's wife.
10. You shall not covet anything that belongs to your neighbor.
(Cf. Deuteronomy 5:5–21.)

538. Why are they called the Commandments of God?

They are called the Commandments of God because he gave them to us by a direct and positive revelation.

539. How did God reveal the Ten Commandments?

God revealed the Ten Commandments when he ordered Moses to gather together the people of Israel at the foot of Mount Sinai. There amid peals of thunder and flashes of lightning, Yahweh proclaimed the Ten Commandments (cf. Exodus 19:16; 20:18).

540. Are the Ten Commandments still binding under the New Law?

Yes, Jesus himself confirmed the Ten Commandments when he said: "Do not imagine that I have come to abolish the Law or the Prophets. I have come not to abolish but to complete them. I tell you solemnly, till heaven and earth disappear, not one dot, not one little stroke, shall disappear from the Law until its purpose is achieved" (Matthew 5:17–18). He brought the Commandments to perfection in the sermon on the Mount.

541. Is it necessary to keep the Commandments?

Yes, it is necessary to keep the Commandments. For to break any of them willfully is to offend God and commit sin. Jesus himself said: "The man who infringes even one of the least of these commandments and teaches others to do the same will be considered the least in the kingdom of heaven; but the man who keeps them and teaches them will be considered great in the kingdom of heaven" (Matthew 5:19).

542. How did Jesus sum up the Ten Commandments?

Jesus summed up the Ten Commandments by reducing them to two fundamental laws: the love of God and the love of neighbor. "Jesus said, 'You must love the Lord your God with all your heart, with all your soul, and with all your mind. This is the greatest and the first commandment. The second resembles it: You must love your neighbor as yourself'" (Matthew 22:37–39).

543. Which Commandments pertain to the love of God?

The Commandments that pertain to the love of God are the first three. They regulate our relation to God and express the fundamental obligations of religion.

544. What are the Commandments that pertain to the love of neighbor?

The Commandments that pertain to the love of neighbor are the last seven. They regulate our relationship with others and express the fundamental obligations of morality.

II.
COMMANDMENTS
OF GOD

First Commandment: "I am Yahweh your God. You shall have no gods except me."

1. The Worship of God

545. What is the first Commandment of God?

The first Commandment of God is: "I am Yahweh your God . . . You shall have no gods except me" (Exodus 20:2–3).

546. What does the first Commandment tell us?

The first Commandment tells us that we are to worship the one, true, and living God and not allow any creature to replace God and his will in our lives.

547. What is the Church's further understanding of the first Commandment?

The Church understands the first Commandment to be a positive precept that obliges us to practice the virtue of religion and a negative prohibition that forbids all sins contrary to this virtue.

548. What is the virtue of religion?

The virtue of religion is a moral virtue by which we are disposed to render to God the worship that he deserves. It is the virtue of justice toward God.

549. Why is the virtue of religion important?

The virtue of religion is important because it draws us nearer to

God. It combines all the virtues and directs them to honor God, who made us to know, praise, and serve the divine Majesty.

550. Are we obliged to worship God?

We are obliged to worship God with the worship of adoration because only the Creator can claim the entire subjection of his creatures as their sovereign Master and Lord.

551. Why are we obliged to worship God?

We are obliged to worship God because he wants us to pay attention to his presence, acknowledge his surpassing greatness, and show in the depths of our being an awareness that he is our God. "Declare the greatness of his name, proclaim his praise with song and with lyre, and this is how you must sing his praises: how wonderful they are, all the works of the Lord!" (Ecclesiasticus 39:20).

552. How is the worship of God put into practice?

The worship of God is put into practice by adoration, prayer, and sacrifice.

553. What is adoration?

Adoration is the honor we give to God in recognition of his infinite perfections, his supreme dominion over all creation, and our total dependence on him.

554. What is prayer?

Prayer is an exercise of the virtue of religion, the lifting up of the mind and heart to God in faith, hope, and charity.

555. Why must we pray?

We must pray because prayer is absolutely necessary for salvation. We must also pray because God wants us to acknowledge his existence and complete reliance on him, to thank him for past favors received, to beg his mercy for having offended him by sin, and ask him for all the graces that we and others need.

556. How should we pray?

We must pray with attention and devotion, that is, with an awareness of God's presence and a desire to be united in spirit with him. Christ taught us in his Sermon on the Mount: "In your prayers do not babble as the pagans do, for they think that by using many words they will make themselves heard" (Matthew 6:7). What is most important is that, during prayer, we are interiorly united in mind and heart with God.

557. When should we pray?

We should pray at regular times during the day, for example, on rising, retiring, and before and after meals. We should pray whenever we are tempted, discouraged, or faced with any trial. We should pray whenever we are uncertain about what to do, or how to do it. We should pray as often as the duties of our life permit. In fact, the Scriptures tell us to pray at all times (cf. Luke 21:36). This means that we are always to pray with our hearts, by our constant readiness to do the will of God.

558. For whom should we pray?

We should pray for anyone who has not yet reached eternal happiness, whether living or dead, for our parents, benefactors, friends, and even our enemies. We should pray for the Church, especially for the pope and bishops, for the faithful and for all mankind.

559. What is sacrifice?

Sacrifice means the surrender of something precious for the love of God.

560. How is sacrifice a fulfillment of the first Commandment?

Sacrifice is a fulfillment of the first Commandment because by it we acknowledge God's majesty and express our total dependence on God. The greatest sacrifice was that of Christ on the Cross: "The Father loves me, because I lay down my life in order to take it up again. No one takes it from me; I lay it down of my own free will, and as it is in my power to lay it down, so it is in my power to take it up again; and this is the command I have been given by my Father" (John 10:17–18).

561. What kinds of sacrifice does God ask of us?

God asks of us both external and internal sacrifices. We sacrifice externally by giving up something we like. We sacrifice internally when we not only deprive ourselves of its possession or use but also let go of it with the affections of the heart. The call to sacrifice applies to all: "Anyone who loves his life loses it;

anyone who hates his life in this world will keep it for the eternal life. If a man serves me, he must follow me" (John 12:25–26). We are as good servants of Christ as we follow his example of total self-sacrifice.

562. What is the most important thing in sacrifice?

The most important thing in sacrifice is the willingness to surrender whatever pleases us in order to please God.

563. How does a person sin against the first Commandment?

A person sins against the first Commandment by failing to give God the acknowledgment he deserves in humble prayer and willing sacrifice.

564. What are the principal sins against the first Commandment?

The principal sins against the first Commandment are by excess or by defect.

565. What are the sins against the first Commandment by excess?

The sins against the first Commandment by excess are superstition, vain observance, and idolatry. Superstition offers worship to God in an improper manner, for example, based on spurious revelations. Vain observance tries to obtain from creatures what only God can confer, for example, through magic or satanism which is worship of the devil. And idolatry means giving divine honors to a creature. Scriptures tells us, "You must not fall into the habit of imitating the detestable practices of the natives . . . the man who does these things is detestable to Yahweh your God" (Deuteronomy 18:9, 12).

566. Are superstition, vain observance, and idolatry serious sins?

Yes, superstition, vain observance, and idolatry are by their nature serious sins. However, ignorance, bad example, or good faith may excuse a person from grave sin—as happens among people who have not been duly instructed in the true faith.

567. What is the sin against the first Commandment by defect?

The sin against the first Commandment by defect is irreligion.

568. What is irreligion?

Irreligion is an assault on the honor of God.

569. How is the honor of God assaulted?

The honor of God is assaulted by tempting God, sacrilege, and simony. To tempt God is to say or do something that tries to find out if God is all wise, almighty, or merciful; as when a person exposes his life to danger to find out if God will work a miracle to save him. Sacrilege is the contemptuous treatment of a person, place, or thing dedicated to God. Simony is the refusal to share, except for a price, such spiritual things as the sacraments, the Mass, blessings, relics, medals, or any object or service that confers supernatural benefits.

570. Does the taking of stipends constitute simony?

Taking stipends does not constitute simony because they are given to help support the priest and are not in payment for service rendered. At the same time, the Church urges her priests to serve the poor and lowly with selfless generosity, after the example of Christ our Lord.

571. What is the worship of false gods?

The worship of false gods is giving creatures the attention and affection that are due only to the one true God. Modern forms of worshipping false gods are secularism, which claims that this world is the only one worth living for; hedonism, which makes earthly pleasure its only aim; and Communism, which denies the existence of God and looks to man's happiness in a classless society in this life and not in the life to come.

2. Veneration of Angels and Saints

572. Why is the veneration of angels and saints pleasing to God?

The veneration of angels and saints is pleasing to God because in this way we praise him in the graces he bestowed on his creatures and recognize his greatness in their holiness. In the spirit of Mary's *Magnificat,* we glorify the Lord for the blessings he conferred on persons who, except for him, would not even exist. God is pleased when we ask them to intercede for us with him, and seek to imitate the virtues they practiced through his help.

573. How does the worship of God differ from the worship of angels and saints?

The worship of God is adoration, that of angels and saints is veneration. Only God is to be adored; all others are to be honored as creatures whose dignity depends entirely on God.

574. Why do we venerate the blessed Mother above all the angels and saints?

We venerate Mary above all the angels and saints because she is full of grace, the most perfect of creatures, the Mother of God and the Church, and the Queen of heaven and earth.

3. Veneration of Images and Relics

575. Of what use are sacred images and pictures?

Sacred images and pictures remind us of the blessings that we have received from God and the saints. They inspire us to follow in their footsteps, to thank God for his great goodness to us, and to lead a holy life.

576. Is there danger of superstition in the use of sacred images?

Yes, people can become superstitious in the use of sacred images. But this does not occur if the teachings of the Church are followed.

577. What is a relic?

A first-class relic is part of the body of a person who has been canonized or beatified by the Church. A second-class relic is an object which belonged to the person during life. And a third-class relic is anything that has been touched to the body of the saint or blessed.

578. Is the veneration of images, pictures, and relics lawful?

The veneration of images, pictures, and relics is lawful because the honor paid to the image passes on to the one it represents. The New Testament describes the use of such objects in the early Church: "So remarkable were the miracles worked by God at Paul's hands that handkerchiefs or aprons which had touched him were taken to the sick, and they were cured of their illnesses, and the evil spirits came out of them" (Acts 19:11–12).

Second Commandment: "You shall not take the name of the Lord your God in vain."

1. Blasphemy and Cursing

579. What is the second Commandment of God?

The second Commandment of God declares: "You shall not utter the name of Yahweh your God to misuse it, for Yahweh will not leave unpunished the man who utters his name to misuse it" (Exodus 20:7).

580. What is the obligation of the second Commandment?

The second Commandment requires the lawful use of God's name and forbids the irreverent use of his name.

581. What does the second Commandment forbid?

The second Commandment forbids blasphemy and cursing.

582. What is blasphemy?

Blasphemy is any speech, thought, or action that shows contempt for God. It is a very grave sin that admits of no light matter. In the Old Testament it was punishable by death: "The one who blasphemes the name of Yahweh must die" (Leviticus 24:16).

583. What is cursing?

Cursing is to call down evil on someone or something.

584. Why is it sinful to curse even irrational objects?

It is more or less sinful to curse irrational objects because of the uncontrolled anger or impatience of the person.

585. What is the greatest evil we can wish on anyone?

The greatest evil we can wish is that a person be condemned to hell. However, wishing spiritual evil on anyone is always sinful.

586. Is cursing always morally wrong?

Cursing is always morally wrong. The gravity of the sin depends on how serious is the spiritual or physical harm that a person wants to befall the one cursed.

587. Is it ever permissible to wish some physical evil on another?

Yes, it is permissible to wish, without cursing, some physical evil on another, provided the intention is the person's spiritual welfare.

588. What is the responsibility of a Christian about cursing?

The responsibility of a Christian about cursing is to watch his tongue, which, as St. James says, "is a pest that will not keep still, full of deadly poison" (James 3:8).

2. Vows, Oaths, and Adjurations

589. What does Catholic tradition associate with the second Commandment?

Catholic tradition associates the making of vows and the taking of oaths with the second Commandment.

590. What is a vow?

A vow is a voluntary promise made to God to do something that is better than what we are obliged to do under pain of sin.

591. Are we obliged to keep or fulfill the vows we make?

We are obliged to keep the vows we make. God himself has commanded us to do so in Sacred Scripture: "If you make a vow to Yahweh your God, you must not be lazy in keeping it; be sure that Yahweh your God requires it, and to withhold it would be a sin" (Deuteronomy 23:22).

592. How does a vow differ from a simple promise?

A vow differs from a simple promise in three ways: in the person to whom it is made, in the intention, and in the duty of living up to it. Vows are covenants made with God, and not merely resolutions to oneself or promises to another person. They are made with a view to obtaining divine grace as God's pledge in response to man's commitment. And they impose the obligation in virtue of religion, to be faithfully carried into effect.

593. Does every vow bind under pain of sin?

Yes, every deliberate failure to keep a vow is sinful.

594. How grave is the obligation of a vow?

The obligation of a vow may be grave or slight, according to the importance of that which is vowed, and the intention of the one taking the vow.

595. Why is a vow pleasing to God?

A vow is pleasing to God because it unites the person to God by a new bond of religion. Moreover, it means offering up to God not only a single act but the will behind all the acts performed under the vow.

596. What is an oath?

An oath is the reverent use of God's name when he is called upon to witness to the truth of what a person is saying. It is lawful to take an oath because swearing has been instituted as an assurance of sincerity. Thus Abraham reassured Abimelech with an oath: "Yes," Abraham replied, "I swear it" (Genesis 21:24). The conditions that make an oath lawful are truthfulness, justice, honesty, and a reasonably grave reason.

597. What is perjury?

Perjury is the deliberate swearing to a falsehood; it is a false oath.

598. Is perjury a serious sin?

Perjury is always a serious sin because it implies a desire to destroy God's truthfulness. "The false witness shall not go unpunished, the man who utters lies will meet his end" (Proverbs 19:9).

599. What is adjuration?

Adjuration is the use of the name of God or of some sacred person or thing in order to strengthen a command or request.

600. Are adjurations permissible?

Adjurations are permissible provided they are made with the

right intention, and the circumstances warrant this kind of solemn invocation.

Third Commandment: "Remember to keep holy the Lord's day."

1. Sundays and Holydays: Mass Obligation

601. What is the third Commandment of God?

The third Commandment of God is, "Remember the sabbath day and keep it holy" (Exodus 20:8).

602. What did the third Commandment require in the Old Law?

In the Old Law, the third Commandment required keeping the Sabbath holy as a day of rest.

603. What does the third Commandment oblige us to do?

The third Commandment obliges us to assist at Mass on Sundays and to abstain from all unnecessary servile work.

604. Why was the Sabbath changed to Sunday?

The Sabbath was changed to Sunday to commemorate the Resurrection of Christ from the dead on the first day of the week. It also commemorates Pentecost Sunday, when Christ sent the Holy Spirit on the disciples in Jerusalem.

605. What is the Church's teaching on the observance of Sunday?

The Church teaches that on Sunday the faithful should assemble to participate in the Eucharist and hear the word of God. Sunday is to be a day of gladness and rest from work. The duty to assist at Mass is a grave obligation.

606. What is the best way to assist at Mass?

The best way to assist at Mass is to unite ourselves with the priest and the congregation all through the Mass and to receive our Lord in the Eucharist.

607. Is bodily presence at Mass necessary and required to fulfill one's obligation?

Bodily presence is necessary and required in order to fulfill one's obligation of hearing Mass.

608. What causes might excuse from assisting at Sunday Mass?

The causes that might excuse from assisting at Sunday Mass are: physical impossibility which applies to those who are unable to hear Mass because they are sick, or who have no priest to say Mass for them; moral impossibility, when it would be very difficult to attend Mass, say because of the absolute necessity of fulfilling other grave duties; and the practice of charity, when Mass is sacrificed to remain at the bedside of the sick or give urgent assistance to someone in great need.

609. Are we obliged to assist at Mass on any other days besides Sunday?

Besides Sunday, we are obliged to assist at Mass on the holydays of obligation. These are special days set aside by the Church for the same reason that Sundays are to be kept holy. They are dedicated to the Lord and his saints to commemorate some outstanding mystery of the Faith.

610. Which are the holydays of obligation?

The holydays of obligation in the United States are:
Solemnity of Mary the Mother of God—January 1
Ascension Thursday—Forty days after Easter
Assumption of the Blessed Virgin Mary—August 15
All Saints Day—November 1
Immaculate Conception—December 8
Christmas—December 25

There are four other holydays of obligation prescribed in the general laws of the Church, namely, Epiphany, St. Joseph (March 19), Corpus Christi, and Sts. Peter and Paul (June 29).

2. Sunday as a Day of Rest

611. Why were the people to rest from labor on the Sabbath?

The people were to rest from labor on the Sabbath because they were to follow the example of Yahweh. He blessed that day as a symbol of his "six days" of work as Creator.

612. Why has the Catholic Church decreed that Christians observe Sunday as a day of rest?

The Church decreed that Christians observe Sunday as a day of rest because our religion and health require some relaxation at regular times. Moreover, Sunday rest indicates that all have the right and duty to enjoy leisure time allowed by divine and human law. They are to use this leisure to cultivate their social, religious, and family life.

613. What kind of work is permitted on Sunday?

So-called liberal work is permitted on Sunday, such as reading, writing, teaching, drawing, or music; common work, such as traveling, hunting, or fishing; daily necessities, like cooking, care of domestic animals; any work having immediate relation with the Church; and acts of charity, like care of the sick and work done for the poor.

614. What kind of work is forbidden on Sundays?

All servile work, such as field labor, mechanical and industrial work is forbidden on Sunday. Public sales and judiciary work are also forbidden.

615. What reasons would allow servile work on Sunday?

Servile work is allowed on Sunday when it is practically necessary as a means of livelihood or when required in strict justice or charity.

616. How serious is the sin of working on Sundays?

It is a grave sin to work on Sunday in contempt of the law or when the work gives grave scandal to others.

Fourth Commandment: "Honor your father and your mother."

Obedience, Love, and Respect for Parents

617. What is the fourth Commandment?

The fourth Commandment is: "Honor your father and your

mother so that you may have a long life in the land that Yahweh
your God has given to you" (Exodus 20:12).

618. What does it mean to honor one's parents?

To honor one's parents means that children are to love, respect, and obey father and mother as the human authors of their
being.

*619. Is the duty of love, respect, and obedience a grave obliga-
tion?*

Yes, the duty of love, respect, and obedience is a grave obligation and sins opposed to this duty are mortal in nature when the
matter is serious.

620. Why must children obey their parents?

Children must obey their parents because God himself is the
source of parental rights. The Scriptures tell us, "Listen, my son,
to your father's instruction, do not reject your mother's teaching:
they will be a crown of grace for your head, a circlet for your
neck" (Proverbs 1:8–9).

621. How should children obey their parents?

Children should obey their parents promptly, respectfully, and
exactly, after the example of Christ who was obedient to Mary
and Joseph at Nazareth.

622. Why should children show a special love for their parents?

Children should show a special love for their parents because,
next to God, they are most indebted to their father and mother.
"With all your heart honor your father, never forget the
birthpangs of your mother. Remember that you owe your birth to
them; how can you repay them for what they have done for you?"
(Ecclesiasticus 7:27–28). Children sin against the love they owe
their parents by not showing marks of affection; by talking about
them uncharitably; by provoking them; by not caring for them in
their need; and by wishing them evil.

623. When is a son or daughter not bound to obey the parents?

A son or daughter is not bound to obey the parents whenever
they command something that is clearly against the Commandments of God or the Church, or when they are unreasonably opposed to the choice of one's state of life, for "Obedience to God
comes before obedience to men" (Acts 5:29).

624. Why must children respect their parents?

Children must respect their parents because they are representatives of God, and elders on whom they depend for so much of their well-being. Children sin against the respect they owe their parents by speaking unkindly to or about them, by striking or insulting them, and being ashamed of them.

625. Must children obey only their parents?

No, children must also obey teachers and anyone who has charge of them.

626. Do children's duties toward their parents cease after they leave home?

Children's duties toward their parents do not cease after they leave home but continue all through life and even after death.

627. Are children obligated to care for parents who are aged or in need?

It is a serious obligation to care for one's parents who are aged or in need, and those who neglect to provide for them adequately, meeting their reasonable needs in a kindly way, sin grievously. The Scriptures tell us, "My son, support your father in his old age, do not grieve him during his life. Even if his mind should fail, show him sympathy, do not despise him in your health and strength; for kindness to a father shall not be forgotten but will serve as reparation for your sins. In the days of your affliction it will be remembered of you, like frost in sunshine, your sins will melt away. The man who deserts his father is no better than a blasphemer, and whoever angers his mother is accursed of the Lord" (Ecclesiasticus 3:12–16).

Fifth Commandment: "You shall not kill."

1. Justice and Charity

628. What is the fifth Commandment of God?

The fifth Commandment of God is: "You shall not kill" (Exodus 20:13).

629. Did the people in the Old Testament respect human life?

Yes, the people in the Old Testament had been forcefully taught to respect human life and avoid killing any innocent human beings, whether born or unborn. "He who sheds man's blood, shall have his blood shed by man, for in the image of God man was made" (Genesis 9:6).

630. How does the New Law differ concerning the fifth Commandment?

The New Law differs from the Mosaic Law regarding the fifth Commandment by its prohibition of interior feelings of hatred and anger and its stress on charity in helping and not only not harming the neighbor. "But I say this to you: anyone who is angry with his brother will answer for it before the court" (Matthew 5:22).

631. What does the fifth Commandment tell us to do?

The fifth Commandment tells us to care for our own life and health and also the life and health of our neighbor.

632. Why must we respect our neighbor?

We must respect our neighbor because Christ's command to love one another implies respect. We are to look upon our neighbor as another self with special concern for all his physical needs. Being redeemed by Christ, we are "one in Christ Jesus" (Galatians 3:28).

633. Why should Christians be outstanding in their concern for others?

Christians should be outstanding in their concern for others because this is the basic way of showing their love for God and their principal witness to the world. "By this love you have for one another, everyone will know that you are my disciples" (John 13:35).

634. How extensive should our charity be today?

Our charity today should be concerned not only for individuals but for the welfare of human society.

635. How should we exercise charity toward others?

We should exercise charity toward others by seeing in them the image of God, for whose sake we love them; and by respecting with great sensitivity their dignity as human persons.

636. Why must we respect the human person?

We must respect the human person because human life is sacred, of and by itself, and apart from any other function it may have in society.

2. Ordinary and Extraordinary Means of Preserving Human Life

637. How are we obliged to care for our own life?

We are obliged to use ordinary means to sustain our life because our body is a gift that God wants us to receive with gratitude.

638. What are the ordinary means to preserve life?

The ordinary means to preserve life are proper food, sleep, clothing, and shelter; they also include such medical care as society can readily provide.

639. What are the extraordinary means of preserving life?

The extraordinary means of preserving life are those that cannot be obtained or used without extreme difficulty in terms of pain, expense, or other burdening factors.

640. Why do we not have to use extraordinary means to keep alive?

We do not have to use extraordinary means to keep alive because God does not demand what is beyond the ordinary power of most people to fulfill.

641. When must extraordinary means be used?

Extraordinary means must be used when a person is very necessary to his family, the Church, or society; in this case, extraordinary means become morally obligatory according to the need for sustaining a person's life.

3. Murder, Genocide, and Organ Transplant

642. What does the fifth Commandment forbid us to do?

The fifth Commandment forbids unjust killing, such as proceeds from human malice or passion; it also forbids doing any harm to the integrity or health of the body.

643. What is murder?

Murder is the direct and deliberate taking of an innocent person's life. It is a grievous sin because it is an invasion of the rights of God, who alone is the master of human life. It is also a most serious injustice to the victim, his family, and to society. When Cain killed his brother Abel, God told him, "Listen to the sound of your brother's blood, crying out to me from the ground. Now be accursed and driven from the ground" (Genesis 4:10–11).

644. What sins lead to murder?

Sins that lead to murder are those opposed to brotherly love; forgetfulness of the revealed truths; loss of respect for human dignity; and, in general, all selfish thoughts and desires inspired by the seven capital sins.

645. Why is human life sacred?

Human life is sacred because it begins by the creative act of God; it is capable of knowing and loving God; it has been redeemed by the Passion and Death of the Son of God, and is destined to possess God for all eternity.

646. Who alone has absolute mastery over human life?

God alone has absolute mastery over human life.

647. When does human life begin?

Human life begins at the moment of conception. The moment the ovum is fertilized, a new human life begins to grow and develop.

648. What is genocide?

Genocide is the deliberate and systematic destruction of a race or class of people on real or alleged grounds of their being harmful to society.

649. Is it sinful to even want to take away the life of an innocent person?

Yes, it is sinful to want to take away the life of an innocent person because this would be murder by intention.

650. May innocent life ever be deliberately terminated?

No, innocent life may never be deliberately terminated because man has an obligation to sustain his own life and the life of those who depend on him.

651. How does the Church look upon the transplanting of vital organs?

The Church looks favorably upon the transplanting of vital organs provided the loss of such organs does not deprive the donor of life itself.

652. What is a special concern regarding the transplant of vital organs?

A special concern regarding the transplant of vital organs is to know when a donor is really dead. There is a medical temptation to anticipate death because it is not certain how effective is the transplant of a vital organ, like the heart, from an authentically dead person.

4. Abortion and Sterilization

653. What is abortion?

Abortion is the direct expelling from the mother's womb of a living fetus that cannot live outside the womb even with the most extraordinary medical care. The Church has always held that abortion, as the deliberate killing of an unborn child, at any time after conception, is a grave sin.

654. Why must Catholics obey this teaching?

Catholics must obey this teaching because the Church is given authority to command in Christ's name. The Church is empowered by Christ to prohibit and prescribe in any area of human conduct that touches on the Commandments of God, whether derived from nature or from supernatural revelation.

655. Is the Catholic Church the only religious body that condemns abortion?

No, many other religious bodies like the Eastern Orthodox Churches, the Orthodox Jews, and the Church of Jesus Christ of Latter-day Saints, also condemn abortion.

656. Why is abortion a grave crime?

Abortion is a grave crime because it is the homicidal intent to kill innocent human life. This is totally independent of the question of when exactly human life begins. Anyone who is willing to kill what may be human is, by his intention, willing to kill what is human. Therefore, the one who performs or consents to abortion is guilty of voluntary homicide.

657. Is abortion also gravely sinful when the unborn child is the result of rape or incest?

Yes, no matter what the cause for a child's conception, the unborn infant has a right to life and therefore to normal birth. Rape or incest as the source of pregnancy does not justify the murder of the innocent child thus conceived.

658. What is abortion on demand?

Abortion on demand is a result of legalized abortion. The law says that a pregnant woman has the "right" to kill the child in her womb whenever continued pregnancy might be injurious to her physical or mental health, or when the child might be born with a physical or mental defect. By implication she can have an abortion when she wants it.

659. What is feticide?

Feticide is the destruction of a living fetus by a variety of physical or chemical means. It is another form of abortion.

660. What is sometimes called indirect abortion?

Indirect abortion is not really abortion. In what is becoming a medical rarity, when a pregnant mother's life is in imminent danger because of some pathological condition, surgery or other radical means may be used to save her life although it is reluctantly foreseen that the unborn fetus will die. This is an application of the principle of the double effect.

661. What is a therapeutic abortion?

In medical terms, a therapeutic abortion is one that safeguards either the life or the health of an expectant mother. But, morally, no therapeutic abortion is allowable except in the rare case where the mother's life is in certain and imminent danger from a pathological condition which is not simply the pregnancy itself.

662. What is sterilization?

Sterilization is the permanent or temporary removal or making inactive of any reproductive organ for the purpose of inducing sterility. Direct or contraceptive sterilization is done with the deliberate intent of avoiding conception. Direct sterilization is a grave sin because it means the unjustified loss of the sacred power of procreation conferred on a person by God. It may never be performed, either as an end, or as a means to some other good action.

663. What is therapeutic sterilization?

Therapeutic sterilization, sometimes called indirect sterilization, is done for the purpose of relieving a person of some pathological condition and, as such, is permitted.

664. What is eugenic sterilization?

Eugenic sterilization is aimed at assuring the elimination of offspring having possible undesirable traits, such as mental retardation. The Church forbids such sterilization and says that public authorities have no power over the bodies of their innocent subjects.

665. What is penal sterilization?

Penal sterilization is done to punish or deter condemned persons from committing further sex crimes. Penal sterilization is not a real punishment or deterrent because it does not deprive the criminal of anything precious in his eyes, and his vicious tendencies remain a threat to society.

5. Suicide

666. What is suicide?

Suicide is the direct taking of one's own life. A person assumes the right to take his own life.

667. Why is suicide a grievous sin?

Suicide is a grievous sin because it is opposed to our nature and to the charity we owe ourselves; because of its scandal to society and the loss of one of its members, and especially because it is an injustice to God, who alone has the right to give life and to take it away.

668. How does the Church view a suicidal death?

The Church views direct suicide as evil in itself and, therefore, no circumstances can ever justify it. Indirect suicide is, generally speaking, unlawful, for man is not only forbidden to take his own life but also forbidden to expose it to unreasonable risk. Suicides are deprived of Church burial unless, as generally happens, they were not fully responsible for their action.

669. May a person deliberately shorten his life?

A person may not deliberately shorten his life because it belongs to God alone to determine our time of probation on earth.

670. Are we ever allowed to perform an act that may lead to our death?

Yes, we are allowed to perform an act that may lead to our death if there is no direct intention of death. There must also be a grave reason for performing the act, and the reason for performing the act must be in proportion to the danger. For example, I may enter a burning building to save someone's life, though I know my own life is in grave danger.

6. Euthanasia and Capital Punishment

671. What is euthanasia?

Euthanasia has two meanings. It is the deliberate termination of human life for the purpose of ending useless pain; and it is the killing of an innocent person who is considered a burden to society.

672. Is euthanasia something new in modern times?

No, euthanasia as the direct killing of innocent but unwanted people is as old as the human race. But in modern times the practice has become legalized on a wide scale.

673. Is euthanasia permissible if the real purpose of causing death is to remove pain?

No, it is not permitted to directly cause death, even to relieve someone of terrible pain.

674. Why has euthanasia become so widespread?

Euthanasia has become so widespread because science has given man a sense of mastery over the universe which includes the unfounded right over human life from conception to the grave. Moreover, modern man is so immersed in the satisfaction of this world that he has become indifferent to whatever lies beyond the experience of his life on earth.

675. Is euthanasia ever permissible?

Euthanasia is never permissible. It is always either willful murder or suicide.

676. Why does Catholic Christianity condemn euthanasia?

Catholic Christianity condemns euthanasia because it is a grave crime against justice, both human and divine. Man is only steward of his own life, and the life of others is their most precious possession of which no one under God may deprive them.

677. Who are disqualified from the divine right to human life?

Disqualified from the divine right to human life are those who are judged to be a grave menace to society, such as criminals and unjust aggressors from whom we may protect ourselves.

678. What is capital punishment?

Capital punishment is punishment by death administered by legitimate civil authority on those who have been lawfully convicted of serious crimes.

679. Who has the right to inflict capital punishment?

The right to inflict capital punishment is invested in public authority. No private person has the right to put a criminal to death.

7. War and Peace

680. What is war?

War is a conflict between two or more nations or between parts of the same nation carried on by force of arms. The Church's position is that, although regrettable, war is not always and necessarily sinful. Participation in war may, on occasion, be praiseworthy.

681. When is a war just?

A war is considered just when declared by proper authority undertaken as a last resort, and when those waging war use no more destructive means than are necessary to achieve an early and just peace. The purpose for which the war is fought must be a good one.

682. Do citizens have a duty to aid their country during a just war?

Citizens have a duty to aid their country to gain victory, but they may not voluntarily provide help if their nation's cause is evidently unjust.

683. How do citizens decide if the cause is just?

Citizens can decide if the cause is just by reflection, prayer, consultation, and, for Catholics, by following the directives of the Church.

684. How has the development of scientific weapons increased the horror of war?

The development of scientific weapons has increased the prospects of wholesale and indiscriminate destruction.

685. What is Vatican II's view on scientific warfare?

The Council teaches that all warfare which tends indiscriminately to the destruction of entire cities or wide areas with their inhabitants is to be condemned.

686. What is the Church's teaching about conscientious objectors?

Conscientious objectors have a right to be excused from bearing arms provided some other form of community service is substituted.

687. Is fear of personal injury or loss of life legitimate grounds for refusing to bear arms?

No, such fear is not of itself legitimate grounds for refusing to bear arms. Citizens have a duty to defend their country in a just conflict. When there is clear evidence of a just cause, personal interests are subordinate to the national welfare.

688. What is peace among nations?

Peace among nations is not only the absence of war but of injustice and hatred that may lead to armed conflict.

689. What does the Church teach about the conditions for peace among nations?

To establish peace among nations it is necessary to root out the causes of disharmony on which war thrives, especially injustice; also a sound economic base must be developed for peaceful coexistence among nations, especially since in our days a serious gap has developed between the prosperous and materially underdeveloped nations.

690. How can peace among nations be achieved?

Peace among nations can be achieved by setting up institutions for international cooperation on every level of human enterprise and actively supporting and improving the institutions already in existence.

691. What is interior peace?

Interior peace is the absence of discord and, when present, is a deep-souled calmness. When we are at peace, we are not troubled or worried; we are not anxious or perturbed; we are not confused or distraught. A peaceful soul is a tranquil soul.

692. How is interior peace related to peace between people?

Interior peace is related to peace between people as cause and effect. There cannot be agreement between people unless there is first tranquillity within people. If we are at peace within, we shall be at peace with others.

Sixth and Ninth Commandments: "You shall not commit adultery. You shall not covet your neighbor's wife."

1. External and Internal Sins Against Chastity

693. What is the sixth Commandment of God?

The sixth Commandment of God is: "You shall not commit adultery" (Exodus 20:14).

694. What is the ninth Commandment of God?

The ninth Commandment of God is: "You shall not covet your neighbor's wife" (Exodus 20:17).

695. How are the sixth and ninth Commandments related?

The sixth and ninth Commandments are related in that they forbid respectively external and internal sins against chastity.

696. What are external sins against chastity?

External sins against chastity are any words, actions, or gestures consciously performed to arouse or indulge sexual pleasure except between husband and wife in their legitimate marital relations. St. Paul reminds us, "Your body, you know, is the temple of the Holy Spirit, who is in you since you received him from God. You are not your own property; you have been bought and paid for. That is why you should use your body for the glory of God" (1 Corinthians 6:19-20).

697. What is adultery?

Adultery is sexual intercourse between a married person and someone other than one's spouse.

698. What is Christ's teaching on adultery in desire?

Christ declared that "if a man looks at a woman lustfully, he has already committed adultery with her in his heart" (Matthew 5:28).

699. What are internal sins against chastity?

Internal sins against chastity are sexual thoughts, desires, or feelings deliberately aroused or indulged, except by husband and wife in their mutual relationships; also included are intentions and desires to perform external sins of unchastity.

700. What does it mean to covet another person's husband or wife?

To covet another person's husband or wife means to desire to have sexual relations with that person's spouse.

2. Virtue of Chastity, Meaning and Practice

701. What is chastity?

Chastity is a form of temperance with regard to sexual pleasure.

702. Who is a chaste person?

A chaste person is one who tempers or restrains the desire for venereal satisfaction by not having the experience except within the divinely ordained precincts of marriage.

703. Why are Christians to be chaste?

A Christian is to be chaste because his body does not belong exclusively to him and because it has been elevated by grace to be the dwelling place of the Holy Spirit. "Didn't you realize that you were God's temple and that the Spirit of God was living among you?" (1 Corinthians 3:16).

704. Why is chastity sacred?

Chastity is sacred because by using the reproductive powers one can cooperate in the procreative work of God to bring another human being into the world, and because by sacrificing their use one can prove one's love for God who is pleased with our willing surrender of what he knows is so pleasing to us.

705. What is the Church's position on premarital sexual relations?

The Church teaches that all nonmarital relations are a serious deviation from divine law. They have been forbidden to the followers of Christ since the beginning of Christianity.

706. Why are nonmarital relations sinful?

Nonmarital relations are sinful because the marital act is legitimate only within the bond of marriage. Intercourse without marriage is an untruth because it belies the total commitment to one another that the marital act expresses between husband and wife. Intercourse without marriage is also an injustice to the children that may be conceived, since they would then lack the dignity, stability, security, and loving care that marriage is expected to provide.

707. How should engaged couples conduct themselves?

Engaged couples should nourish and foster their love for each other with a chaste love which means the mastery, with God's help, of their sexual emotions as a promise of happiness in married life.

708. What is fornication?

Fornication is voluntary sexual intercourse between an unmarried man and an unmarried woman. It is always gravely sinful. If the two people are closely related, there is the further malice of incest.

709. What is the best preparation for Christian marriage?

The best preparation for Christian marriage is the practice of chastity before marriage. Then the selfless love between the couple who plan to marry can sustain them after they are married. Hence, the urgent need for parents to train their sons and daughters from childhood in the practice of this difficult Commandment.

710. What is the virtue of chastity for the unmarried?

The virtue of chastity for the unmarried is total abstinence from any deliberate sexual desire or indulgence in sexual pleasure.

711. What is the virtue of chastity for the married?

The virtue of chastity for the married means the grateful enjoyment of marital pleasure between themselves, as husband and wife. But they may not seek or indulge sexual satisfaction either alone (masturbation) or with another person of the opposite sex (adultery), or of the same sex (homosexuality), or with each other while interfering with conception (contraception).

712. Why is sexual experience in marriage sacred?

Sexual experience in marriage is sacred because it is divinely intended to encourage married people to fulfill their marital obligations and help them to grow in mutual love.

713. What are the principal means of preserving chastity?

The principal means of preserving chastity are vigilance and prayer.

714. How does vigilance help preserve chastity?

Vigilance helps preserve chastity internally by keeping watch over our pride, intemperance, and idleness; socially by keeping check on the persons we associate with and the people we allow to influence us; and externally by avoiding needless stimulation through indecent reading, movies, television and, in general, the communications media.

715. How does the practice of prayer help to preserve chastity?

The practice of prayer helps to preserve chastity because it obtains for us the grace of God, without which it is impossible to be chaste.

716. What practices of prayer are most useful to preserve chastity?

The practices of prayer most useful to preserve chastity are: a humble devotion to the blessed Virgin; the thought of the presence of God and of our last end; frequent confession in the sacrament of penance which purifies the soul and strengthens it against temptation; and frequent Holy Communion which increases our love for God and weakens our inclination to sin.

717. When is sex used for selfish purposes?

Sex is used for selfish purposes when its ultimate purpose is deliberately frustrated by contraception; when intercourse is had in circumstances where children would be brought into the world without proper care for their upbringing, as in adultery or fornication; and when sexual pleasure is sought for one's own self-indulgence, as in masturbation or even marital relations that ignore the rights or reasonable wishes of one's spouse.

718. What are direct sexual actions?

Direct sexual actions are those whose immediate and exclusive intention is to arouse or encourage sexual pleasure. These are the privilege only of married partners between themselves.

719. What are indirect sexual actions?

Indirect sexual actions are those whose purpose is not to arouse sexual stimulation but some other good reason. If there is such a reason, the actions are not sinful, provided a person neither intends the sexual pleasure nor consents if it spontaneously arises.

720. What is the Church's attitude toward sexual experience?

The Church praises and blesses legitimate sexual experience. "The sexual activity by which married people are intimately and chastely united is honorable and worthy; and, if done in a truly human fashion, it signifies and fosters the self-giving by which the couple gladly and gratefully enrich each other" (Second Vatican Council, The Church in the Modern World, 49).

721. What is Christian maturity?

Christian maturity is the attainment of a fully developed personality, whose features are a balanced control of the sex impulse and a harmonious unity of all the experiences of one's personal, social, and spiritual life.

722. Why should young people be instructed in purity and in married love?

Young people should be instructed in purity and married love because they must know how to cope with the widespread non-Christian attitudes toward sexual promiscuity and marital instability.

3. Unnatural Sex Experience: Masturbation, Homosexuality, and Contraception

723. What sexual experiences are unnatural?

The sexual experiences that are unnatural are masturbation and homosexuality.

724. What is masturbation?

Masturbation is the act of stimulating the sexual organs by oneself for the purpose of obtaining emotional satisfaction.

725. What is homosexuality?

Homosexuality is sexual activity with a person of the same sex.

726. Why are masturbation and homosexuality contrary to the will of God?

Masturbation and homosexuality are contrary to the will of God because by their very nature they are selfish actions which cannot fulfill the divinely ordained purpose of the reproductive powers.

727. What is contraception?

Contraception is any action deliberately taken before, during, or after intercourse in order to prevent conception.

728. Why is contraception sinful?

Contraception is sinful because the conjugal act is of its very nature designed for the purpose of procreating children. Therefore, those who deliberately interfere with the natural act of procreation do that which is essentially immoral and contrary to the will of God.

729. How sinful is contraception?

Contraception is seriously sinful because it contradicts the divinely ordained purpose of marital intercourse which is the fostering of procreative love.

730. In what sense is the procreation of children primary in marriage?

The procreation of children is primary in marriage in the sense that married people may not deliberately frustrate this purpose for any reason whatever; procreation is naturally primary because human nature provides the kind of care and nourishment that children require in marriage; and it is primary because one of the main reasons why people have the moral right to enter marriage is to be able to have children and rear them as the physical and spiritual image of themselves. God himself commanded our first parents, and through them tells all married people to "Be fruitful, multiply, fill the earth and conquer it" (Genesis 1:28).

731. What is the Church's teaching on contraception?

The Church's teaching on contraception is that direct interruption of the generative process is to be absolutely excluded as a licit means of regulating birth.

732. Why is contraception morally inseparable from abortion?

Contraception is morally inseparable from abortion because selfish indulgence of sex can become murderous. People who practice contraception are strongly tempted to resort to legalized abortion if an unwanted child is conceived.

733. Why is contraception contrary to the natural law?

Contraception is contrary to the natural law because it deliberately interferes with the divinely ordained purpose of marital intercourse.

734. Why is contraception so common today?

Contraception is so common today because there is a fear that the world population is growing more rapidly than the resources that are available. Working and living conditions, together with pressures in the economic and educational fields, have made the rearing of a large family more difficult than it used to be. The status of women is changing, with greater insistence on their freedom from the duties associated with rearing a normal family. Above all, man's progress in dominating the forces of nature now gives him a new sense of power to regulate the transmission of life on his own terms and independent of the laws of God.

735. Do these reasons justify their use?

These reasons do not justify the use of contraception. They merely help to explain the rise of the modern contraceptive society.

4. True Conjugal Love

736. Why is marital intercourse sacred?

Marital intercourse is sacred because its purpose is to deepen the mutual affection of husband and wife, and because in this way they cooperate with God in bringing new human life into the world. As Christ explained, "the two become one body" (Mark 10:8).

737. What are the two love functions of marital intercourse?

The two love functions of marital intercourse are the unitive and procreative.

738. What is unitive love?

Unitive love is the selfless charity fostered between husband and wife in their physical embrace. It merits an increase of divine grace to live out their marriage in lifelong fidelity.

739. What is procreative love?

Procreative love is love communicated from husband-with-wife to their potential offspring. It is love that wants to go beyond the communion between husband and wife; it wants to raise up new human life.

740. When is conjugal love authentically Christian?

Conjugal love is authentically Christian when it is selfless and self-giving. True conjugal love must involve self-sacrifice, just as the love that Christ had for us meant a lifetime of self-oblation even to his death on the Cross.

741. When is conjugal love selfish?

Conjugal love is selfish when each spouse is seeking his or her own interests while using the other as a means to heighten one's own satisfaction. The true concept of Christian marriage excludes this selfishness. St. Paul teaches that "husbands must love their wives as they love their own bodies; for a man to love his wife is for him to love himself" (Ephesians 5:28).

5. Natural Family Planning

742. What is periodic continence?

Periodic continence is abstinence from marital intercourse, for legitimate reasons, during the days each month when the wife is naturally fertile.

743. How may Catholics limit the number of offspring?

Catholics may limit the number of their offspring by using the wife's natural cycles of fertility and sterility; provided the husband and wife mutually agree; provided they are not liable to fall into masturbation, contraception, or adultery; and they have serious justifying reasons for spacing out the children.

744. What is the difference between natural family planning and contraception?

Natural family planning makes legitimate use of what nature provides, namely long periods each month when the wife is sterile, while abstaining from intercourse when she is fertile. But contraception contradicts nature by having intercourse during fertile periods and deliberately interfering with the natural life process.

745. How is the exclusion of children justified in natural family planning?

The exclusion of children is justified because the means used are legitimate. Those who practice natural family planning renounce marital intercourse during fertile periods with a good reason. They have intercourse during the wife's sterile periods in order to manifest their affection and to safeguard their marital fidelity.

746. Why is the exclusion of children by contraception sinful?

The exclusion of children by contraception is sinful because the means used are contrary to the purpose for which God gave us the faculties of generation.

747. How can married couples grow spiritually in today's contraceptive atmosphere?

Married couples can grow spiritually in today's contraceptive atmosphere by developing deep convictions concerning the true values of life and family. This calls for education with regard to the meaning of chastity and demands growth in self-mastery. It mainly calls for the deepening of virtue through prayer and the frequent use of the Mass and the sacraments.

Seventh and Tenth Commandments: "You shall not steal. You shall not covet anything that belongs to your neighbor."

1. Justice and Private Property

748. What is the seventh Commandment of God?

The seventh Commandment of God is: "You shall not steal" (Exodus 20:15).

749. What is the tenth Commandment of God?

The tenth Commandment of God is: "You shall not covet anything that belongs to your neighbor" (cf. Exodus 20:17).

750. How are the seventh and tenth Commandments related?

The seventh Commandment stresses the practice of justice in external conduct; the tenth requires justice in one's interior disposition.

751. What kind of right is implied by these two Commandments?

These two Commandments imply the right to own private property.

752. What is the right to own private property?

The right to own private property is the moral power a person has to keep or dispose, to use or to change material possessions according to his needs and independently of others, provided there is no violation of the rights of others.

753. How do we know that the right to own property is divinely approved?

The right to own property is divinely approved because the seventh Commandment forbids theft, which would be meaningless unless ownership were a prior and natural right that was approved by God.

754. Why has God given man the right to private ownership?

God has given man the right to private ownership as part of his natural right to be a person with divinely ordained individual and social responsibilities. Private ownership gives man the freedom and incentive to fulfill these responsibilities.

755. How is justice a two-edged sword?

Justice is a two-edged sword that obliges others to respect the property of an individual and condemns anyone who takes what does not belong to him.

756. How does the Catholic Church view the right to private property?

The Catholic Church has always viewed the right of private property as a natural right that, even when abused, does not disappear. At the same time the Church insists on the rights of society which are equally binding on the individual to respect.

2. Stealing, Dishonesty, and Gambling

757. What does the seventh Commandment forbid?

The seventh Commandment forbids the taking of another's goods against his reasonable wishes. This includes thievery, robbery, unjust acquisition of goods, and all deliberate destruction of property.

758. What is theft?

Theft is the secret taking of an object against the rightful owner's reasonable wish for the purpose of gain. If the object is taken openly and without secrecy theft becomes robbery; and if something is stolen by means of deception and fraud, it is cheating.

759. Who are guilty of theft or robbery?

Not only robbers and thieves but all those who 1) advise or assist them; 2) buy, sell, or keep stolen goods; 3) do not return what they have found or borrowed; 4) do not pay their just debts; and 5) beg without need and thus defraud those who are really poor.

760. What is cheating?

Cheating is any gain, whether material, social, or psychological, obtained by fraud. The most common form of cheating is committed by injuring another's property or business, whether openly or secretly. Thus cheating is practiced by giving false weight or measure, or practicing any other deceit in buying or selling, and by misrepresenting an object or product in order to attract buyers or users.

761. How may servants and employees be guilty of fraud?

They are guilty of fraud by 1) disposing of their employer's property or possessions without his approval; 2) by wasting time, equipment, or material; and 3) by ignoring just agreements or contracts made with employers.

762. What duty do we have regarding found articles?

Found articles should be returned as soon as possible to the owner. If not known, the first duty is to make a reasonable effort to find the owner. For items of great value, the civil authorities should be contacted.

763. What governs the right relations between employer and employees?

The principle that governs the right relations between employer and employees is the Christian concept of work.

764. In the light of faith, what is the value of work?

In the light of the Christian faith, work is not something to be looked down on; it is not an evil to be avoided as though leisure were more worthy of man's dignity. Work ennobles our character as persons and helps us become like the Savior who labored with his hands and became tired. Even in the beginning, man's work was blessed by God: "Yahweh God took the man and settled him in the garden of Eden to cultivate and take care of it" (Genesis 2:15). Because of our fallen human nature, we now find work difficult and tiresome. But with God's grace, we can offer up the effort and fatigue in expiation of our sins, and to become more like Christ who became tired from his strenuous labors.

765. Do workers have a right to form labor unions?

Workers have a right to form labor unions that truly represent them and are designed to protect the rights of working people. The unions should help labor cooperate with management for the welfare of the workers, the business and the industry or service in which they work, and for the common good of society.

766. What is the Christian responsibility with regard to strikes?

Before any strike, labor must first bargain with management in a fair and just way. The efforts at arbitration must be sincere. During the strike, there may be no deliberate violence or force used, and the strike must not be prolonged or pursued in such a way that it begins to injure the welfare of the workers it was intended to benefit.

767. What is a necessary purpose of amendment after theft?

A necessary purpose of amendment after theft is the willingness to make restitution. Without it, forgiveness cannot be expected.

768. What is gambling?

Gambling is staking money or valuables on chance, or a future or possible event that is unknown or uncertain to the participants. It is sinful when the means used are dishonest, or when the gambler risks losses that he cannot afford, or his family will suffer, or if others will be scandalized. Gambling is permissible if there is no fraud, and if all who participate have basically the same chance of winning.

769. What is betting?

Betting is a form of agreement in which two or more people contract to give a prize to whichever one correctly guesses some future fact or event. It can be illicit if certain conditions are not fulfilled.

770. What are the conditions that must be fulfilled to make betting licit?

For betting to be morally licit: all parties must clearly understand the conditions of the agreement in the same way; they must be sincerely uncertain about the outcome of the event; they must honestly want to pay if they lose the bet; and the bet cannot be an encouragement to do something evil or sinful.

771. What are the dangers involved in betting and gambling?

The dangers involved in betting and gambling are that they

tend to induce a fatalistic outlook on life, unlike the Christian view that the universe is controlled by the loving providence of God.

772. What is lottery?

Lottery is a scheme in which chances are sold and prizes are distributed to those whose names are drawn, by chance, from among the participants.

773. What problems arise from the State's involvement in betting and lottery?

The problems arising from the State's involvement in betting and lottery are the danger of dishonest manipulation, of creating a community tolerance of gambling, and of weakening the citizens' sense of responsibility for the necessary support of public services and institutions.

774. Are lotteries sponsored for a charitable cause permissible?

Lotteries sponsored for a charitable cause are permissible if there is no deception and if there is some proportion between the hope of winning and the amount each person pays.

3. Social Justice

775. What is social justice?

Social justice is the virtue which regulates the mutual relations between human individuals and society.

776. What are the two wrong extremes of social justice?

The two wrong extremes of social justice are individualism, which denies or minimizes the social and public character of the right of private property; and collectivism, which rejects or minimizes the private and individual character of ownership.

777. How can one maintain a Christian balance between individualism and collectivism?

A Christian balance between individualism and collectivism respects private ownership as divinely ordained but also believes that ownership is not absolute, that society too has rights for which the Author of man's social nature equally demands recognition.

778. What does the Church say about the great disproportion between the very rich and the very poor?

Concerning the great disproportion between the very rich and the very poor, the Church says that the rich must share or give some of their wealth to the poor. In doing this, they are not making a gift of their possessions but handing out what already belongs to the poor.

779. Does everyone have a right to share in earthly goods?

Yes, everyone has a right to a just share in earthly possessions. This means an amount sufficient for the decent livelihood of an individual and his family.

780. Do the rich need special counsel with regard to their possessions?

The rich need special counsel regarding their possessions. As Christ told us, riches can suffocate the human heart and be a menace to the spiritual life; but with counsel and divine grace, the wealthy can do the humanly impossible, and not only save their souls but be sanctified.

781. Is a poor person justified in stealing to gain a fair share in the earth's goods?

No, a poor person may not steal to gain what he considers a fair share of the earth's goods. Stealing is never allowed. It is not a disgrace to be honestly poor, as we know from the Holy Family at Nazareth.

782. Should governments confiscate the surplus wealth for distribution among the poor?

Governments may not directly confiscate what they consider surplus wealth for distribution among the poor. Even rich people have a right to private property they have justly acquired. But governments may, with the consent of their citizens, so redistribute the wealth of a country that the people will have a fair share in the nation's material possessions.

783. Is everyone bound to see that others have a just share in earthly possessions?

Everyone is bound to see that others have a just share in earthly possessions. Consequently, all are obliged to share what they have and not only when they have more than they need. Christ commanded us to "Give, and there will be gifts for you: a full measure, pressed down, shaken together, and running over, will be poured into your lap; because the amount you measure out is the amount you will be given back" (Luke 6:38).

4. Greed

784. Why does God forbid not only stealing but also greed?

God forbids not only stealing but also greed because we are obliged not only to keep our hands but also our hearts off other people's possessions.

785. What is greed?

Greed is the inordinate desire to possess material things. It is the basis of covetousness which leads to stealing.

786. What does it mean to "covet"?

To "covet" means to set one's heart or desire on anything that belongs to another.

787. Why is covetousness sinful?

Covetousness is sinful because evil thoughts and desires defile the human heart; in this case they are against the divine commandment to be satisfied with what we possess or can justly acquire.

788. Is it always wrong to desire what another person possesses?

No, it is not always wrong to desire what another person possesses. However, what we desire must be according to God's will for us, and we must intend to use only lawful means to acquire what we want.

Eighth Commandment: "You shall not bear false witness against your neighbor."

1. Telling the Truth

789. What is the eighth Commandment of God?

The eighth Commandment of God is: "You shall not bear false witness against your neighbor" (Exodus 20:16).

790. What does the eighth Commandment tell us to do?

The eighth Commandment tells us how we are to use our tongue and always to tell the truth.

791. What does the eighth Commandment forbid?

The eighth Commandment directly forbids telling an untruth about another person, whether the untruth is told in a court of law or in personal matters. Indirectly it forbids all deliberate lying (cf. Proverbs 12:22).

792. What does the Bible teach about telling the truth?

The Bible teaches that those who speak the truth can be believed, that what they say can confidently be followed, that their statements produce conviction, and their friendship brings peace. Thus, "Lips that tell the truth abide firm for ever, the tongue that lies lasts only for a moment" (Proverbs 12:19).

793. How should we use our tongue?

We are to use our tongue according to the will of God who is the truth. We are to control our tongue in all circumstances. Those who will do this can control every part of themselves (cf. James 3:2).

794. What does it mean to tell the truth?

To tell the truth means not only saying what is on one's mind but also communicating what should be said.

795. Why is it necessary to tell the truth?

It is necessary to tell the truth in order that people may live together in human society. As social beings we need to know what people are thinking and they should know what is on our minds.

796. Why is it important for people to tell the truth?

It is important for people to tell the truth because truth is the foundation of love. We cannot love what we do not know. And we come to love people because of the good that we know about them. Our main source of knowledge of others is what they tell us about themselves; the same is true about others knowing us. As the proverb has it, "Speak that I may know who you are," so our speech is the principal means of self-manifestation. It is the foundation of mutual love and therefore of human society.

797. What is lying?

Lying means deliberately speaking contrary to what is on a person's mind. One can lie by either verbal or nonverbal communication, that is, by means of spoken or written words, body language, or through the circumstances of a situation. One need not have the intention to deceive in order to lie.

798. How sinful is lying?

Lying is traditionally held to be a venial offense against God. It may, however, become grave under certain circumstances, such as telling a lie under oath or denying one's religion as a Catholic.

799. What is mental reservation?

A mental reservation consists in withholding a part of what is in one's mind.

800. What is the difference between broad and strict mental reservation?

In strict mental reservation, one limits the meaning of the words used but without leaving a reasonable clue about what is intended, whereas in broad mental reservation one leaves a clue to what the speaker means. Strict mental reservations are lies, because there is no way the listener can read the speaker's mind. Broad mental reservations are used in order to preserve secrets, when the benefit to the common good (not revealing the confidence) is greater than would be the manifestation of something that is sure to cause harm.

801. How must broad mental reservations be used?

Broad mental reservations must be used with great prudence. There is always the risk of creating mistrust if people cannot be sure that what they are told is what they can believe.

802. How do hypocrisy, flattery, and boastfulness amount to lies?

Hypocrisy is a lie by which a person pretends to be virtuous in order to win the esteem of others. Flattery is the insincere praise of a person or thing with the hope of gaining praise for one's self in return. Boasting is a form of deceit in which a person claims to have qualities that are not actually possessed.

2. Media of Social Communication

803. What are the modern means of social communication?

The modern means of social communication are: the press, cinema, radio, television, telephone, telegraph, radar, computer, and photography—along with their many combinations and derivatives.

804. What are the benefits of social communications?

Social communications facilitate the rapid, widespread, and persuasive interchange of ideas and information beyond anything ever before possible in the history of mankind.

805. What are the dangers of social communications?

Social communications can be manipulated contrary to the will of God. Instead of the truth, error can be communicated. And instead of raising moral and religious principles the media can be used to indoctrinate people in secularism and a disregard for Christian values.

806. What is the main condition for the proper use of the media?

The main condition for the proper use of the media is that those who control the means of social communication know the laws of sound morality and are willing to apply them.

807. What are the laws of morality governing mass communication?

The laws of morality governing mass communication are that the media must be operated in the interest of the common good, the information and ideas communicated should be true and within the limits of justice and charity, and there must be a prudent and balanced judgment in choosing what is both useful and aesthetically appealing.

808. Do people have a right to information through the media?

People have a right to information through the media about matters which affect their welfare, both as individuals and as members of society.

809. What are the duties of those who receive information?

Those who receive information should be discriminating about what they are being told, should protest when omission or distortion occurs, and should develop effective means for insuring that the truth is communicated to the public.

810. What is the morality of leisure in the right use of the media?

The morality of leisure in the right use of the media requires that we recognize the value of time and do not waste it in useless exposure to the attractive and often seductive mass communications.

811. What is the function of advertising?

The function of advertising is to announce publicly the desirable qualities of a thing so as to arouse a desire in someone to purchase or invest in what has been advertised.

812. How is advertising beneficial to society?

Advertising is beneficial to society because it helps people know beforehand what they are asked to buy or invest in, enables them to compare the different items advertised, gives them a right to expect (and demand) what has been advertised, stimulates healthy competition for excellence among advertisers, and assists the economy by encouraging people to prudently want what they might otherwise not have desired.

813. How can advertising be harmful to society?

Advertising harms society when it urges people to spend money beyond their available means, when it fosters a consumer mentality that believes happiness consists in having more material possessions and comforts, when it lowers the dignity of men and women by using sex to promote what is advertised, when it distorts the public image of a people by stressing the luxuries and nonessentials of human living, when it publicizes the sale of products or services that are immoral to use, and when it falsifies the quality or value of a commodity or investment.

814. Is the formation of public opinion justified?

The formation of public opinion is justified when the true leaders of a society are enabled to contribute to this formation, when the process of shaping the mind of a people serves the truth, when its objectives and methods accord with the dignity of man, and when it promotes causes that are consistent with the laws of God and the best interests of a society.

815. What is propaganda?

Propaganda is the conscious and organized forming of public opinion.

816. What types of propaganda are morally wrong?

Propaganda is morally wrong when it harms the true public welfare, or allows no response from the people, or withholds essential facts, falsifies in order to protect or promote some preconceived ideas or policy, or diminishes man's legitimate freedom of decision.

3. Keeping Secrets

817. What is a secret?

A secret is hidden knowledge that may not be revealed unless some higher right prevails.

818. What is a natural secret?

A natural secret is one that our reason tells us we should keep confidential.

819. How do I recognize a natural secret?

I can recognize a natural secret by asking if I would want this particular hidden fault, or defect, or sin, or mistake of mine revealed to anyone else.

820. What is a promised secret?

A promised secret is one that a person has promised to keep after having received or come upon confidential knowledge.

821. What are entrusted secrets?

Entrusted secrets are those a person is obliged to keep in virtue of his professional position.

822. What is our responsibility to keep secrets?

Secrets should be kept because each person has exclusive right to his own ideas and ingenuity and, if the confidential matter pertains to his reputation, the right to his good name. Natural and promised secrets may not be revealed unless keeping the knowledge hidden would cause grave damage or injury. Entrusted secrets must be kept unless the grave harm caused by withholding the information is imminent. Should one reveal a secret unjustly, the gravity of the sin depends on how serious the matter is.

823. May we read another person's letters, notes, or diaries?

We may not read another person's letters, notes, or diaries. It is sinful to do so unless permission has been given by the owner of the writing, or it may reasonably be presumed he would not mind. On the other hand, letters and similar written confidences may be read if it is considered necessary in order to prevent grave harm to the writer, oneself, or society.

824. What is meant by the seal of confession?

By the seal of confession is meant the absolute obligation to keep secret whatever is disclosed in sacramental confession. This applies to any confession, regardless of the circumstances of the sacrament. The confessor himself and anyone else who intentionally or unintentionally obtains knowledge of a confessional matter are bound by the seal.

825. What is reputation?

Reputation is the good opinion that one person has about another. Next to life it is the most precious of earthly possessions. Both the dead and the living have a right to good esteem. Reputation is the object of an acquired right, and to take it away from a person or lower it is an act of injustice. "A good name," we are told, "is more desirable than great wealth, the respect of others is better than silver or gold" (Proverbs 22:1).

826. How can a person's reputation be injured?

A person's reputation can be injured by detraction, calumny, or slander, and interiorly by rash judgments and suspicion.

4. Detraction, Calumny, Rash Judgment, and Vengeance

827. What is detraction?

Detraction is the unjust violation of the good name of another by revealing something true about him. The essence of detraction is the unwarranted disclosure of a hidden failing, which implies that there are occasions when the disclosure can and even should be made.

828. When may we disclose a person's hidden failings?

We may disclose another's hidden failings in order to help the person or to protect oneself or someone else from harm.

829. What is calumny?

Calumny, sometimes called slander, differs from detraction in that what is said or attributed to the person is not true. We are warned, "Brothers, do not slander one another. Anyone who slanders a brother, or condemns him, is speaking against the Law and condemning the Law" (James 4:11).

830. How sinful is calumny?

Calumny is by its nature a mortal sin. It immediately attacks truth, justice, and charity. It is venial only when the matter is light.

831. What are rash judgments?

Rash judgments are acts of the mind in which we go beyond the evidence available to judge the sinfulness of a person's action, attribute evil motives, and decide against the character of the one whose conduct we observed. People make rash judgments because they are inclined to see evil in what other people do and see only the good in their own conduct.

832. Are rash judgments wrong?

Rash judgments are wrong because of the hasty imprudence with which a critical judgment is reached. They are also wrong because of the loss of reputation that the person suffers in our estimation, since everyone has a right to the good esteem of his fellow men.

833. Who alone has the right to judge?

God alone has the right to judge the intention of the hearts of men. Jesus said to "Be compassionate as your Father is compassionate. Do not judge, and you will not be judged yourselves" (Luke 6:36–37).

834. What is meant by suspicion?

Suspicion is the tendency to consider the evil we think of others as true without believing it to be certain.

835. What is an insult?

An insult is any word, action, or gesture that tells a person he is not respected. It is also a failure to show someone those marks of esteem which he deserves. Should one person be insulted by another, he may never seek vengeance.

836. Why is vengeance wrong?

Vengeance is wrong because it serves no other purpose than to give selfish satisfaction to the injured party. To inflict punishment on a person in return for another's offense is forbidden by Christ, who wants us to forgive others even as he has forgiven us: "I say this to you: love your enemies and pray for those who persecute you; in this way you will be sons of your Father in heaven, for he causes his sun to rise on bad men as well as good, and his rain to fall on honest and dishonest men alike" (Matthew 5:44–45).

837. If vengeance is wrong, why does the Bible teach retaliation, that is, an eye for an eye, a tooth for a tooth?

The Old Testament teaches that those who do harm to others should be punished according to the measure of their crime. But this punishment may be inflicted only by legitimate civil authority and not by private individuals. Moreover, if some people in the Old Testament believed in private retaliation, this was changed by Christ. He told his followers to forgive their offenders and to show charity even toward their enemies.

III.
THE BEATITUDES

1. *The New Covenant*

838. What does everyone desire to obtain?
Everyone desires to obtain happiness.

839. What is happiness?
Happiness is the experience of having one's desires satisfied.

840. How is true happiness achieved?
True happiness is achieved by doing the will of God. This is the teaching of divine revelation in the Old and New Testaments, and it is summarized in the Beatitudes.

841. What are the Beatitudes?
The Beatitudes are God's covenant with his chosen people in the New Testament. He promises them not only heaven in the world to come but joy on earth. In the Beatitudes, Christ explains how the joy foretold by the angels at Bethlehem is to be attained.

842. How many Beatitudes are there?
There are eight Beatitudes which our Lord proclaimed in his Sermon on the Mount. They may be called the eight commandments of the New Law. Each commandment carries the promise of a distinctive form of happiness (cf. Matthew 5:1–12).

843. Is it possible to practice the Beatitudes?
It is possible for any of the faithful, no matter what their state of life, to practice the Beatitudes. But they must pray and trust in God. Christ tells us, "my yoke is easy and my burden

light" (Matthew 11:30). Doing the will of God is a yoke but love makes it easy, and denying oneself to follow Christ is a burden but divine grace makes it light.

844. Why are they called Beatitudes?

They are called Beatitudes because they begin with the word "blessed" or "happy" and end with the assurance of a reward for the practice of a certain virtue.

2. *Eight Sources of True Happiness*

845. What is the first Beatitude?

The first Beatitude is: "How happy are the poor in spirit; theirs is the kingdom of heaven."

846. Who are the poor in spirit?

The poor in spirit are those who voluntarily become poor to follow Christ more closely, those who are detached in spirit from the material goods of this life, those who maintain a low opinion of themselves while others esteem them, and those who are satisfied with what they have and accept it without impatience.

847. What is the kingdom of God promised to the poor in spirit?

The kingdom of God promised to the poor in spirit is the state of grace by which God now lives in us and the beatific vision in the world to come.

848. What does Christ advocate in the first Beatitude?

In the first Beatitude, Christ advocates poverty, while the world despises the poor and canonizes the rich.

849. What is the second Beatitude?

The second Beatitude is: "Happy the gentle: they shall have the earth for their heritage."

850. What is gentleness?

Gentleness is love when faced with provocation; it is acting toward others with charity and humility, without sharpness, without contempt, and without ever becoming impatient with their short-comings.

851. What heritage is promised to the gentle?

The heritage promised to the gentle is the land of their own hearts of which they have control, the land of the hearts of others which they have conquered by their goodness, and the land of heaven.

852. What does Christ praise in the second Beatitude?

In the second Beatitude, Christ praises gentleness while the world belittles meekness and extols those who succeed by crushing anyone who stands in the way.

853. What is the third Beatitude?

The third Beatitude is: "Happy those who mourn: they shall be comforted."

854. What kind of mourning is praised by Christ?

Christ especially praises the mourning of repentance for one's own sins and of reparation for the sins of others; and the mourning of sorrow over the loss, by death or separation, of someone who is loved.

855. What is Christ's promise to those who mourn?

Christ's promise to those who mourn is the spiritual strength they need to remain firm in their tribulation and, in fact, to grow in God's friendship because of their trial.

856. What does Christ mainly encourage in the third Beatitude?

Christ mainly encourages sorrow for sin while the world revels in pleasure and the noise of empty laughter.

857. What is the fourth Beatitude?

The fourth Beatitude is: "Happy those who hunger and thirst for what is right: they shall be satisfied."

858. Who are the ones that hunger and thirst for what is right?

Those that hunger and thirst for what is right are those who desire what they should. They want what God wants; and their desires are always satisfied.

859. How are those who hunger and thirst for what is right satisfied?

Those who hunger and thirst for what is right are satisfied because their desires are in agreement with God's will. And God always gives a deep spiritual joy to those who do his will in spite of trial and difficulty. Indeed, there is no true happiness even in this life, except in conformity with the divine Will.

860. What does Christ promise in the fourth Beatitude?

In the fourth Beatitude, Christ promises joy only to those who seek justice and holiness, while the world offers satisfaction in the enjoyment of sin.

861. What is the fifth Beatitude?

The fifth Beatitude is: "Happy the merciful: they shall have mercy shown them."

862. Who are the merciful?

The merciful are those who forgive injuries and pardon those who offend them. Mercy is love shown to the unlovable, and charity to those who have been unjust and ungrateful.

863. What is the reward of the merciful?

The reward of the merciful is that they will obtain mercy from God.

864. What does Christ command in the fifth Beatitude?

In the fifth Beatitude, Christ commands us to forgive and show mercy to those who have offended us while the world seeks vengeance and its law courts are filled with demands for retribution.

865. What is the sixth Beatitude?

The sixth Beatitude is: "Happy the pure in heart; they shall see God."

866. Who are the pure in heart?

The pure in heart are those who observe chastity according to their state of life. They are all whose hearts are free from sinful attachment to creatures.

867. What reward is given to the pure in heart?

The reward given to the pure in heart is a clear faith in the divine mysteries in this life, and the promise of the vision of God in the life to come.

868. Whom does Christ bless in the sixth Beatitude?

In the sixth Beatitude, Christ blesses those who are pure in heart while the world scoffs at chastity and makes an idol of creatures.

869. What is the seventh Beatitude?

The seventh Beatitude is: "Happy the peacemakers: they shall be called sons of God."

870. Who are the peacemakers?

Peacemakers are those who love peace and labor to establish peace all around them; they try to heal discord between people and especially seek to reconcile sinners who are estranged from God.

871. What are the rewards promised to peacemakers?

The rewards promised to peacemakers are the grace now of being specially loved by God as his dearest children and the attainment of heavenly glory, as part of God's family, in eternity.

872. What is the eighth Beatitude?

The eighth Beatitude is: "Happy those who are persecuted in the cause of right: theirs is the kingdom of heaven."

873. Who are those persecuted in the cause of right?

Those are persecuted in the cause of right who are opposed and criticized for their loyalty to Christ and his Church and who persevere in doing God's will in spite of not being accepted or even being rejected by others.

874. What does Christ teach in the eighth Beatitude?

Christ teaches the humanly impossible doctrine of accepting persecution with patience and resignation to God's will, while the world dreads nothing more than criticism and rejection; and human respect, which means acceptance by society, is the world's moral norm.

875. What is the reward for suffering persecution?

The reward for suffering persecution on earth is the possession of the kingdom of God in heaven.

IV.
COMMANDMENTS
OF THE CHURCH

Principal Obligations of Catholics

876. Are we obliged to keep only the Commandments of God?

We are also to keep the commandments of the Church, which are called the precepts of the Church.

877. By what authority does the Church make commandments?

The Church makes commandments by the authority given to her by Christ, as when he told the apostles, "All authority in heaven and on earth has been given to me. Go, therefore, make disciples of all the nations" (Matthew 28:18–19). To St. Peter, the head of the apostles, he said, "I will give you the keys of the kingdom of heaven; whatever you bind on earth shall be considered bound in heaven" (Matthew 16:19).

878. What obedience do we owe the laws of the Church?

The obedience we owe the laws of the Church is not merely external conformity but internal submission of will. It is not enough to keep the letter of the law; we must understand the spirit of the law and put it into practice.

879. Why did the Church make commandments?

The Church made commandments to enable the faithful to better observe the Commandments of God and to follow the teachings of the Gospel.

880. What are the principal commandments of the Church?

1. To keep holy the day of the Lord's Resurrection: to worship God by participating in Mass every Sunday and holyday of obligation; to avoid those activities that would hinder renewal of soul and body, e.g., needless work and business activities or unnecessary shopping.

2. To lead a sacramental life: to receive Holy Communion frequently and the sacrament of penance regularly—minimally, to receive the sacrament of penance at least once a year, between the First Sunday of Lent and Trinity Sunday.

3. To study Catholic teaching in preparation for the sacraments of penance, the Eucharist, and confirmation; to be confirmed; and then to continue to study the Catholic faith.

4. To observe the marriage laws of the Church: to give religious training (by example and word) to one's children; to use parish schools and religious education programs.

5. To strengthen and support the Church, one's own parish community and parish priests, the worldwide Church and the Holy Father.

6. To do penance, including abstaining from meat and fasting from food on the appointed days.

7. To join in the missionary spirit and apostolate of the Church.

881. What rights does the Church have regarding the Commandments of God and her own precepts?

The Church has the right to interpret the Commandments of God and her precepts for the faithful. She is divinely authorized to protect the faithful from misinterpretation of the divine and ecclesiastical laws. She is to watch over the observance of the Decalogue and her own precepts. And she may legitimately punish those who are disobedient, for example, by excluding them from the sacraments, from Christian burial, and, in extreme cases, even from visible communion with the rest of the faithful.

882. Why has the Church given us these commandments?

They are given to the faithful to explain the Commandments of God more precisely and determine more particularly how they are to be observed.

883. Are these the only commandments of the Church?

No, there are many other laws of the Church, of which these are only the more common ones that affect most of the people. A complete collection of the Church's laws, unified and synthesized, is in the Code of Canon Law.

V.
KNOWLEDGE OF GOD'S WILL

Meaning, Types, and Formation of Conscience

884. How do we know the divine will in our regard?

We know the divine will from the natural and revealed laws of God.

885. How does each person individually know God's will in all the circumstances of life?

Each person knows God's will individually through the voice of conscience.

886. How do we form our conscience?

We form our conscience by learning what God wants us to do from the Church's moral teaching as expressed by the hierarchy in communion with the bishop of Rome. We further form our conscience by the practice of frequent prayer asking God to enlighten us, not only in times of crisis but often during the day. We finally form our conscience by faithfully putting into practice what we know is God's will, no matter what the observance may cost us.

887. What is conscience?

Conscience is the practical judgment of our intellect deciding, from the general principles of reason and faith, on the goodness or badness of our human actions.

888. Must we always follow our conscience?

Yes, we must always follow our conscience, provided we made an honest effort to know our duty and are certain that something is the right thing to do.

889. What are the functions of conscience?

The functions of conscience are twofold. The operation of the mind before we perform a human action either commands or forbids, counsels or permits the act, according to whether it is right or wrong. After the act is performed, the conscience passes judgment on what we have done, telling us whether it was good or bad.

890. What kind of conscience is necessary for growth in Christian virtue?

To grow in Christian virtue, our conscience should be alert to fulfill the divine will, not only in matters of strict obligation, but in whatever would be pleasing to God.

891. How can our conscience become more spiritually sensitive?

Our conscience can become more spiritually sensitive by the regular practice of examining our conduct during the day to see how well we have cooperated with the will of God.

892. What is a scrupulous conscience?

A scrupulous conscience is a timid and fearful conscience. Its tendency is to judge something to be wrong when it is lawful. It is an unbalanced conscience.

893. What should a person do who is troubled by a scrupulous conscience?

A person with a scrupulous conscience should consult a prudent confessor and follow his advice with trustful obedience.

894. When is a conscience perplexed?

A conscience is perplexed when it sees sin in both the performance and the omission of some act.

895. What is a lax conscience?

A lax conscience decides on insufficient grounds that a sinful act is permissible or that something gravely wrong is not serious. A lax conscience sees virtue where there is sin.

896. What is a pharisaic conscience?

A pharisaic conscience minimizes grave sins but magnifies matters of little importance. It is called "pharisaic" because it is like that of the Pharisees in the Gospels. Of them, Jesus said, "This people honors me only with lip service, while their hearts are far from me. The worship they offer me is worthless; the doctrines they teach are only human regulations" (Matthew 15:8–9). The Pharisees observed the external precepts of the Jewish law and were proud and self-righteous men who looked down on others as publicans and sinners.

897. What is a hardened conscience?

A hardened conscience judges that either all or certain grave sins are trivial or not wrong at all. It is acquired by the habit of sinning mortally, until a person's mind makes virtue out of vice.

898. When is a conscience certain?

A conscience is certain when it has no prudent fear of being wrong but firmly decides that some action is right or wrong.

899. What is a doubtful conscience?

A conscience is doubtful when a person cannot decide for or against a course of moral action. We may never act on a doubtful conscience.

900. What is an erroneous conscience?

An erroneous conscience tells a person that a good action is bad or a bad action is good.

901. How is a doubtful conscience to be resolved?

A doubtful conscience should be resolved by personal reflection, seeking wise counsel and, above all, asking for divine light in prayer. Christ tells us to seek for illumination in prayer: "Ask, and it will be given to you; search and you will find; knock, and the door will be opened to you" (Matthew 7:7).

VI.
VIOLATION OF GOD'S WILL

1. Capital Sins: Pride, Lust, Anger, Covetousness, Envy, Sloth, and Gluttony

902. What is sin?

Sin is the willful transgression of a divine law, that is, we knowingly and freely go beyond the limits that God has imposed on our moral liberty.

903. Why are we led into sin?

We are led into sin because we want our own personal satisfaction rather than submit to the will of God. "But they would not pay attention; they turned a petulant shoulder; they stopped their ears rather than hear; they made their hearts adamant rather than listen to the teaching and the words that Yahweh Sabaoth had sent by his spirit through the prophets in the past" (Zechariah 7:11–12).

904. What sins are the basis of all human failings?

The sins that are the basis of all human failings are the capital sins.

905. What is the common origin of all capital sins?

The common origin of all capital sins is original sin.

906. What are the capital sins?

Capital sins are the perverse inclinations of our fallen human nature, namely, pride, lust, anger, covetousness, envy, sloth, and gluttony.

907. What is pride?

Pride is an excessive love of our own superiority. It blinds a person to the truth that all our good qualities are gifts from God and that others have the same or even greater gifts. It begets a spirit of independence that is impatient with subjection to authority, whether human or divine. Humility is the virtue opposed to pride. St. Paul reminds us of our place, "What do you have that was not given to you? And if it was given, how can you boast as though it were not?" (1 Corinthians 4:7).

908. What is lust?

Lust is the inordinate desire for sexual pleasure. The desire is inordinate when sought outside the bonds and laws of marriage. Christ warned us against lust, even in our desires, "If a man looks at a woman lustfully, he has already committed adultery with her in his heart" (Matthew 5:28). Chastity is the virtue opposed to lust.

909. What is anger?

Anger is a disorderly emotion that inclines a person to repel whatever displeases him; if not controlled it can become hatred and lead one to seek revenge.

910. When is anger unjust or sinful?

Anger is sinful when the feeling of displeasure is not justified or goes beyond what the situation requires. Anger is especially wrong when it inflicts pain on another person who does not deserve to be punished, or the punishment exceeds the fault, or punishment is inflicted to satisfy a spiteful feeling or revenge. The virtue contrary to anger is gentleness or meekness.

911. How is covetousness defined?

Covetousness is an excessive love of temporal goods, usually in terms of money. It makes a person hard-hearted, miserly about sharing what he owns with others, eager to accumulate riches and indifferent about the means he uses to acquire wealth and power. The opposite virtue is liberality.

912. What is envy?

Envy is the sadness experienced in seeing the talents, achievement, property, or success of others that a person feels outshines or obscures his own. The contrary virtue is love. "It was the devil's envy that brought death into the world, as those who are his partners will discover" (Wisdom 2:24).

913. What is the difference between envy and jealousy?

The difference between envy and jealousy is the motive. Envious people are sad because someone else has what they themselves lack; jealous people are slow or unwilling to share with others what they themselves possess.

914. What is sloth?

Sloth is an inordinate love of ease, that leads a person to omit or neglect recognized duties. It is more or less sinful depending on the duty neglected and the scandal it gives. Another name for sloth is laziness, which may be either spiritual or physical. In spiritual laziness we are unwilling to exert our minds and wills; in physical laziness we fail to exert our bodies. The virtue contrary to sloth in diligence.

915. What is gluttony?

Gluttony is an inordinate love of eating or drinking. It means eating or drinking to excess, taking more than is needed or healthy, or indulging the appetite merely for pleasure, or beyond one's means. The virtue opposed to gluttony is temperance.

916. What is the difference between sin and vice?

Sin is an evil action, whereas vice is an evil habit. Therefore, it is possible to commit a sin against a certain virtue without having the vice opposed to the virtue.

2. Personal Sins, Mortal and Venial

917. What is personal sin?

Personal sin is the sin of each individual.

918. How many kinds of personal sin are there?
There are two kinds of personal sin, actual and habitual.

919. What is actual sin?
Actual sin is any deliberate thought, word, deed, or omission contrary to God's eternal law.

920. How can we commit actual sins?
We commit actual sins by evil thoughts when they become sinful desires; by words which may be spoken, written, or expressed in some other way; by deeds which involve some voluntary external action; and by omission which is a failure to do what should be done in a given situation.

921. How are actual sins classified in their effect on the soul?
Actual sins are either mortal sins or venial sins, depending on whether they deprive a person of supernatural life or not.

922. What is mortal sin?
Mortal sin is an actual sin that destroys sanctifying grace in the soul. It is called mortal since it causes the supernatural death of the soul.

923. What are the conditions for a mortal sin?
There are three conditions for a mortal sin. First, the matter or what is done must be seriously wrong, either in itself or because of the circumstances, as telling a lie under oath; or because of the purpose, as telling others something bad about someone in order to ruin that person's character. Second, there must be clear awareness of the serious nature of the act at the time it is performed. And third, there is full consent of the will, so that a person deliberately wants to do what he knows is gravely sinful.

924. What are the effects of mortal sin?
The effects of mortal sin are the loss of divine friendship, past supernatural merits, and the right to enter heaven unless the sinner repents. St. James says, "When sin is fully grown, it too has a child, and the child is death" (James 1:15).

925. How can the supernatural life of the soul be restored?
The supernatural life of the soul, lost by mortal sin, can be restored by the sacrament of penance or by a perfect act of contri-

tion. In the sacrament of penance a person confesses the mortal sin(s) and receives absolution from the priest. In a perfect act of contrition, the person is sorry for having offended God who is all good and deserving of all our love; and resolves to confess the mortal sin(s) in the sacrament at his early convenience.

926. What is venial sin?

Venial sin is an offense against God that does not deprive the sinner of sanctifying grace. As the psalmist writes, "He may fall, but never fatally, since Yahweh supports him by the hand" (Psalms 37:24).

927. Why are some sins called venial?

Some sins are called venial from the Latin word *venia,* which means "pardon." A person in venial sin still has the principle of supernatural life that allows healing (or pardon) from within. Mortal sins require the special intervention of God's mercy to restore a supernaturally dead soul to spiritual life. Venial sins are also called minor, or ordinary, or daily sins. They may best be called harmful sins, compared to those that are deadly or mortal. Of venial sin, St. John wrote, "Every kind of wrongdoing is sin, but not all sin is deadly" (1 John 5:17).

928. When does a person commit a venial sin?

A person commits a venial sin when he transgresses a divine law that is not grave, or when he transgresses a grave precept but without awareness of its gravity or without full consent. St. James says, "Every one of us does something wrong, over and over again" (James 3:2).

929. What are the effects of venial sin?

Venial sin darkens the mind in its perception of virtue, weakens the will in its pursuit of holiness, lowers one's resistance to temptation, and causes a person to deviate from the path that leads to heavenly glory.

3. Occasions of Sin, Temptation, Situation Ethics, and Fundamental Option

930. How are people led into doing wrong?

People are led into doing wrong through occasions of sin.

931. What is meant by occasion of sin?

An occasion of sin is any external circumstance—a person, place, or thing—that of its own nature or because of man's weakness inclines and leads one to sin. Associating with dishonest people can be the occasion to sins of dishonesty; watching television programs or reading books that make light of Christian marriage or family life can lead to sins of adultery; and living in surroundings that are preoccupied with this world can weaken a person's religion and faith in life after death.

932. What are the kinds of occasion of sin?

There are two kinds of occasion of sins: a proximate occasion will certainly or at least probably lead a person into sin; and in a remote occasion the danger of committing sin is only slight.

933. Are we obliged to avoid the occasion of sin?

We are not obliged to avoid a remote occasion of sin unless there is danger that it will likely become a near occasion of sin. We are obliged to avoid all voluntary proximate occasions of sin.

934. What is temptation?

A temptation is any urge or incitement to sin, either by offering a person some satisfaction or by persuading a person's will. Temptations arise from the world, the flesh, and the devil.

935. How does temptation arise from the world?

Temptation arises from the world when other human beings solicit us to sin. They do so by what they are (their evil but attractive life), by what they say (in speech, writing, or audiovisual media), or by what they do (their sinful actions which invite imitation).

936. How does temptation arise from the flesh?

Temptation arises from the flesh insofar as we have sinful tendencies due to our fallen human nature. These tendencies come from within ourselves and they are both bodily, as with gluttony or lust, and spiritual, as in envy or pride.

937. How does temptation arise from the devil?

Temptation arises from the devil who is permitted by God to try to deceive us by stressing the benefits of something that is sinful.

938. What is habitual sin?

Habitual sin is the sinful state of a soul resulting from actual sin.

939. What kinds of habitual sin are there?

There are two kinds of habitual sin. More properly, habitual sin refers to the state of soul in unrepented mortal sin. Habitual sin, however, may also mean the weakened state of soul of a person, with unforgiven venial sins, who is still in the grace of God.

940. What is the habit of sin?

The habit of sin is the ease of committing certain sins that a person acquires by repeatedly doing some particular action that is morally wrong.

941. What is situation ethics?

Situation ethics is a purely subjective theory of conduct. It holds that the final standard of conduct is not an objective norm found outside of man and independent of his subjective persuasion, but an immediate internal illumination and judgment of each person for himself in whatever situation he finds himself. Thus, according to situation ethics, adultery is permissible when a person finds marital fidelity difficult to practice; and contraception is permissible when periodic continence would be inconvenient; and abortion is allowable when the mother's reputation is at stake.

942. What is the Church's position on situation ethics?

The Church teaches that situation ethics does not conform to the objective principles of Catholic morality.

943. How are the principles of Christian morality objective?

The principles of Christian morality are objective because they are independent of the personal judgment of each person. Right and wrong do not exist only in the mind. They are also objective because their validity is not conditioned by changing circumstances or times. And they are objective in their capacity to evoke great moral courage and generosity.

944. What is the theory of the fundamental option?

The theory of the fundamental option holds that the only mortal sin a person can commit is to choose to reject God. No matter how objectively grave a sin may be, e.g., adultery, it is not a mortal sin unless a person makes a radical decision (fundamental option) against serving God.

945. What is the Church's teaching on the fundamental option?

The Church's teaching on the fundamental option is that mortal sin, which is opposed to God, does not consist only in the explicit resistance to the divine commandment of charity. It is equally present in every deliberate choice of a creature that a person knows is gravely opposed to the will of God. In other words, mortal sin is committed whenever a person deliberately does anything which is seriously contrary to the law of God. It is God and not man who decides what deprives man of divine friendship.

946. Does the practice of morality include other particular precepts besides love?

Yes, the practice of morality includes other particular precepts. Therefore a person sins mortally not only when his action comes from direct contempt for love of God and neighbor, but also when he consciously and freely, *for whatever reason,* chooses something which is seriously disordered. For in this choice, there is already included contempt for the divine commandment.

VII.
THE VIRTUES

1. Theological Virtues

947. What is a virtue?

A virtue is a good habit, as opposed to a vice, which is a bad habit. Habit refers to the ease, readiness, satisfaction, and effectiveness with which we perform human actions. Habits reside in the faculties of the mind and the will. They may be acquired either by personal effort, or directly infused into the soul by God. Infused virtues are those supernatural virtues directly produced by God in the faculties of man.

948. What are the theological virtues?

They are the infused virtues of faith, hope, and charity, which supply for the mind and will what neither faculty has of itself, namely, the salutary knowledge, desire, and love of God and his will that lead to heaven. Without these there could be no supernatural order, which means the voluntary choice of the right means to reach our heavenly destiny.

949. What is the difference between natural and supernatural virtues?

Supernatural virtues differ from the natural because they are powers directly infused in the soul by God to enable one to act on a supernatural level; natural virtues, acquired by human activity, are habits of the soul which incline it to do good.

950. How can we grow in virtue?

We can grow in all the virtues in the same way that we grow in grace, namely by prayer, participation in the Liturgy and reception of the sacraments, and good works. We also grow in the virtues by practicing them with the help of God's grace.

951. How are infused virtues diminished or even lost?

Infused virtues are diminished by not performing acts of faith, hope, and charity, and by venial sin; depending on the virtue, they are lost when a person commits a mortal sin. Thus supernatural charity is lost by every mortal sin, hope is lost by the sin of despair, and faith by a grave sin of disbelief in whatever God has revealed.

2. *Faith as a Virtue*

952. What is the virtue of faith?

Faith is a supernatural virtue by which we believe all the truths which God has revealed.

953. Why is faith called a supernatural virtue?

Faith is called a supernatural virtue because it is directly infused in the soul by God, because what we believe is the revealed truth, and because it is necessary for our salvation.

954. What is the authority of God as the basic motive for our faith?

The authority of God as the basic motive for our faith is his infinite wisdom and his truthfulness.

955. How is God's wisdom a motive for divine faith?

God's wisdom is a motive for divine faith because we are ready to believe in God who knows all things and therefore cannot be deceived.

956. How is God's truthfulness a motive for our faith?

God's truthfulness is a motive for our faith because we are also ready to believe in God who is all good and therefore would not deceive us.

957. How do we know that our motive for faith is reasonable?

We know that our motive for faith is reasonable because we can know from reason that God exists and that he actually made a revelation.

958. Is the virtue of faith necessary for salvation?

Yes, the virtue of faith is absolutely necessary because no one can be saved without sanctifying grace; and sanctifying grace cannot exist without habitual faith. Christ himself said, "he who does not believe will be condemned" (Mark 16:16).

959. How can the gift of faith be lost?

The gift of faith can be lost by neglecting to know what we are bound to believe; by not making an honest effort to understand what we believe and why; by not performing acts of faith, through internal belief and external profession of what we believe; and by failing to strengthen our faith through the sacraments of penance and the Eucharist and through constant prayer.

960. What are the principal means of persevering in the faith?

The principal means of persevering in the faith are fidelity to grace and especially the grace of prayer; combating pride, avarice, and sensuality; humble reflection on the mysteries of faith; associating with people who have a deep faith; and regular reading of authors who are loyal to the teaching authority of the Catholic Church.

961. What are the sins against faith?

Sins against faith by omission are the willful neglect to learn what should be believed. Sins by commission are heresy if anything that God has revealed is doubted or denied, or apostasy if everything is doubted or denied.

962. What are doubts against the faith?

Doubts against the faith are deliberate inclinations not to accept whatever a person knows God has revealed. This is seriously sinful, for God wants us to believe unhesitatingly with complete submission to his revealed word.

963. What are difficulties about the faith?

Difficulties about the faith are problems that one has in understanding why or how something revealed is true. Nevertheless, in spite of the difficulties, one firmly believes.

964. How are difficulties different from positive doubts?

Unlike difficulties in the faith, positive doubts are a willful refusal to fully assent to what God has revealed. Unlike positive doubts, difficulties are not sinful; they can arise in the mind of any sincere believer because he cannot comprehend what God has revealed. For this reason, we must pray for a strong faith to believe even though we do not fully understand. Otherwise difficulties can lead to doubts, when a person willfully admits the possibility that a revealed truth may be false.

3. Supernatural Hope

965. What is the virtue of hope?

The virtue of hope is a supernatural virtue by which we firmly trust that God will give us heaven in the life to come, and in this life will provide all the means we need to reach heaven. The foundation of hope is our belief that God is faithful to his promises.

966. Why is hope a supernatural virtue?

Hope is a supernatural virtue because of its purpose and the way it is received. Its purpose is to lead us to the eternal salvation to which we have no natural right or claim. It can be received only by a special gift of God's grace, and not by any merely natural effort on our part.

967. Does hope in a future life lessen the importance of our earthly life?

Hope in a life to come does not lessen but rather increases the importance of this life by giving us new motives for performing our earthly duties. Without hope of eternity, our life on earth would lose most of its dignity and meaning.

968. What is the object of our hope?

The main object of our hope is everlasting happiness, that is, the possession of God in heaven. The secondary object is the means of obtaining eternal happiness, namely, sanctifying and actual grace. Anything else is to be hoped for only insofar as it leads to the possession of God in eternity. "For you alone are my hope, Lord" (Psalms 71:5).

969. Is the virtue of hope necessary?

Yes, the virtue of hope is necessary because it is the link between faith and charity. We must believe (with the mind) in something before we can hope (with the will) to obtain it. Our hope enables us to love what we are looking forward to attain. St. Paul says, "We must hope to be saved since we are not saved yet" (Romans 8:25).

970. Is hope sufficient for salvation?

The virtue of hope is not sufficient for salvation. It must also be animated by supernatural charity.

971. When are we obliged to make acts of hope?

We are obliged to make acts of hope when we reach the age of reason and understand sufficiently what God has promised us. We should make acts of hope often in life, at the point of death, and whenever we are tempted to discouragement.

972. How can a person sin against hope?

A person can sin against hope by presumption and despair.

973. How do we sin by presumption?

We sin by presumption by acting as though we can save our souls without God's help. This is shown by neglect of prayer and by a foolhardy exposure to moral dangers and temptations to the faith. At the other extreme it reflects the mistaken notion that God will save us in spite of ourselves with the consequent postponement of conversion. Presumption is a serious sin because it implies contempt for the order that God has provided for man to be saved.

974. What is meant by the sin of despair?

The sin of despair means that salvation is believed to be impossible because God might withhold grace; or grace is recognized but cooperation with grace is considered practically impossible. Convinced that God, salvation, or grace are unattainable, the will gives up in despair. Despair is a serious sin because it implies the denial of God's mercy.

4. Love of God and Our Neighbor

975. What is the virtue of charity?

Charity is the supernatural virtue by which we love God above all things for his own sake, and our neighbor as ourselves, indeed, as Christ has loved us.

976. Why is charity a supernatural virtue?

Charity is a supernatural virtue because it is not naturally acquired but specially infused into the soul at baptism. It is also supernatural because it enables us to do what is naturally impossible to attain the eternal vision of God by loving him, our neighbor, and ourselves with the same love as he has been showing us.

977. What is the object of charity?

The main object of charity is God; the secondary objects are ourselves and our neighbor.

978. What does charity toward God involve?

As Jesus said, "You must love the Lord your God with all your heart, with all your soul, and with all your mind" (Matthew 22:37). We must love God above all other things, and be ready to lose everything rather than offend him. Charity toward God, expressed by frequent acts of love, is necessary for salvation. In perfect charity, we are not motivated by any benefit, but simply by the desire to please the all-good God. This is pure love.

979. How can a person sin against charity toward God?

A person sins against charity toward God by failure to make acts of the love of God, by inordinate love of creatures, by ungrateful murmurings against God, by a dislike or hatred of God, and by every sin committed, especially mortal sin.

980. How should we love ourselves?

We should love ourselves with a holy love, that is, for God's sake; with a just love, that is, within the limits of what is pleasing to God; and with a true love, that is, desiring only what is supernaturally good for us.

981. Can self-love be disorderly?

Self-love can be disorderly whenever we prefer ourselves and the things of this world to God and his divine will.

982. What is the remedy for disorderly self-love?

The remedy for disorderly self-love is a constant struggle against pride, by practicing humble obedience, against sensuality, by abstinence from unlawful pleasures, and against greed, by detaching our desires from the things of this world.

983. What is meant by love of neighbor?

By love of neighbor we mean that we share with others what we possess. The command to love our neighbor is actually the profoundest human need. It is a positive hunger of the spirit to exercise its freedom, by freely giving of ourselves, for the love of God, in order to benefit others, and in the process we imitate the perfect sharing among the divine Persons in the Holy Trinity. Christ told us that the love we have for one another would identify us as his disciples: "By this love you have for one another, everyone will know that you are my disciples" (John 13:35).

984. Who is our neighbor?

Our neighbor is any person who is able to enjoy everlasting happiness or who already enjoys it. Therefore our neighbor is any person on earth, the souls in purgatory, and the angels and saints in heaven.

985. Can we love God and not love our neighbor?

No. Jesus Christ has declared that the precept which commands us to love our neighbor as God loves us is like that which commands us to love God. We are obliged to love God *and* our neighbor.

986. What is Christ's command about loving our neighbor?

Christ commanded us to love one another as he has loved us. "I give you a new commandment: love one another; just as I have loved you, you also must love one another" (John 13:34).

987. Why did Christ call this a new commandment?

Christ called this a new commandment because it is higher than even the highest precept of charity in the Old Testament.

988. What was the highest precept of charity of the Old Law?

The highest precept of charity of the Old Law was to "love your neighbor as yourself" (Leviticus 19:18).

989. Did Christ do away with this precept of the Old Law?

No. He repeated and confirmed it. But he also gave us his own new commandment of love.

990. How does Christ's new commandment of love surpass the Old Testament precept of charity?

Christ's new commandment of love surpasses the Old Testament precept of charity in two ways: in giving us a higher motive and standard for loving others, and in bidding us love one another mutually.

991. What is the higher motive we now have for loving others?

The higher motive we now have for loving others is to show our love for God, who became man to show his love for us.

992. What is the higher standard we now have for loving others?

The higher standard we now have in loving others is the measure of Christ's love for us.

993. How is Christ's love for us a higher standard?

Christ's love for us is a higher standard because Christ loved (and loves) us more than we love ourselves. He loved us even to dying for us, and he loves us with the selfless generosity of God.

994. What did Christ mean when he commanded us to love one another mutually?

When Christ gave us this commandment, he was laying the foundation of the Christian community. The selfless love of his followers for one another brought into existence a new Society, the Church, whose members would do what is humanly impossible. With Christ's grace, each would love the other with self-sacrificing generosity after the example of the Son of God who became man and died on the Cross out of love for us.

995. How is fraternal charity put into practice?

Fraternal charity is put into practice by wishing our neighbor well out of love of God, and by performing the spiritual and corporal works of mercy.

996. What are the spiritual works of mercy?

The spiritual works of mercy are: to admonish the sinner, instruct the ignorant, counsel the doubtful, comfort the sorrowful, bear wrongs patiently, forgive all injuries, and pray for the living and the dead.

997. What are the corporal works of mercy?

The corporal works of mercy are: to feed the hungry, give drink to the thirsty, clothe the naked, ransom the captive, shelter the homeless, visit the sick, and bury the dead.

998. Who are our enemies?

Our enemies are those who needlessly cause us pain, who have been unjust to us, or who, out of hatred or dislike, oppose or persecute us.

999. How must we love our enemies?

We must love our enemies by forgiving them the wrong they have done to us, relieving their needs when we can do so, and treating them as Christ treated his enemies, that is, with great mercy and compassion. At the Sermon on the Mount, Christ commanded: "Love your enemies and pray for those who persecute you; . . . For if you love those who love you, what right have you to claim any credit? Even the tax collectors do as much, do they not?" (Matthew 5:44, 46).

1000. How do we sin against charity toward our neighbor?

We sin against fraternal charity internally by hatred, envy, and discord. We can sin externally by dispute, scandal, and cooperation in the sins of others. Hatred is wishing someone evil, envy is sadness at another's possession or achievement, discord is the conflict brought on by self-will, scandal is any evil act or omission that becomes the occasion of spiritual harm to another, and cooperation in the sins of another means agreeing with another person's sinful action or helping someone to do wrong.

1001. How does Christian charity include the sharing of spiritual possessions with others?

Christian charity includes the sharing of spiritual possessions, notably one's thoughts and the deepest sentiments of one's heart. This means the desire to communicate with others in conversation, especially about matters religious and other important things in life.

5. Moral Virtues: Prudence, Justice, Fortitude, and Temperance

1002. What are moral virtues?

They are those virtues whose immediate object is not God, the final end of all things, but human activities that lead one to God. They are acquired virtues because they are normally developed by human effort, and facility is achieved through repetition. But the moral virtues can also be supernaturally infused. The four moral virtues—prudence, fortitude, temperance, and justice—are also called cardinal virtues, because they are primary in human conduct.

1003. How can moral virtues be diminished or lost?

The moral virtues can be diminished or lost just as they are acquired: directly, by the repetition of acts that are opposed to the virtues, which may not only destroy the virtue but replace it with the opposite vice; or indirectly, by not performing the acts which produce and maintain the virtues. When we fail to practice a good habit, it weakens and dies out.

1004. What is the virtue of prudence?

Prudence is a moral virtue of the mind which enables us to decide what is the right thing to do in a given situation.

1005. What are the functions of prudence?

The functions of prudence are to *deliberate* on the means and circumstances needed to perform a morally good action; to *judge* whether the means and circumstances are as good as they should be; and to *command* the will to put into practical effect the decisions that have been made.

1006. What are the virtues allied to prudence?

The virtues allied to prudence are good counsel, which profits from the advice of others when confronted with difficult affairs; common sense, which judges things according to the ordinary rules of conduct; and good judgment, which is attentive to the mind of the lawmaker.

1007. What is the virtue of justice?

Justice is the moral virtue that constantly disposes the will to give everyone what is his or her due. It is an all-balanced fairness in dealing with others. Of justice the Scriptures say: "If you pursue justice you will achieve it and put it on like a festal gown. Birds consort with their kind, justice comes home to those who practice it" (Ecclesiasticus 27:8–9).

1008. What are the principal virtues that complement justice?

The virtues that complement justice are religion, which is the worship we owe to God; obedience, which we owe to those in authority in a society; truthfulness in communicating our thoughts; gratitude for benefits received; zeal in protecting others from evil; and restitution in repairing injuries caused.

1009. What is fortitude?

Fortitude is the moral virtue which inspires us to undergo suffering and to undertake difficult tasks. It therefore enables us to suffer great evils, even death itself, for the purpose of accomplishing good. And it strengthens us to begin and carry to completion enterprises that demand great endurance.

1010. What virtues accompany fortitude?

There are four virtues that accompany fortitude: magnanimity which means greatness of soul and inclines us to heroic acts of every kind of virtue; magnificence which inclines us to do great things at great expense; patience which enables us to keep our souls in peace, in spite of trials and opposition; and perseverance which helps us pursue a good cause to the end, no matter what obstacles stand in the way.

1011. What is temperance?

Temperance is the moral virtue which enables us to use according to right reason the things that are pleasant and agreeable to the senses.

1012. Why is the virtue of temperance important?

Temperance is important because it regulates our bodily appetites.

1013. What are the principal bodily appetites?

The principal bodily appetites are the desire to live as an individual and the desire to propagate the human race.

1014. How are bodily appetites controlled?

Bodily appetites are controlled by abstinence and sobriety, diligence, and chastity. Abstinence is moderation in the consumption of food for one's spiritual welfare; sobriety is regulating food, and especially drink, according to the dictates of right reason; diligence regulates our desire for ease and comfort; and chastity controls our desire for sexual pleasure in conformity with reason and the teachings of Christ.

1015. To what vices are these virtues opposed?

Abstinence is opposed to gluttony, sobriety is opposed to intemperance, diligence is opposed to laziness, and chastity is opposed to lust.

1016. What virtues coincide with temperance?

The virtues that coincide with temperance are clemency that remits the punishment due to a guilty person; meekness that restrains even justified anger; modesty that controls internal affections and bodily movements within the limits of right reason; moderation that tempers curiosity and the excessive desire for knowledge; and humility, based on profound self-knowledge, that leads people to regard themselves as small and undeserving of praise or recognition.

1017. How do the cardinal virtues guide our moral actions?

The cardinal virtues guide our moral actions by keeping our faculties in order: prudence is for the mind, justice is for the will, temperance controls the urge to what is pleasant, and fortitude enables us to bear with what is painful.

1018. How can we overcome our dominant moral failings?

We can overcome our dominant moral failings by honestly admitting what these failings are in our personality and character, then, concentrating on one failing at a time, we seriously strive to practice the corresponding virtue. All the while, we must ask God to help us and trust that his grace will be available.

1019. How do we develop good moral habits?

We develop good moral habits by first recognizing our sinful tendencies and, by overcoming them, cultivate the contrary virtues. In fact, our principal weaknesses are God's way of telling us that he expects us to grow especially in the opposite virtues.

VIII.
GIFTS AND
FRUITS OF THE
HOLY SPIRIT

1. Seven Gifts or Instincts of the Divine Indwelling

1020. Why do we appropriate the divine indwelling to the Holy Spirit?

We appropriate the divine indwelling to the Holy Spirit because this greatest manifestation of divine love in the created world is comparable to the Holy Spirit who is the personal love proceeding from the Father and the Son in the Holy Trinity. "The proof that you are sons," we are told, "is that God has sent the Spirit of his Son into our hearts" (Galatians 4:6).

1021. What are the gifts of the Holy Spirit?

The gifts of the Holy Spirit are supernatural habits which perfect the soul beyond the virtues, by making it ready and responsive to divine grace.

1022. How many gifts of the Holy Spirit are there?

There are seven gifts of the Holy Spirit: wisdom, understanding, counsel, fortitude, knowledge, piety, and fear of the Lord.

1023. Explain the seven gifts of the Holy Spirit.

The gift of wisdom makes the soul respond to the Holy Spirit in the contemplation of divine things; understanding enables us to believe the truths of faith more clearly, deeply, and with greater certainty; knowledge helps us see everything in life from the viewpoint of eternity; counsel makes us more prudent in guiding ourselves and others in doing the will of God; piety increases the virtue of justice by disposing us to honor God as our Father and others as children of God; fortitude deepens our courage in overcoming obstacles in the practice of virtue; and the fear of the Lord strengthens our hope to protect us from doing whatever might displease the Lord.

1024. How do we know of the gifts of the Holy Spirit?

We know of the gifts of the Holy Spirit from the prophecy of Isaiah, who foretold them of the Messiah: "A spirit of wisdom and insight, a spirit of counsel and power, a spirit of knowledge and the fear of Yahweh" (Isaiah 11:2). We receive a share in these gifts of Christ when we are baptized.

1025. What special effects does the Holy Spirit produce by means of the gifts?

The fruits of the Holy Spirit are produced by means of his gifts.

2. Twelve Fruits or Benefits of God's Friendship

1026. What is the difference between the virtues and the gifts?

The difference between the virtues and the gifts lies in the need for having a supernatural counterpart to the natural instincts of mind and will. The virtues are the faculties through which divine life operates—we receive light to see and strength to carry out an action; gifts are reactive instincts that answer to the divine impulse almost without reflection. They are higher promptings of the Holy Spirit.

1027. What are the fruits of the Holy Spirit?

The fruits of the Holy Spirit are the result of his presence in a believing soul, much as the produce of a tree is the evidence of its fruit-bearing quality.

1028. How do we know of the fruits of the Holy Spirit?

We believe in the fruits of the Holy Spirit because they are revealed in St. Paul. He is comparing the effects of the Holy Spirit to the works of the flesh. He says: "What the Spirit brings is very different: love, joy, peace, patience, kindness, goodness, trustfulness, gentleness and self-control" (Galatians 5:22–23).

1029. Explain the fruits of the Holy Spirit.

The fruit of charity inclines our heart to the love of God because he is all good and urges us to a selfless love of others; joy is the satisfaction of doing the will of God; peace is the quiet serenity of a soul conformed to the divine will; patience controls the daily troubles we have in the practice of Christian virtue; benignity is a deep kindness of character; goodness is all the blessings we obtain for others by the witness of virtue that we give; continence is the restraint acquired of our bodily desires, especially the sexual appetite; mildness is strength tempered by love, moderating severity and showing itself more ready to forgive than to punish; fidelity is loyalty to God and the persons we have committed ourselves to out of love for God; longanimity is long-suffering or enduring pain over a long period of time; modesty is moderation in our actions, especially conversation and external behavior; and chastity is a deep respect for the sexual faculties as divinely ordained means of procreating the human race.

1030. How are the fruits of the Holy Spirit divided?

The fruits of the Holy Spirit are divided into those which make us more perfect interiorly and those which make us more perfect exteriorly.

1031. What fruits of the Holy Spirit make us more perfect interiorly?

The fruits of the Holy Spirit that make us more perfect interiorly are charity, joy, and peace—for doing good; patience and longanimity—for strength against evil.

1032. What are the fruits of the Holy Spirit that make us more perfect exteriorly?

The fruits that make us more perfect exteriorly are goodness, benignity, mildness, and fidelity—with reference to our neighbor; modesty, continence, and chastity—with reference to our own body.

IX.
CHRISTIAN
PERFECTION

1. The Call to Holiness

1033. What is holiness?

Holiness is being Christlike, which means the imitation of Jesus Christ. The more we become like Christ the more holy we are. As St. Paul says, "Try, then, to imitate God, as children of his that he loves, and follow Christ by loving as he loved you, giving himself up in our place as a fragrant offering and a sacrifice to God" (Ephesians 5:1–2).

1034. Who are called to become holy?

All Christians, regardless of their age, ability, or rank in society, are called to become holy. "Before the world was made, he chose us, chose us in Christ, to be holy and spotless, and to live through love in his presence" (Ephesians 1:4).

1035. Why are all Christians called to become holy?

All Christians are called to become holy because this is why God became man, not only to redeem us from sin but also to lead us to become perfect. In Christ's own words, "You must therefore be perfect just as your heavenly Father is perfect" (Matthew 5:48).

1036. Why is Christian holiness especially necessary in the modern world?

Christian holiness is especially necessary in the modern world because it takes sanctity to cope with seductive temptations, and the pressures to conformity.

1037. How are bishops called to holiness?

Bishops are called to holiness whose distinctive features are promptness, humility, and courage in carrying out their service in the care of souls. As successors of the apostles they must not be afraid to lay down their lives for their sheep.

1038. How do priests grow in the holiness of Christ?

Priests grow in the holiness of Christ by devotion to the Eucharist and their life of sacrifice in the service of the Church.

1039. What is the road of sanctity for married people?

The road of sanctity for married people is for husband and wife to support each other with their faithful love, to accept with gratitude the children God wishes to send them, and to teach their children how to prepare for time and eternity.

1040. How are the widowed and those in the single state called to holiness?

The widowed and the single are called to holiness by recognizing their state in life as a true vocation from God. This vocation enables them to labor generously in the apostolate through the practice of the spiritual and corporal works of mercy.

2. States of Perfection

1041. What are the states of perfection?

The states of perfection are mainly religious communities and secular institutes. Their principal purpose is to witness to holiness.

1042. How are religious to grow in holiness?

Religious are to grow in holiness by freely accepting Christ's invitation, "If you wish to be perfect." They vow themselves to a lifetime practice of the Beatitudes that go beyond the precepts necessary for salvation.

1043. Who are religious?

Religious are men and women who are called to follow Christ with greater liberty, and to imitate him more closely by practicing the evangelical counsels. They voluntarily consecrate their whole lives to God, according to the different charisms of each founder of a religious institute as accepted and approved by the Church's hierarchy under the holy see.

1044. Why are they called religious?

They are called religious because their primary purpose is to practice the virtue of religion. Everything else in their lives is to be subordinated to this end.

1045. What is the religious state?

The religious state is a state of perfection that consists of four essential elements: a fixed or stable mode of life, community living, observance of the evangelical counsels, and profession of the vows of poverty, chastity, and obedience.

1046. How is the religious state a witness to the world?

The religious state is a witness to the world by testifying to the value of things spiritual over things material, of the power of grace over weak human nature, and of the treasures of heaven over the temporal possessions of this life.

1047. Does the world need the witness of religious life?

Yes, the Church tells us this is the principal role of religious. They are to show the world that Jesus Christ is alive and active on earth today, by transforming into his own likeness those who follow his example and invoke the help of his grace.

1048. Why choose religious life if all are called to holiness?

Provided one has the vocation, religious life is chosen in order to assist in the sanctification of others. Thus, within the Church, religious communities are specially called to sanctify the people of God. They are to contribute to the Church's holiness by their example, their instruction, and by their merit of grace in the sight of God.

1049. In what way is religious life essentially different from other states of life?

Religious life is essentially different from other states of life because, unlike other people, religious bind themselves to a lifetime practice of the evangelical counsels. "In this way," declared Pope Paul VI, "a person is totally surrendered to God, loved above all things. It is true that through baptism he dies to sin and is consecrated to God. But that he might be able to derive more abundant fruit from this baptismal grace, he intends, by the profession of the evangelical counsels in the Church, to free himself from those obstacles which could draw him away from the fervor of charity and the perfection of divine worship. Thus he is more intimately consecrated to the divine service" (Apostolic Exhortation, *Gospel Witness,* 7).

1050. What is the mind of the Church about a religious habit?

The Church explicitly teaches that religious are to wear a distinct and recognizable habit. It is a sign of consecration to God. It should be simple and modest and at once poor and becoming; hence distinguished from forms of dress that are obviously secular. In this way the religious gives a greater witness of poverty and externally identifies the interior dispositions of the person who wears it. (Cf. Second Vatican Council, Decree on the Up-to-date Renewal of Religious Life, 17.)

1051. What is a secular institute?

A secular institute is a society, whether clerical or lay, whose members profess the evangelical counsels in the world in order to attain Christian perfection and to exercise the apostolate among the people with whom they work and live. They need not be recognizable as members of an institute of Christian perfection.

1052. Why are they called secular institutes?

They are called secular institutes because their holiness and apostolate are pursued in the world (*saeculum*), in general outside the cloister and common life.

3. Laity and the Lay Apostolate

1053. Who are the laity?

The laity are all the faithful, except those in holy orders or states of perfection, who are called to be holy and witness to Christ in the world.

1054. Scripture speaks of the royal priesthood of the laity. Does this mean they are equal to ordained priests?

No, the laity are not equal to ordained priests. Their royal priesthood refers to the privilege received at baptism to offer themselves, with Christ, in the Eucharistic Sacrifice and to obtain from Christ the graces he confers on the Church as his Mystical Body.

1055. What is the special task of lay people in the Church?

The special task of the laity is to make the Church present and fruitful in the world. It is through them that she can become the salt of the earth. Incorporated into Christ by baptism, they share in their own way the priestly, prophetic, and kingly office of the Savior. Their lives of sacrifice help to sanctify the whole people of God; they proclaim Christ and teach him by word and example; and they are in a position to bring others to Christ as parents and leaders in the family and civil society.

1056. Is the apostolate of the laity necessary to the Church?

The apostolate of the laity is necessary because the Church depends mainly on the laity to bring Christ to the secular world, where they are most numerous, most familiar, and can be the most influential.

1057. How do we know the lay apostolate is necessary?

We know the lay apostolate is necessary from the frequent teaching of the Church. She recognizes as a manifest action of the Holy Spirit the growing awareness by the laity of their responsibility to serve Christ and the Church with dedicated zeal and generosity. Since the Second Vatican Council, the lay apostolate may be one of three types: apostolic work done by the laity but totally supervised by the hierarchy; apostolic work conducted by the laity but officially responsible to the hierarchy; and apostolic work totally conducted by lay men or women but approved by the hierarchy.

1058. Should women take an active part in the apostolate of the laity?

Yes, it is very important that the participation of women in the Church's apostolate develop far beyond what it has been until now. This is consistent with the increasingly active share that women are taking in the whole life of modern society.

1059. Does the apostolate of women make them eligible for ordination to the priesthood?

No, women are not eligible for ordination to the priesthood because Christ decided to ordain only men. The Church teaches that his will in this regard is the universal norm for all time.

1060. What is the specific task of young people?

The youth must become the first apostles among their peers. By their good example, they exercise a powerful influence on the youth among whom they live.

1061. Is there an apostolate for children?

Yes, in their own way they are true living witnesses to Christ among their companions. As the Savior tells us, "Unless you change and become like little children you will never enter the kingdom of heaven" (Matthew 18:3). Children, therefore, by their good example are an inspiration not only to other children but also to adults.

PART THREE

SOURCES OF THE CHRISTIAN LIFE

I.
DIVINE GRACE

1. Meaning and Kinds

1062. How does God show his goodness to mankind?

God shows his goodness to mankind in two ways: naturally, by bringing us into existence out of nothing and giving us the divine image of intellect and will; and supernaturally, by raising us to participate in the Holy Trinity.

1063. What, then, is supernatural life?

Supernatural life is a share in the life of God, who communicates himself to us here on earth by faith in order that we might possess him by vision in the final beatitude of heaven.

1064. What is grace?

Grace is a supernatural gift that, through the merits of Jesus Christ, God freely bestows on human beings in order to bring them to eternal life. Nature is what we are born with and into, when we enter this world; grace is what we still need to enter heaven in the world to come.

1065. Why is grace called a supernatural gift?

Grace is called a supernatural gift because we have absolutely no claim or right to it, and because its purpose is to lead us to heaven, which is our supernatural destiny.

1066. Why do we say that divine grace is available to all?

Divine grace is available to all because Christ died for all mankind. All are in fact called to the same destiny, which is heaven. The Holy Spirit offers everyone the possibility of salvation. Even the most hardened sinner receives at least the grace to pray and ask for God's help.

1067. How is grace a communication of divine love?

Grace is a communication of divine love because God gives us, by his grace or favor, a share in all the treasures of infinite goodness which the Father, Son, and Holy Spirit possess by nature in the Holy Trinity.

1068. How many kinds of grace are there?

There are two kinds of grace, uncreated and created.

1069. What is the gift of uncreated grace?

The gift of uncreated grace is God himself. Another name for this is the divine indwelling.

1070. How does the divine indwelling take place?

The divine indwelling takes place through justification.

1071. What is justification?

Justification is the passing from a state of sin to the state of grace and adoption as children of God. "Now you have been washed clean," says St. Paul, "and sanctified, and justified through the name of the Lord Jesus Christ and through the Spirit of our God" (1 Corinthians 6:11).

1072. What are the further effects of justification?

Besides the divine indwelling, through justification we receive the created gift of habitual or sanctifying grace.

1073. How does God abide in the justified soul?

God abides in the justified soul in a special manner that we cannot fully understand. But it can be experienced through the intimate knowledge and ardent love of God that becomes available to the soul in whom he dwells, as in a temple.

2. Sanctifying or Habitual Grace

1074. What is habitual or sanctifying grace?

Habitual or sanctifying grace is a supernatural quality that dwells in the human soul, by which a person shares in the divine nature, becomes a temple of the Holy Spirit, a friend of God, his adopted child, an heir to the glory of heaven, and able to perform actions meriting eternal life. As St. Paul writes: "The Spirit himself and our spirit bear united witness that we are children of God. And if we are children we are heirs as well: heirs of God and coheirs with Christ, sharing his sufferings so as to share his glory" (Romans 8:16–17).

1075. What is sanctifying grace compared with the divine indwelling?

Compared with the divine indwelling, sanctifying grace is the principal created gift of God.

1076. Is sanctifying grace necessary to reach heaven?

Yes, sanctifying grace is absolutely necessary for everyone, even for infants, to reach heaven and the eternal vision of God.

1077. How does sanctifying grace manifest itself in practice?

Sanctifying grace manifests itself in practice through the theological and moral virtues and the gifts of the Holy Spirit.

1078. Can sanctifying grace be increased?

Yes, sanctifying grace is increased by every good action we perform in the state of grace. Every act of virtue, every prayer, every reception of the sacraments by a person already in the friendship of God increases that person's habitual or sanctifying grace.

1079. Can sanctifying grace be lost or lessened in the soul?

We lose sanctifying grace by committing mortal sins. This means the soul is spiritually dead because it is no longer united with God. Sanctifying grace is lessened in the soul through giving in to temptation by committing venial sins.

1080. How is sanctifying grace regained?

Sanctifying grace is regained by sincere sorrow for the sins committed, and receiving the sacrament of penance or anointing.

1081. Is sanctifying grace the only created grace that we receive?

No, sanctifying grace is not the only created grace that we receive. We also receive actual graces.

3. Actual Graces

1082. What is actual grace?

Actual grace is a supernatural help from God by which he enlightens a person's mind and moves the will to do good and avoid evil for the sake of eternal life. Unlike sanctifying grace, actual grace is not a quality that dwells in the soul. It is rather a holy thought or holy desire from God that leads a person to perform a supernatural action that is naturally impossible to do.

1083. How does sanctifying grace differ from actual grace?

Sanctifying grace differs from actual grace in several ways. Actual grace is a transient gift which lasts only during the action; sanctifying grace remains with us unless lost by mortal sin; actual grace is still communicated even if we do not possess sanctifying grace; if sanctifying grace is lost it cannot be recovered without actual grace, nor can sanctifying grace be preserved for any length of time without the assistance of actual grace.

1084. What do sanctifying and actual grace have in common?

Sanctifying and actual grace are both supernatural, since both are far above the powers of unaided nature. They are directly given by God out of sheer love for us.

1085. What are the two forms of actual grace?

Actual graces are illuminations for the mind and inspirations for the will.

1086. Why are these graces called actual?

They are called actual because they actually enlighten the mind to know and inspire the will to choose what God wants a person to do. Moreover, they are meant to be acted upon. They are passing supernatural aids and therefore distinct from sanctifying grace which is an abiding possession of the soul.

1087. What are divine illuminations?

Divine illuminations are, first of all, actual graces insofar as they enlighten the mind to see what is already there. Illuminations also confer knowledge not yet possessed and that, except for grace, the mind would not possess. "I will instruct you," says the Lord, "and teach you the way to go; I will watch over you and be your adviser" (Psalms 32:8).

1088. What are divine inspirations?

Divine inspirations are actual graces for the will to help it reach a decision. They also strengthen the will to embrace and persevere in what we have already chosen. "It is God, for his own loving purpose, who puts both the will and the action into you" (Philippians 2:13).

1089. Is actual grace necessary?

Yes, actual grace is absolutely necessary for a person to recover sanctifying grace that has been lost by mortal sin. It is also necessary for those in the state of grace to perform actions pleasing to God and leading to heaven. Christ tells us, "For cut off from me you can do nothing" (John 15:5); and St. Paul tells Christians, already in God's friendship, "May Our Lord Jesus Christ himself, and God our Father who has given us his love and, through his grace, such inexhaustible comfort and such sure hope, comfort you and strengthen you in everything good that you do or say" (2 Thessalonians 2:16–17).

1090. How do we know that grace is absolutely necessary for salvation?

We know that grace is absolutely necessary for salvation from the teaching of Christ and the Church. We can also conclude to the need of grace from the fact that our human faculties of themselves are capable only of natural acts. Therefore, actions must be raised by grace to a supernatural level to become means of salvation. "Both Jew and pagan sinned and forfeited God's glory, and both are justified through the free gift of his grace by being redeemed in Christ Jesus" (Romans 3:23–24).

1091. Can we do anything without the assistance of divine grace?

We can do nothing in the supernatural order without the assistance of divine grace. Only in God can we do all things. As Christ said, "I am the vine, you are the branches. Whoever remains in me, with me in him, bears fruit in plenty; for cut off from me you can do nothing" (John 15:5).

1092. Can we resist grace?

Yes, we can resist grace because we are free to accept or reject the grace God gives us to save our souls.

1093. Does God give his grace at every moment of our lives?

Yes, God gives us grace at every conscious moment of our lives. He does so especially in time of temptation, illness, imminent death, on the occasion of a good example, and in time of suffering and trial.

1094. What is the difference between internal and external graces?

Internal graces are actual graces directly received from God in the human intellect or will. External graces are the ordinary means God uses to confer actual graces. In this sense, every person, place, or thing in our lives is an external grace by which God intends to lead us to our eternal destiny.

4. Human Freedom and Merit

1095. What is supernatural merit?

Supernatural merit is that quality of a good act which gives the one who performs it the right to be rewarded by God, in this life and in the life to come. We are assured that "God would not be so unjust as to forget all you have done, the love that you have for his name or the services you have done, and are still doing, for the saints" (Hebrews 6:10).

1096. What can we merit supernaturally?

We can supernaturally merit for ourselves an increase of sanctifying grace and the infused virtues, actual graces and a title to them, the right to enter heaven if we die in the divine friendship, and an increase of happiness in heaven.

1097. Can we also merit supernaturally for others?

Yes, we can merit supernaturally for others but not in the same way as for ourselves. Our merit for others does not depend on a strict promise of God to repay our good deeds, but rather on his goodness in the way that he responds to our prayers. Merit for others, therefore, is like a petition made to God rather than a reward for the good works performed.

1098. What are the conditions for gaining supernatural merit?

The two conditions for gaining supernatural merit are the state of grace and the performance of a morally good action.

1099. What factors determine the degree of our merit?

The degree of our merit first and mainly depends on the will of God. On our part, however, other things being equal, we gain more or less merit depending on the intensity of our sanctifying grace, the love by which we are motivated, the willingness and freedom with which we act, and the dignity of the action we perform. The hardship experienced in doing something good does not, of itself, increase merit. But if we are not sinfully responsible for the difficulties, they increase our merit because they evoke more effort in the service of God.

1100. Can a person perform good works while in mortal sin?

A person in mortal sin can perform good works. Although these good actions do not merit heaven, yet with the help of actual grace they dispose a sinner for a return to God's friendship.

1101. What is the grace of final perseverance?

The grace of final perseverance is the grace of actually dying in the friendship of God and therefore reaching heaven. This grace cannot be strictly merited but must be earnestly and constantly prayed for. Thus, every Our Father is a prayer for the grace of final perseverance; and in every Hail Mary we ask, "Holy Mary, Mother of God, pray for us sinners, now and at the hour of our death."

1102. What is the main purpose of our human freedom?

The main purpose of our human freedom is to cooperate with the graces that God gives to us. Fidelity to grace gives joy to the heart and merits further grace. Infidelity to grace has the opposite effect. It discourages the soul and deprives persons of the graces they would have gained had they been faithful to the graces already received.

1103. Are we free only to choose between good and evil?

No, we can choose between good and evil, between one good action and another, and between the good and something better. Our highest use of freedom is to choose what is most pleasing to God.

II.
THE SACRAMENTS
IN GENERAL

Institution by Christ, Number, Administration, and Reception

1104. What is a sacrament?

A sacrament is a sensible sign, instituted by Jesus Christ, which confers the grace it signifies.

1105. What does the word "sacrament" mean?

Literally "sacrament" means something sacred. In the Catholic vocabulary it is a mystery of faith and the external sign of an interior grace.

1106. What elements are necessary to constitute a true sacrament?

The elements necessary to constitute a true sacrament are: a sensible sign, instituted by Christ, and the power to produce grace.

1107. What is a sensible sign?

A sensible sign is something perceived by the senses that leads one to know something else not perceived by the senses. For example, the pouring of water in baptism is perceived by the senses. This signifies the internal cleansing of soul from sin, which is known only by faith. The sensible sign consists of the matter and form of the sacrament.

1108. How are the sacraments signs?

They are signs in two ways: they indicate externally what takes place within the soul of the one receiving the sacrament, and they actually produce the grace which they signify.

1109. What is the matter of a sacrament?

The matter of a sacrament is the external action performed by the minister of the sacrament. It normally involves the use of some material thing like oil, water, bread, or wine.

1110. What is the form of a sacrament?

The form is the essential words pronounced by the one who administers or performs the sacrament. Thus, in baptism the form is: "I baptize you in the name of the Father, and of the Son, and of the Holy Spirit." And in penance it is: "I absolve you from your sins."

1111. Must the matter and form be united?

Yes, to constitute a sacrament the matter and form must be joined together in a single action. The same person must unite the matter and form, without notable interruption between using the matter and pronouncing the words.

1112. Why should the faithful strive to better understand the sacraments?

The faithful should strive to better understand the sacraments because 1) they are mysteries of faith that God wants us to grow in appreciating, 2) this will better dispose us to receive the sacraments more fervently, 3) a deeper understanding will lead to more frequent reception, and 4) this will enable us to explain the value of the sacraments more effectively to others.

1113. How many sacraments did Christ institute?

Christ instituted seven sacraments, namely, baptism, confirmation, Holy Eucharist, penance, orders, matrimony, and anointing of the sick.

1114. How do we know the sacraments were instituted by Christ?

We know the sacraments were instituted by Christ from Sacred Tradition and the teaching of the Church. Only Christ can infallibly join grace to the performance of a sensible sign.

1115. Why did Christ institute the sacraments?

Christ instituted the sacraments because he instituted the New Law. The demands of his law, notably of selfless love of God and one's neighbor, require extraordinary grace that only he can give. He confers this grace on his followers mainly through the sacraments, as indispensable means of salvation and sanctification. "Cut off from me," Christ tells us, "you can do nothing" (John 15:5).

1116. Why are there seven sacraments?

The final reason is hidden in the mind of God. But humanly speaking we can say there are seven sacraments because they correspond in things of the spirit to the needs we have in the order of nature. We must be born in the life of grace by baptism, strengthened in this life by confirmation, nourished to sustain the supernatural life by the Eucharist, healed by the sacrament of penance, guided in the supernatural society of the Church by priests who receive sacred orders, the Church is perpetuated by the sacrament of matrimony, and we are prepared for eternity by the sacrament of anointing.

1117. Were there sacraments in the Old Law?

There were equivalent sacraments in the Old Law. They were such ceremonies as circumcision, the eating of the paschal lamb, numerous sacrifices and purifications.

1118. How do the sacraments of the Old Law differ from those of the New Law?

The sacraments of the Old Law signified grace to come that would be bestowed through the Passion of Jesus Christ. The sacraments of the Old Law did not produce grace of themselves in virtue of the rite being performed, but by faith in God. They were signs of faith. Christian sacraments confer the grace they symbolize on all who place no obstacle in the way.

1119. Are the sacraments necessary for salvation?

According to the way God has willed that we be saved, the sacraments are necessary for salvation. Not all the sacraments, however, are equally necessary for everyone. Two of the sacraments, baptism and the Eucharist, on the words of Christ, are absolutely necessary (cf. John 3:5; 6:47–53), at least by desire. Moreover, once God became man in the person of the Savior, and decided to give us the means of salvation, it was necessary that these means should correspond to his twofold nature. They are at the same time visible signs (like Christ who is human) and confer invisible grace (like Christ who is divine).

1120. Who is the minister of a sacrament?

The minister of a sacrament is the one who has the power to administer it. The ordinary minister is one who dispenses the sacrament by right of his office. An extraordinary minister is one who confers the sacrament either in virtue of a special privilege or of delegated power. The minister of a sacrament, in order to administer it validly, must have the intention of doing what the Church wants.

1121. Why must the minister intend to do what the Church wants?

Without this intention a person would not perform a sacred action, or draw on the graces intended by Christ. He would be acting in his own name and not as a minister of God.

1122. Why are faith and the state of grace not required to confer the sacraments validly?

Faith and the state of grace are not required to confer the sacraments validly because the sacraments communicate grace in virtue of the rite itself. Jesus Christ is their principal agent. Thus the power of administering the sacraments is a grace given freely by God, even on persons who are sinners.

1123. Can everyone receive all the sacraments?

Only baptized persons can receive any of the other sacraments. Children who have not reached the age of reason cannot receive the sacraments of penance, anointing of the sick, or matrimony; those who are not sick or aged cannot receive the sacrament of anointing; women cannot receive the sacrament of orders; those in sacred orders, bound by celibacy, and solemnly professed religious cannot receive the sacrament of matrimony, without a special dispensation from the holy see.

1124. What conditions are necessary for the valid reception of a sacrament?

For the valid reception of a sacrament adults must have the intention to receive because no one can be sanctified without the consent of his will. For infants and those who never had the use of reason the intention is supplied by the Church.

1125. What dispositions are necessary for the lawful and profitable reception of baptism, penance, and anointing?

For the lawful and profitable reception of baptism, penance, and anointing, faith, hope, and at least imperfect sorrow are necessary. Moreover, to receive penance and anointing validly, a person must have been previously baptized.

1126. What disposition is necessary for the lawful and profitable reception of the remaining sacraments?

For the lawful and profitable reception of the remaining sacraments the state of grace is necessary. This is a grave obligation.

1127. What sin does one commit who, through his own fault, does not have these dispositions?

A person who, through his own fault, does not have the proper dispositions for the reception of the sacraments commits a sacrilege, because he profanes a sacred thing.

1128. When is the reception of a sacrament said to be null?

The reception of a sacrament is said to be null if the person is not fit to receive it, or has no intention to receive, or lacks an essential disposition. When the person is fit, and has the intention to receive, the reception is said to be valid. The reception of the sacrament is said to be fruitful when the person has, in addition to the necessary fitness and intention, the proper disposition of will. The grace proper to the sacrament is then received.

1129. When is the reception of a sacrament said to be unfruitful?

The reception of a sacrament is said to be unfruitful when it is valid but does not produce grace due to the absence of the necessary disposition on the part of the one receiving.

1130. What are the effects of the sacraments?

The effects of the sacraments are grace and the sacramental character.

1131. How many kinds of grace do the sacraments produce?

The sacraments produce or increase sanctifying grace, and they give a distinctive sacramental grace which differs with each sacrament.

1132. How do the sacraments give sanctifying grace?

They confer sanctifying grace on a person who lacks the supernatural life, as in the case of baptism, or, when needed, through the sacraments of penance and anointing. In other cases, the sacraments increase sanctifying grace every time they are received.

1133. What is sacramental grace?

It is a special grace that gives a person the right to those actual graces necessary to attain the end for which the sacrament was instituted, since each of the sacraments produces what it signifies.

1134. Does everyone receive the same sacramental grace?

No, the grace we receive from a sacrament varies with the dispositions of each person. The more detached we are from sinful creatures, and the more devoted we are to God, the greater the grace we receive from the sacraments.

1135. What is the sacramental character?

The sacramental character is a permanent, spiritual sign, imprinted on the soul, which makes it impossible to repeat the sacrament.

1136. Has the understanding of the sacramental character developed in the Church's teaching?

The understanding of the sacramental character has been greatly developed in the Church's teaching in two main directions: to bring out the likeness to Christ that the character confers, and to show how the character unites the members of the Mystical Body with their Head and among themselves.

1137. Which of the sacraments imprint a character?

Baptism, confirmation, and sacred orders imprint the sacramental character. They establish a person in a perpetual state proper to the sacrament. Thus baptism gives us a place in the family of Jesus Christ, confirmation enlists us in the army of the Savior, and sacred orders constitutes certain men as ministers of Jesus Christ, to consecrate his body and blood, offer Mass, and forgive sins in his name.

1138. What are the ceremonies of a sacrament?

The ceremonies of a sacrament are those external acts of religion established by the Church to give excellence to divine worship, to administer the sacraments with becoming respect and dignity, to instruct the faithful and to deepen their faith and devotion.

1139. What kinds of ceremonies are associated with the sacraments?

Three kinds of ceremonies are associated with the sacraments, namely words, such as prayers and the reading of Scripture; gestures, like the sign of the cross, bows, and genuflections; and the use of material objects, as holy water, incense, vestments, and sacred vessels.

III.
THE SEVEN SACRAMENTS

Baptism

1. Meaning and Conferral

1140. What is baptism?

Baptism is the sacrament of spiritual rebirth. Through the symbolic action of washing with water and the use of appropriate ritual words, the baptized person is cleansed of all his sins and incorporated into Christ. It was foretold in Ezekiel, "I shall pour clean water over you and you will be cleansed; I shall cleanse you of all your defilement and all your idols. I shall give you a new heart, and put a new spirit in you" (Ezekiel 36:25–26).

1141. When did Christ command the sacrament of baptism?

Christ commanded the sacrament of baptism when he said: "Go, therefore, make disciples of all the nations; baptize them in the name of the Father and of the Son and of the Holy Spirit, and teach them to observe all the commands I gave you. And know that I am with you always; yes, to the end of time" (Matthew 28:19–20).

1142. What does the word "baptism" mean?

The word "baptism" literally means immersion, in the sense of dipping under water. It also means to bathe.

1143. Who may receive the sacrament of baptism?

Any living person who has not yet been baptized may receive the sacrament of baptism.

1144. When should baptism be received?

Baptism should be received as soon after birth as is conveniently possible, certainly within a month.

1145. What is the sign of baptism?

The sign of the sacrament of baptism is the external pouring of the water or immersion into water, along with the invocation of the Holy Trinity.

1146. What is the meaning of the baptismal sign?

The baptismal sign means that a person is reborn in Jesus Christ.

1147. What is called the matter of baptism?

The matter of baptism is natural water, commonly recognized as such, even though other things may be dissolved in it. Except in case of urgent necessity, the water should be specially blessed for baptism.

1148. How is the water of baptism to be applied?

The water of baptism is to be applied to the person's head. This is commonly done by pouring or ablution; but it may also be done by dipping under water or immersion; and, in exceptional cases, by sprinkling or aspersion. In every case, however, the water must flow on the person's head.

1149. What is the form of baptism?

The necessary and sufficient form of baptism is the invocation of the Blessed Trinity: "I baptize you in the name of the Father, and of the Son, and of the Holy Spirit."

1150. How are the matter and form united in baptism?

The matter and form are united when the water and words of baptism are combined in one ritual act. While the water is flowing on the head, one and the same person applies the water and pronounces the invocation of the Trinity.

2. Spiritual Effects

1151. What are the effects of baptism?

The effects of baptism are the removal of the guilt of sin and all punishment due to sin, conferral of the grace of regeneration and the infused virtues, incorporation into Christ and his Church, receiving the baptismal character and the right to heaven.

1152. What sins does baptism take away?

Baptism remits the guilt of all sins, that is, it takes away all sins, whether original sin as inherited from Adam at conception, or actual sin as incurred by each person on reaching the age of reason. No matter how frequent, or how grave the actual sins may be, their guilt is all removed at baptism. All of this is the pure gift of God, since St. Paul writes, "It was for no reason except his own compassion that he saved us, by means of the cleansing water of rebirth" (Titus 3:5).

1153. What penalties does baptism remove?

Baptism removes all the penalties, eternal and temporal, attached to original and actual sin.

1154. If all penalties due to sin are removed, why do we have to suffer so much from infancy to death?

It is the will of God that we suffer through life until death though all penalties are removed by baptism. Also by baptism, we become united to Christ and should therefore be likened to him, who suffered and died, though he had never sinned. As St. Paul wrote, "It makes me happy to suffer for you, as I am suffering now, and in my own body to do what I can to make up all that has still to be undergone by Christ for the sake of his body, the Church" (Colossians 1:24). Moreover, by our patient endurance of the trials of life, we are enabled to grow in virtue because of the superabundant grace received from Christ. We can give God more glory and attain to a greater happiness in heaven as the result of struggling successfully with our fallen human nature.

1155. What is the grace of regeneration?

The grace of regeneration infuses into our souls the life of grace that Christ won for us by his Death and Resurrection. It is the new birth of which Christ spoke to Nicodemus (cf. John 3:3) and the new creation described by St. Paul (cf. 2 Corinthians 5:17).

1156. What virtues are infused into the soul at baptism?

The virtues infused into the soul at baptism are faith, hope, and charity. Among the gifts of grace infused at baptism are the peace and joy of the Holy Spirit, which make possible the practice of the Beatitudes.

1157. How does baptism incorporate us into Christ?

By baptism we become members of Christ's Mystical Body, which is the Church. That is why "By the sacrament of baptism, whenever it is properly conferred in the way the Lord determined and received with the proper dispositions of soul, man becomes truly incorporated into the crucified and glorified Christ and is reborn to a sharing of the divine life, as the apostle says: 'For you were buried together with him in baptism, and in him also rose again through faith in the working of God who raised him from the dead' (Romans 6:4)" (Second Vatican Council, Decree on Ecumenism, 22).

1158. Do all baptized persons belong to the Church?

All baptized persons belong to the Church. "It remains true," says the Second Vatican Council, "that all who have been justified by faith in baptism are incorporated into Christ; they therefore have a right to be called Christians, and with good reason are accepted as brothers by the children of the Catholic Church" (Decree on Ecumenism, 3).

1159. What is the baptismal character?

The baptismal character is a permanent, irremovable change produced by the sacrament of baptism. It imparts to those who receive it a likeness to Christ in his priesthood, grafts them onto Christ, the Vine, so that they participate in a unique way in the graces of his humanity. It imprints on their souls an indelible seal that nothing, not even the loss of virtue or faith itself, can eradicate.

1160. Does a baptized person always remain a Christian?

A baptized person always remains a Christian because the baptismal character confers a permanent relationship with Christ.

1161. Is a Catholic always a Catholic?

Yes, once a Catholic a person always remains a Catholic in the fundamental sense of having the baptismal character. One cannot cease to be a Catholic because, once baptized, he cannot be un-baptized. The seal of baptism continues in this life and endures into eternity.

1162. Does baptism restore us to the state in which Adam was created?

Baptism does essentially restore us to the state in which Adam was created. As St. John says, "To all who did accept him he gave power to become children of God" (John 1:12). But baptism does not give back to us the special gifts possessed by our first parents.

1163. What effects of original sin, therefore, remain after baptism?

The effects of original sin that remain after baptism are suffering and death, concupiscence and ignorance. However, baptism gives us the grace to cope with suffering in this life; the promise of deliverance from suffering after death and of bodily immortality after the Resurrection; the grace to resist concupiscence and thereby grow in holiness; and the infused virtue of faith, which enables us to believe all that God has revealed.

3. Ceremonies, Sponsors, Ritual Changes, and Catechumens

1164. What is solemn baptism?

Solemn baptism is conferred when all the liturgical ceremonies prescribed by the Church are performed.

1165. Who is the ordinary minister of solemn baptism?

The ordinary minister of solemn baptism is the pastor of the parish (or bishop) within whose territory the person to be baptized lives. The delegated minister for the administration of solemn baptism is any priest or deacon in good standing who has been authorized to confer the sacrament.

1166. What are the ceremonies of solemn baptism?

The ceremonies are essentially the same for the baptism of children and adults. In children's baptism, the sequence is as follows: 1) Reception, during which the sponsors (and parents) declare they want the child baptized; 2) Celebration of God's word, with readings from the New Testament and intercessions; 3) Exorcism and first anointing; 4) Conferral of the sacrament, preceded by renunciation of Satan and profession of faith; 5) Anointing with chrism, clothing with the white garment, receiving the lighted candle, the *ephphetha* or prayer over ears and mouth, concluding song and blessing. Adult baptisms are conferred during Mass.

1167. What are the baptismal promises?

Baptismal promises are the spiritual obligations that a baptized person assumes. They consist in renouncing Satan, his works and pomps, that is, all thoughts, desires, words, and deeds contrary to the law of God, and all that the world loves, for these are the things Satan uses to lead people away from God. By our baptismal promises we bind ourselves to live according to the teachings of Christ and to follow his example. We do this by giving ourselves to Christ, listening to what the Church he directs tells us to do, and imitating the virtues he practiced during his visible stay on earth.

1168. What is emergency or private baptism?

Emergency or private baptism takes place when there is danger of death and no priest or deacon is available. In case of emergency, anyone, even a non-Catholic, who has the use of reason, may validly baptize. The intention of the one who does the baptism must be to do what the Church intends.

1169. What must be the dispositions of a person being baptized after reaching the age of reason?

A person being baptized after reaching the age of reason must believe the basic truths of the Christian faith, be sorry for his sins, at least out of fear of God's just punishments, and sincerely want to receive baptism.

1170. Does the Catholic Church recognize the baptism of other Christian Churches?

Yes, the Catholic Church recognizes as valid baptism the ceremony properly performed by other Christian Churches. It is properly performed when: 1) water is used; 2) the water is applied to the person's head by pouring, immersion, or sprinkling; 3) the same person pronounces the words, "I baptize you in the name of the Father, and of the Son, and of the Holy Spirit" while applying the water; and 4) even though mistaken about the true meaning of baptism, the one baptizing has the intention of doing what Christ wants.

1171. Are sponsors required for valid baptism?

At least one sponsor or godparent is required for baptism. However, sponsors are not necessary for valid conferral of the sacrament. The sponsors must be of the Catholic faith, and willing to fulfill the obligations of a godparent.

1172. What is the sponsors' role?

The sponsors' role is second only to that of the parents. Sponsors are official representatives of the community of faith and, with the parents, request baptism for the child. They are to take the place of the parents if the parents are unable or fail to provide for the religious training of the child.

1173. Why should the child receive the name of a saint at baptism?

The child should receive the name of a saint at baptism because it symbolizes newness of life in Christ and entrance into the Christian community. The saint whose name is taken at baptism thus becomes a heavenly patron who exercises special lifelong care over the one baptized with his or her name.

1174. What is the parents' duty regarding baptism?

Parents are gravely bound to see that no child should die without baptism. As defined by the Council of Trent, justification from original sin is not possible "without the washing unto regeneration or the desire for the same." After baptism, parents are to teach their children the true faith, and train them in the practice of the Catholic religion.

1175. Why have there been changes in the baptismal rite?

The changes in the baptismal rite were introduced by the Church to make the reception of the sacrament more meaningful to all who participate and, in the case of adults, to better dispose them for the blessings that are conferred. The Church wants parents to pray and reflect on the sacrament their children are to receive. Baptism may be conferred along with the celebration of Mass, to bring out more clearly that the Eucharist sustains us in the supernatural life received in the first sacrament.

1176. What are catechumens?

Catechumens are persons, especially in mission countries, who are being instructed in the Catholic faith in preparation for baptism and admission into the Church.

1177. How are catechumens introduced into the life of the Church?

Catechumens are introduced into the life of the Church by being admitted with liturgical rites to the catechumenate. This is not a mere explanation of doctrine and morality, but a period of formation in the whole Christian life, an apprenticeship of sufficient duration, during which the disciples will be joined to Christ their Teacher. The catechumens should be properly initiated into the mystery of salvation and the practice of Christian virtue and they should be introduced into the life of faith, liturgy, and charity of the people of God by successive rites. (Cf. Second Vatican Council, Decree on the Church's Missionary Activity, 14).

1178. Are catechumens joined to the Church?

Catechumens who, moved by the Holy Spirit, desire to be incorporated into the Church are by that very intention joined to her. With love and solicitude Mother Church already embraces them as her own (Second Vatican Council, Dogmatic Constitution on the Church, 14).

4. Necessity for Salvation

1179. Is baptism of water necessary for salvation?

It is commonly taught by the Church that baptism of water is necessary for salvation for those who have not reached the use of reason.

1180. What is baptism of desire?

Baptism of desire is the implicit desire for baptism of water by a person who makes an act of perfect love of God, based on faith and with a sincere sorrow for one's sins. Such was the case in the Acts of the Apostles, when Peter encountered pagans who, moved by the grace of the Holy Spirit, proclaimed the greatness of God. "Peter himself then said, 'Could anyone refuse the water of baptism to these people, now they have received the Holy Spirit . . . ?'" (Acts 10:46–47).

1181. Is baptism of desire a sacrament?

Baptism of desire is not a sacrament; it does not imprint the baptismal character or enable a person to receive the other sacraments. Nevertheless, it does confer sanctifying grace.

1182. What is the fate of unbaptized infants?

The fate of the unbaptized infants is left to the mercy of God. It is generally taught that the souls of those who depart this life with original sin on their souls, but without actual sin, go to limbo.

1183. What is limbo?

According to St. Thomas, limbo is a place of perfect natural happiness but without the supernatural vision of God to which we have no natural right.

1184. When is baptism invalid?

Baptism is invalid when true natural water is not used; when the water does not touch the body of the one being baptized; when the entire form is not pronounced or a different form is used; when the form is not pronounced as the water is being poured or is not pronounced by the one pouring the water.

1185. What must be done if a baptism is doubtful?

If a baptism is even slightly doubtful, the baptism must be repeated conditionally, because this sacrament is necessary for salvation. "Unless a man is born through water and the Spirit, he cannot enter the kingdom of God" (John 3:5). There is no question of rebaptizing anyone. In a conditional baptism, the priest says, "N.N., if you are not baptized, I baptize you in the name of the Father, and of the Son, and of the Holy Spirit."

1186. Is it a serious obligation to baptize a person in danger of death?

It is a grave duty, based on charity, to baptize a person who is in danger of death. This presumes, in the case of an adult, that he would want baptism. In case of infants, it normally (but not necessarily) presumes the willingness of the parents to have their child baptized.

1187. How is baptism to be administered in case of emergency?

In case of emergency the one baptizing takes some form of natural water and pours it in the form of a cross on the head of the person to be baptized, while pronouncing the invocation to the Trinity. If the baptized person survives, the ceremonies for solemn baptism (without conferring the sacrament) are to be performed later on by a priest in church.

Confirmation

Nature, Administration, and Sacramental Effects

1188. How do we know that Christ instituted the sacrament of confirmation?

We know that Christ instituted the sacrament of confirmation because of the evidence in the New Testament. The ancient prophets had foretold the outpouring of the Spirit of God over the whole of mankind, as a sign of the Age of the Messiah (cf. Joel 3:1, Isaiah 44:3–5, Ezekiel 39:29). Jesus promised his apostles and all the future faithful to send them the Holy Spirit (cf. John 14:16, Luke 24:49, Acts 1:5, John 7:38). On the feast of Pentecost, he fulfilled his word to the first Christian community. "They were all filled with the Holy Spirit" (Acts 2:4). Later on, the apostles communicated the Holy Spirit by the outward rite of imposition of hands on the baptized (cf. Acts 8:14–17). St.

Paul communicated the Holy Spirit to some twelve disciples in Ephesus after they had received Christian baptism (cf. Acts 19:6) and the early converts from Judaism were told that the imposition of hands, which brings the communication of the Holy Spirit, belongs to the foundation of the Christian religion (cf. Hebrews 6:2, 4).

1189. What is the sacrament of confirmation?

Confirmation is the sacrament of spiritual strengthening. It is the sacrament in which, through chrism and the imposition of hands together with the use of certain sacred words, a baptized person receives the Holy Spirit, is strengthened in grace, and signed as a soldier of Christ.

1190. Why does confirmation presuppose baptism?

Confirmation presupposes baptism because it is a completion of the grace of baptism. A person must be regenerated by baptism in order to mature through confirmation in the life of grace.

1191. How is confirmation a sacrament of initiation?

Confirmation is a sacrament of initiation as a stage in the sacramental progress of a Christian. Confirmation is to baptism what growth is to birth. In baptism we are reborn to share in the divine nature. We are strengthened in this divine life by the sacrament of confirmation, and nourished by the food of Christ's body and blood through the Holy Eucharist.

1192. Who is the usual minister of confirmation?

In the Western Church, the usual minister of confirmation is the bishop. However, priests may confirm under certain conditions. In the Eastern Rite all priests can confer the sacrament.

1193. When may a priest administer confirmation?

Priests may confirm in case of emergency and when they have received permission to do so. Hospital chaplains and parish priests may confirm adult converts. Priests in the Latin Rite, in accordance with the faculties which they have, may administer to the faithful in the Eastern Churches.

1194. How is the sacrament of confirmation conferred?

The sacrament of confirmation is conferred through the anointing with chrism on the forehead, which is done by laying on of the hand, and through the words "Receive the seal of the gift of the Holy Spirit." Anointing with chrism along with the second imposition of the hand (during the anointing) are essential. The new formula was adopted from the Byzantine rite to express more clearly that in confirmation, as on Pentecost, "the gift of the Holy Spirit himself" is received.

1195. What does the anointing with chrism signify?

The anointing with chrism signifies the spiritual anointing by the Holy Spirit who is given to the faithful. Anointing with chrism, which is a mixture of olive oil and balsam consecrated by the bishop on Holy Thursday, is a sign of strengthening.

1196. What does the laying of hands signify?

The laying of hands is a sign of communicating what one has. Hands are laid on someone to show that what one person has he passes on to another. It is a common sign of encouragement and, in the custom of all nations, is a sign of solidarity and acceptance.

1197. What are the major changes in the rite of confirmation since the Second Vatican Council?

There are three changes in the rite of confirmation prescribed since the Second Vatican Council. Confirmation is now preceded by the formal renewal of baptismal promises; it is conferred during the Sacrifice of the Mass, at which Holy Communion is received; and a new formula for administering the sacrament was introduced, taken from the ancient Eastern liturgy.

1198. What does the Church wish to manifest by the sacrament of confirmation?

By the sacrament of confirmation, the Church wishes to manifest the transmission of the Holy Spirit. He is communicated by apostolic genealogy going back to Pentecost, through the symbolism of consecrated hands being laid on the head of the one receiving the gift of God.

1199. Who may receive the sacrament of confirmation?

Confirmation may be received validly and fruitfully by any baptized person who has not already been confirmed. A person who has reached the age of reason must have at least the intention of receiving the sacrament. But to receive the full effects of confirmation, one must be in the state of grace and should have received instruction in the principal truths of the faith, especially those pertaining to this sacrament.

1200. What are the effects of confirmation?

Confirmation increases the possession of divine life, confers actual graces, a special sacramental grace, and gives a unique sacramental character. The divine life becomes more resilient, and better able to resist dangers and overcome opposition to its existence and growth. Confirmation gives us grace to fulfill Christ's command: "You must therefore be perfect just as your heavenly Father is perfect" (Matthew 5:48).

1201. What virtues and gifts are increased in confirmation?

While confirmation increases all the infused virtues and the gifts of the Holy Spirit, it mainly strengthens the virtue of faith in the mind and the gift of fortitude in the will.

1202. What actual graces are received?

The actual graces received through confirmation are illuminations of the mind to believe more firmly and inspirations of the will to do battle against the enemies of divine truth.

1203. What is the sacramental grace of confirmation?

The sacramental grace of confirmation brings to perfection the supernatural life infused at baptism by giving it the power to withstand opposition from within, which is human respect and fear, and from without, which is physical or psychological coercion to deny or compromise what the faith demands.

1204. What sacramental character is imprinted on the soul in confirmation?

The sacramental character imprinted on the soul in confirmation is a permanent gift that assimilates us to Christ in three ways. We are able to become 1) like Christ the priest, in bearing suffering patiently and sacrificing courageously; 2) like Christ the teacher, by acquiring a strong will to keep the faith and a strong mind to understand and share the faith; and 3) like Christ the king, in developing qualities of leadership to withstand what is alien to the Gospel and draw others to follow Christ in extending the kingdom of Christ on earth.

1205. Why is the sacrament of confirmation referred to as the sacrament of martyrdom?

The sacrament of confirmation is referred to as the sacrament of martyrdom because it is the sacrament of testifying to Christ, in the Church, before the world. The character of this sacrament empowers us to testify publicly to our faith in Christ as Catholics, even to suffering death rather than compromise in our loyalty to the Master.

1206. Why is confirmation called the sacrament of witness?

Confirmation is called the sacrament of witness because it enables us to profess our faith not only courageously but also effectively. Our strong allegiance to Christ and his Church, with patience and loving kindness, will help convince others of the truth of what we believe.

1207. What is the responsibility of every baptized person who is confirmed?

Every baptized person who is confirmed has a mission to bring others to Christ. Baptism and confirmation confer the grace of zeal to convert unbelievers to the Christian faith and to make strong believers of those who are now weak.

1208. How are all the graces of confirmation related to divine faith?

The graces received in confirmation are related to faith in several ways. Confirmation makes the virtue of faith more clear, by enabling us to better recognize what we are to believe and why, and to see the difference between religious truth and error. It makes our faith more intelligible, by enabling us to understand our faith more deeply. Confirmation makes the faith more certain by increasing our certitude that what we believe is the truth. It makes our faith more zealous by inspiring us to share what we believe with others. It makes the faith more constant, by giving us the strength to withstand criticism of the Catholic faith, and opposition or indifference from others. Finally, confirmation makes our faith more vital, by giving us the grace to live up to what we believe, especially in the practice of charity.

1209. Is confirmation valid if received in mortal sin?

Yes, the sacrament is valid and the character is imprinted, even if confirmation is received in mortal sin. But the special graces of the sacrament are not conferred until the person is once again in the grace of God. One who consciously receives the sacrament of confirmation in the state of mortal sin commits the grave sin of sacrilege.

1210. When is confirmation administered in the Eastern Church?

In the Eastern Church, confirmation is conferred in infancy immediately after baptism.

1211. When is confirmation administered in the Western Church?

In the Western Church, confirmation is administered to baptized persons after they have reached the age of reason and normally after they have for some time been receiving the sacraments of penance and the Holy Eucharist.

Eucharist

1. The Real Presence

1212. What is the center of the whole Catholic liturgy?

The center of the whole Catholic liturgy is the Eucharist. The Eucharist is most important in the life of the Church because it is Jesus Christ. It is the Incarnation continued in space and time. The other sacraments and all the Church's ministries and apostolates are directed toward the Eucharist.

1213. What does the word "Eucharist" mean?

Eucharist means "thanksgiving." The name is explained by the fact that Christ "gave thanks" when he instituted the Eucharist and this is the supreme act of Christian gratitude to God.

1214. What is the sacrament of the Eucharist?

The Eucharist is a sacrament which really, truly, and substantially contains the body and blood, soul, and divinity of our Lord Jesus Christ under the appearances of bread and wine. It is the great sacrament of God's love in which Christ is eaten, the mind is filled with grace, and a pledge is given to us of future glory.

1215. When was the sacrament of the Eucharist instituted?

The sacrament of the Eucharist was instituted at the Last Supper the night before Christ died. This is recorded by St. Paul in his letter to the Corinthians (cf. 1 Corinthians 11:23–26) and in the Synoptic Gospels of Matthew (26:26–28), Mark (14:22–24), and Luke (22:19–20). St. John omitted the institution because he wrote his gospel to supplement what the other evangelists had already written.

1216. How did Christ institute the Holy Eucharist?

The Eucharist was instituted in this way: "Jesus took some bread, and when he had said the blessing he broke it and gave it to the disciples. 'Take it and eat'; he said, 'this is my body.' Then he took a cup, and when he had returned thanks he gave it to them. 'Drink all of you from this,' he said, 'for this is my blood' " (Matthew 26:26–28).

1217. Is the Eucharist necessary for salvation?

The Eucharist is necessary for salvation, to be received either sacramentally or in desire. Christ's words, "if you do not eat the flesh of the Son of Man and drink his blood, you will not have life in you" (John 6:53), mean that Holy Communion is necessary to sustain the life of grace in a person who has reached the age of reason. Those who, through no fault of their own, do not realize this can receive the necessary grace to remain in God's friendship through other means. This is similar to what happens with the baptism of desire to first receive the state of grace.

1218. What is the sensible sign in the Eucharist?

The sensible sign in the Eucharist is the appearance of bread and wine, that is, anything in these elements that falls under the senses, such as size, color, shape, taste, weight, and texture.

1219. What is contained in this sign?

After consecration, this sign contains the whole Christ, his body and blood, his soul and divinity.

1220. What is the matter of the sacrament of the Eucharist?

The matter of the sacrament is wheaten bread and wine. In the Latin Rite, the bread must be unleavened; in the Eastern Rites of the Catholic Church, leavened bread is used. The wine is mixed with a little water before consecration.

1221. Why did Christ choose bread and wine for the matter of this sacrament?

Christ chose bread and wine for the matter of the sacrament in order to teach that as we daily partake of food for the body so we should daily receive this heavenly food for the soul.

1222. What is the form of the sacrament of the Eucharist?

The form of the sacrament of the Eucharist consists in the words: "This is my body. This is my blood."

1223. Is only the substance of Christ's human nature present in the Eucharist?

Christ is present in the Eucharist not only with everything that makes him man, but with all that makes him this human being. He is therefore present with all his physical properties, hands and feet and head and human heart. He is present with his human soul, with his thoughts, desires, and human affections.

1224. How does Christ become present in the Eucharist?

Christ becomes present in the Eucharist by means of transubstantiation. Transubstantiation is the term used to identify the change that takes place at the consecration.

1225. What remains of the bread and wine after consecration?

After the consecration, nothing remains of the bread and wine except their external properties. Their substance becomes the living body and blood of Christ.

1226. Is Jesus Christ contained under each particle of the species of bread and wine?

Yes, it is a matter of faith that Jesus Christ is contained under each particle of the species of bread and wine. No matter how great the number of parts into which the species are divided, the whole Christ is present in every portion.

1227. Is Jesus Christ present in the Eucharist as long as the species remain?

Yes, Jesus Christ is present in the Eucharist as long as the species remain. Therefore, we worship the Blessed Sacrament as we would worship the person of Jesus himself.

1228. Why is the Eucharist the most excellent of all the sacraments?

The Eucharist is the most excellent of all the sacraments because it contains Christ himself. All the other sacraments are channels of grace but they do not actually possess Jesus Christ, the Author of grace. Moreover, the other sacraments point to the Eucharist as their purpose or end. Baptism enables us to receive the Eucharist; confirmation perfects the Christian so that his faith in the Eucharist may remain strong; penance and anointing of the sick cleanse the soul from weakness and sin and dispose it for the reception of the Eucharist; holy orders ordains the priests necessary to consecrate and offer the Eucharist; and matrimony is the earthly sign of the purpose of the Eucharist, to unite the faithful with Christ in selfless love.

1229. What perfections of God does the Eucharist reveal?

In the Holy Eucharist God reveals his power, his wisdom, and his infinite goodness.

1230. How does the Eucharist reveal God's power?

The Eucharist reveals God's power because it is a compendium of miracles: the change of substance of bread and of wine into the body and blood of Christ; the remaining appearances of bread and wine, after the bread and wine have ceased to exist; the presence of Christ at the same time in heaven and under the sacramental species in many different places; the presence of Christ, whole and entire and living under the sacred elements; the presence of the Trinity in the Eucharist as a result of the union of the two natures in Christ, and the union of the Son of God with the Father and the Holy Spirit; and the multiplication of his presence in every particle of the species.

1231. How does the Eucharist reveal God's wisdom?

The Eucharist reveals God's wisdom in that God has made this sacrament the center on which all other mysteries converge, especially those of redemption and sanctification. It is also in the light of the Eucharist that everything else in the faith takes on a deeper meaning. By this marvelous invention of his divinity, Christ remains among us and unites himself to us in Communion, even while he is in heaven.

1232. How does the Holy Eucharist reveal God's goodness?

The Holy Eucharist reveals God's goodness in that Christ gives us not only his grace, but all that he is and all that he has. Since goodness means giving, in the Eucharist God gives himself to the limit of divine love.

1233. Which virtues of Christ can we imitate in the Eucharist?

In the Eucharist, we can especially imitate Christ's humility and obedience.

1234. How is the virtue of humility portrayed in the Eucharist?

In the Eucharist, Christ empties himself, as it were, twice over: once in having become man and thus hiding his divinity; and once again in hiding his humanity behind the sacramental veils of bread and wine. It is especially in the Eucharist that he invites us, "Come to me . . . for I am gentle and humble in heart, and you will find rest for your souls" (Matthew 11:28–29).

1235. How is Christ's obedience seen in the Eucharist?

Christ's obedience is seen in the Eucharist in that he obeys promptly and perfectly the words of consecration spoken by the priest at Mass. The moment these words are pronounced, Christ becomes present on the altar. Moreover, he allows himself to be placed where those who handle the Eucharist wish him to be.

1236. Name the kinds of ministers for the Eucharist.

There are two kinds of ministers for the Eucharist: one for consecrating the sacrament and the other for distributing it.

1237. Who are the ministers for consecrating the sacrament?

The ministers for consecrating the sacrament are bishops and priests. Our Lord gave to the apostles and their successors alone the power to consecrate when he said, "Do this as a memorial of me" (Luke 22:19).

1238. Who are the ministers for distributing the Eucharist?

The official ministers for distributing the Eucharist are the priests and deacons. "Acolytes duly appointed, moreover, may, as extraordinary ministers, distribute Holy Communion when no priest or deacon is available, when neither priest nor deacon is able to distribute it on account of ill health or advanced age, or because of the pressure of other pastoral duties. Acolytes may similarly distribute Holy Communion when the number of the faithful approaching the altar is so large that the celebration of Mass or other sacred ceremony would be unduly prolonged." Besides, "The local ordinary may give to other extraordinary ministers the faculty to distribute Holy Communion whenever this seems necessary for the pastoral good of the faithful and when no priest, deacon, or acolyte is available" (Sacred Congregation for Divine Worship, *Eucharistiae Sacramentum,* III, 17).

1239. What change takes place when the priest pronounces the words of consecration in the Mass?

When the priest pronounces the words of consecration, Jesus Christ becomes present on the altar at that very moment. We perceive the presence of Christ in the Eucharist by faith alone.

1240. How is the dogma of the Real Presence proved?

The dogma of the Real Presence is proved from Sacred Scripture, from Sacred Tradition, and from the infallible teaching of the Church.

1241. How is the Real Presence proved from Sacred Scripture?

The Real Presence is separately proved from Sacred Scripture in the narrative of the Last Supper, and in the sixth chapter of the Gospel of St. John.

At the Last Supper, Christ simply declared that he was giving the disciples his body and blood. Nothing in the context of his words indicates he was speaking figuratively, whereas everything shows he meant it to be taken literally (cf. Matthew 26:26–28; Mark 14:22–25; Luke 22:19–20).

In the Gospel of John, when Christ foretold he would give his body to eat and blood to drink, many of his disciples left him because they would not believe this. Yet, so far from taking back what he said or qualifying his statement, he repeated the promise and even asked the apostles if they also wanted to leave him (cf. John 6:47–67).

1242. What is the teaching of Sacred Tradition about the Real Presence?

Sacred Tradition from the earliest times teaches the Real Presence with absolute clarity. St. Ignatius of Antioch wrote in A.D. 107, "The Eucharist is the flesh of our Savior Jesus Christ" (Smyrneans, 6:2). And St. Justin wrote in A.D. 145, "As Jesus Christ our Savior was made incarnate by the word of God and had both flesh and blood for our salvation, so too, as we have been taught, the food which has been made into the Eucharist by the Eucharistic prayer set down by him . . . is both the flesh and the blood of that incarnated Jesus" (I Apology, 66).

1243. What is the teaching of the Church on the Real Presence?

The teaching of the Church on the Real Presence is defined revealed doctrine according to the Council of Trent. It declares that the whole Christ is truly, really, and substantially present in the sacrament of the Holy Eucharist immediately after consecration. It also declares that the whole Christ is present under each form, and under each part or particle of each species of both bread and wine.

1244. What is meant by the "whole Christ" in the Eucharist?

By the "whole Christ" in the Eucharist we mean he is present in the fullness of his divine and human natures. He is present under the sacramental veils with the fullness of his divine attributes as well as all his human qualities.

1245. When may the Eucharist be administered?

The Eucharist should normally be administered during the Mass, but it may be distributed to the faithful also outside of Mass. It is desirable, however, when it is to be distributed outside of Mass, that fixed times be appointed for the distribution of Holy Communion, with due consideration for the convenience of the faithful.

1246. Where should Holy Communion be distributed outside of Mass?

Holy Communion should be distributed outside of Mass in a church or oratory in which Mass is habitually celebrated, or where the Blessed Sacrament is habitually reserved. In case of real necessity, however, Holy Communion may be distributed in other places, not excluding private homes.

1247. When does the Church's precept oblige us to receive Holy Communion?

The Church's precept obliges us to receive Holy Communion at Easter time.

1248. Why are the faithful encouraged to receive Holy Communion during Mass?

The faithful are encouraged to receive Holy Communion during Mass because in this way they share more perfectly in the celebration of the Eucharist. At the Last Supper, Christ gave the apostles Holy Communion immediately after he offered the first Mass, to be completed on Calvary. By receiving the body and blood of the Lord after the priest's Communion, the faithful likewise signify more clearly their participation in the same sacrifice.

1249. Why should we worship Jesus in the tabernacle?

We should worship Jesus in the tabernacle because he is present there under the appearance of bread and wine as truly as he is in heaven. We should give him the adoration given to God alone on account of his infinite perfection and his supreme dominion over all things created.

1250. How does the Church foster devotion to the Real Presence?

The Church fosters devotion to the Real Presence through public veneration of the Holy Eucharist, notably Exposition of the Blessed Sacrament, Benediction, and Forty Hours Devotion.

1251. What is Benediction of the Blessed Sacrament?

Benediction of the Blessed Sacrament is a special devotion that dates from at least the fifteenth century. It consists of Exposition of the Blessed Sacrament, hymns, readings, prayers, and the blessing of the people with the Holy Eucharist.

1252. What is Exposition of the Blessed Sacrament?

This is the solemn placing of a consecrated Host in a monstrance, on the altar, to be viewed and venerated by the faithful. The exposition is opened with a hymn and incensing by the priest. During the exposition, public or private prayers are said, and the ceremony is commonly concluded with Benediction of the Blessed Sacrament.

1253. Why should the faithful assist at Benediction of the Blessed Sacrament?

Benediction of the Blessed Sacrament inspires the faithful to a deeper awareness of the marvelous presence of Christ in the Eucharist and encourages them to spiritual communion with the Savior.

1254. How is prayer before the Blessed Sacrament related to the Eucharist as liturgy?

Prayer before the Blessed Sacrament is related to the Eucharist as liturgy because it draws the faithful into an ever deeper participation in the Paschal Mystery. It also leads them to respond gratefully to the gift of him who, through his humanity, constantly pours divine life into the members of his body. The faithful are also better disposed to profit from their participation in the Mass and reception of Holy Communion through devotion to the Blessed Sacrament reserved on the altar.

1255. How should the Blessed Sacrament be honored?

The Blessed Sacrament should be honored with extraordinary festive celebration and carried solemnly from place to place and should be publicly exposed for the people's adoration.

1256. What is the Forty Hours Devotion?

Forty Hours Devotion is the public exposition of the Blessed Sacrament in the monstrance for forty hours, either consecutively or over a period of three days.

1257. What is the sign by which the people know that Christ is present in the tabernacle?

The sign by which the people know that Christ is present in the tabernacle is the sanctuary light which burns night and day before the tabernacle. Also a tabernacle veil or other suitable means may be prescribed by competent authority.

1258. How do we manifest our adoration outwardly?

We manifest our adoration outwardly by genuflecting before the place where the Blessed Sacrament is reserved.

1259. Is Christ present in other ways besides the Real Presence?

Christ is present when the Church prays. He is present when the Church performs her work of mercy. He is present in the

Church as she governs the people of God. He is present in the pastors who exercise their priestly and episcopal power. He is specially present in the Church when she offers in his name the Sacrifice of the Mass, and he is present when the Church administers the sacraments. But the Real Presence is absolutely unique. It is the physical presence of Christ in our midst, no less truly present than he is now present at the right hand of the Father in heaven.

1260. Why is Christ's presence in the Blessed Sacrament called the "Real Presence"?

It is called the "Real Presence" because it is presence in the fullest sense possible. It is a substantial presence by which Christ, the God-Man, is now on earth, no less truly than he was during his visible presence in history, in the first century in Palestine.

2. The Mass

1261. Is the Sacrifice of the Cross the only perfect sacrifice?

The Sacrifice of the Cross is the only perfect sacrifice, in which the one offered and the one offering the sacrifice is God himself.

1262. How was the Sacrifice of the Cross a true sacrifice?

The Sacrifice of the Cross was a true sacrifice because it fulfilled all the necessary conditions. The external offering was a visible human being, Jesus Christ. It was offered to God alone by an authorized priest, Jesus Christ. The object offered was immolated since Christ was put to death. The purpose of the sacrifice was accomplished because the sovereign dominion of God over the human race was acknowledged.

1263. How did Christ prepare for the Sacrifice of the Cross?

Christ prepared for the Sacrifice of the Cross by making his life one long sacrifice and by submitting most perfectly his will to the will of his Father.

1264. How is the Sacrifice of the Cross continued on earth?

The Sacrifice of the Cross is continued on earth through the Sacrifice of the Mass.

1265. What is the Sacrifice of the Mass?

The Sacrifice of the Mass is the true and properly called Sacrifice of the New Law. It is the Sacrifice in which Christ is offered under the species of bread and wine in an unbloody manner. The Sacrifice of the altar, then, is no mere empty commemoration of the Passion and Death of Jesus Christ, but a true and proper act of sacrifice. Christ, the eternal High Priest, in an unbloody way offers himself a most acceptable Victim to the eternal Father, as he did upon the Cross.

1266. What is a sacrifice?

A sacrifice is the surrender of something precious to God to acknowledge his dominion over us as Creator, and our total dependence on him as our Lord.

1267. What are the essentials of every sacrifice?

The essentials of every sacrifice are the object offered and the act of surrender by which the object is offered to God. Thus in martyrdom, a human life is the object and the voluntary giving up of one's life is the act of surrender to God.

1268. How are the Mass and Calvary related?

The Mass and Calvary are related in three ways: as re-presentation, as memorial, and as effective application to mankind of the merits gained by Christ's Death on the Cross.

1269. How does the Mass re-present Calvary?

The Mass re-presents Calvary by continuing Christ's sacrifice of himself to his heavenly Father. In the Mass, no less than on Calvary, Jesus really offers his life to his heavenly Father. This is possible because in the Mass is the same priest, Jesus Christ, who with his human will (united to the divine) offers himself; and it is the same victim, Jesus Christ, whose human life (united with the divinity) is sacrificed. The only difference is that, being now glorified, Christ cannot die a physical death as he did on the Cross. St. Paul writes of Christ's self-offering: "Since men only die once, and after that comes judgment, so Christ, too, offers himself only once to take the faults of many on himself" (Hebrews 9:27–28).

1270. How is the sacrifice of Christ manifested in the Mass today?

The sacrifice of Christ is manifested in the Mass today by the separate consecration which symbolizes the actual separation of his body and blood, or death.

1271. How is the Mass a memorial of Calvary?

The Mass is a memorial of Calvary because the apostles have handed down what Jesus ordered them to do when he said, "Do this as a memorial of me" (Luke 22:19). Consequently, in the Mass we not only call to mind what Jesus did at the Last Supper and completed on Calvary. We have reenacted what took place between Holy Thursday and Good Friday.

1272. Is the Mass then truly the same Sacrifice as Calvary?

The Sacrifice of the Mass is substantially the same as the Sacrifice of the Cross. However, the Mass differs from the Sacrifice of the Cross in the following ways: *In the manner of offering:* on the Cross Christ was offered in a bloody manner. On the altar he offers himself in an unbloody manner; *By reason of the One offering:* on the Cross Christ offered himself alone and directly. In the Mass he offers himself along with us through the ministry of priests; *By reason of the Victim:* on the Cross his humanity was visible while in the Mass Christ's humanity is hidden; *By reason of the effects:* on the Cross Christ merited once and for all the price of Redemption for a fallen mankind. On the altar nothing new is merited, but now the satisfaction and merits of the Cross are applied to us.

1273. How does Christ offer the Sacrifice of the Mass?

Christ offers the Sacrifice of the Mass as Head of the Mystical Body. This means that he offers the Mass not only as one physical person, but united with the members of the Church. The Mass, therefore, is the sacrifice of Head and members of the Mystical Body of Christ.

1274. By whom, then, is the Sacrifice of the Mass offered?

The Sacrifice of the Mass is offered by Christ himself, by the ordained priest, by each person assisting and by the whole Church. However, each one offers the Mass in a different way, and always dependent on and united with the great High Priest, Jesus Christ.

1275. How do the faithful offer the Holy Sacrifice?

The faithful offer the Holy Sacrifice from the fact that the minister at the altar is offering Mass in the name of all of Christ's members, since he represents Christ in the fullness of his Mystical Body. The ordained priest represents the Savior, who is Head of the Church. The people unite their sentiments of praise and petition, of expiation and gratitude with the prayers and intentions of the priest, who is acting in the name of Christ.

1276. Is there any sense in which the Mass can be considered a bloody sacrifice?

The Mass can be considered a bloody sacrifice insofar as some members of the Mystical Body even now are shedding their physical blood in martyrdom. Moreover, all the faithful are to offer what may be called the "spiritual blood" of their sufferings and trials, which they unite with the sacrifice of Christ on the altar.

1277. Does the Mass detract from the one, unique Sacrifice of the Cross?

The Mass in no way detracts from the one, unique Sacrifice of the Cross because the Mass is the same Sacrifice as that of the Cross, to continue on earth until the end of time. Christ not only was the priest who offered himself to his heavenly Father. He is the priest whose intercession for sinful mankind continues, only now he communicates the graces he had won for us by his bloody Passion and Death. The Mass, therefore, no less than the Cross, is expiatory for sins; but now the expiation is experienced by those for whom, on the Cross, the title of God's mercy had been gained.

1278. Why is the Sacrifice of the Mass offered?

The Sacrifice of the Mass is offered to glorify God and obtain his blessings for those who have not yet reached heaven, whether on earth or in purgatory.

1279. How are the merits of Calvary dispensed through the Holy Sacrifice of the Mass?

The merits of Calvary are dispensed through the Mass in that the graces Christ gained for us on the Cross are communicated by the Eucharistic Sacrifice. The degree of this communication of grace depends on 1) how often the Mass is offered, 2) the dispositions of the priest at the altar, 3) the dispositions of those who join the priest in offering Mass, 4) the dispositions of those for whom the Mass is offered, and 5) the mysterious dispositions of divine Providence.

1280. To whom do we offer the Sacrifice of the Mass?

We offer the Mass to God alone. However, we also celebrate the Mass in honor of the angels and saints.

1281. How do we celebrate the Mass in honor of the angels and saints?

Through the Mass we thank God for the graces he bestowed on the angels and saints before they reached heaven, and for the glory they now enjoy in the beatific vision.

1282. What are the ends or purposes for which we offer the Mass to God?

We offer the Mass to God as a sacrifice of adoration to his divine majesty; as a sacrifice of thanksgiving for all the benefits we have received from him; as a sacrifice of expiation for the sins we have committed in offending him; and as a sacrifice of petition, to obtain from his bounty all that we need for ourselves, for all the living on earth and the souls in purgatory.

1283. What are the liturgical divisions of the Mass?

The liturgical divisions of the Mass are: the penitential rite, the liturgy of the word, the liturgy of the Eucharist, the communion rite, and the concluding rite.

1284. Within these liturgical divisions what are the principal parts of the Mass?

Within the liturgical divisions of the Mass the principal parts are the offertory, the consecration, and the communion.

1285. What is the offertory?

The offertory is that part of the Mass in which the unconsecrated bread and wine are offered to God. While separately offering the bread (on a paten) and the wine (in the chalice) the priest says: "Blessed are you, Lord God of all things, because we have received bread [wine] from your bounty. We offer this fruit of the earth [wine] and of men's labor, that it may become for us the Bread of Life [Spiritual Drink]."

1286. What is the consecration?

The consecration is the words of institution pronounced by the priest at Mass, by which the bloody Sacrifice of Calvary is renewed in an unbloody manner on the altar.

1287. What is communion?

Communion is the reception of the body and blood of Christ first by the priest and then by the people during the Sacrifice of the Mass.

1288. Is the Mass, then, both a form of worship and a sacrament?

Yes, the Mass is a form of worship as an act of adoration and thanksgiving to God; it is a sacrament as a means of obtaining grace from God, in reparation for sins committed in the past and in petition for favors needed in the future.

1289. What are the graces conferred by the Mass as a sacrament?

The graces conferred by the Mass as a sacrament are twofold. Through the Mass we obtain forgiveness for venial sins and the remission of temporal punishment still due for past sins; we also obtain for ourselves and others the grace of repentance and the desire to expiate offenses against God. Looking to the future, the Mass is the single most effective source of grace by which Christ distributes the blessings of Calvary.

1290. For whom may the Holy Sacrifice of the Mass be offered?

The Holy Sacrifice of the Mass may be offered for all the living, whether they are in the state of grace or estranged from God; and for the dead, that is, those who died in God's grace and yet have sins to atone in purgatory.

1291. How do the benefits of the Mass differ in their application?

The general benefits are applied to the whole Church, both living and dead. The special benefits are mainly applied to the priest or priests who offer Mass, then those for whom a Mass is particularly offered, those who are actively participating in the Mass, and finally for all the faithful, and, indeed, for the whole human race.

1292. Is the Sacrifice of the Mass only for the expiation of sins?

No, the Sacrifice of the Mass, no less than Calvary, is at once a sacrifice of adoration, to praise the majesty of God; of thanksgiving, to thank God for his blessings in the past; of petition, to ask him for spiritual and temporal favors in the future; and of expiation, to obtain his mercy for sinners and remission of his just punishment for their sins.

1293. Is only the Death of Christ commemorated in the Mass?

In the Mass not only the Death of Christ is commemorated. The Church teaches that the Mass is also a memorial of his Resurrection. The Risen Savior, who is now in heaven, is also the principal priest at the altar.

1294. Is the Sacrifice of the Mass of infinite value?

The Sacrifice of the Mass is of infinite value, no less than that of the Cross. However, the merit received depends on a person's dispositions.

3. Holy Communion

1295. What is Holy Communion?

Holy Communion is the sacrament in which we receive the body and blood of Jesus Christ as the spiritual nourishment of our souls.

1296. What are the spiritual effects of Holy Communion?

The spiritual effects of Holy Communion are an increase of sanctifying grace, a title to actual graces, forgiveness of venial sin as to guilt and the penalty due to sin, preservation from mortal sin, and reception of the special sacramental grace of Holy Communion.

1297. What is the special sacramental grace of Holy Communion?

The special sacramental grace of Holy Communion is an increase of the supernatural virtue of charity, in a greater love for God, closer union with Jesus Christ, and a greater love of one's neighbor.

1298. What are the bodily effects of Holy Communion?

The bodily effects of Holy Communion are a corporeal union with Christ, the weakening of concupiscence through a growing mastery of the passions, and an increase of one's title to eternal happiness after the resurrection of the body in heavenly glory.

1299. On what do the effects of the Eucharist depend?

The effects of the Eucharist depend on the dispositions of the recipient. Therefore, the reception of Holy Communion should be preceded by serious preparation and followed by a suitable thanksgiving according to circumstances and a person's freedom from other pressing responsibilities.

1300. What are the dispositions for receiving Holy Communion?

The principal dispositions necessary for Holy Communion are the state of grace and having the right intention.

1301. What is the right intention?

A right intention means that the one who approaches the Holy Table does not do so out of routine or vainglory or human respect. His purpose is rather to please God, to become more closely united with God by charity, and to use this divine remedy for one's moral weaknesses and defects.

1302. What is the difference between strictly necessary and praiseworthy dispositions for Holy Communion?

The one strictly necessary disposition for Holy Communion is to be free from mortal sin. It is praiseworthy, however, to be free also from venial sins, especially those which are fully deliberate. Moreover, it is highly desirable that a person also be free from all deliberate attachment to anything sinful.

1303. What does it mean to receive Christ unworthily?

To receive Christ unworthily means to receive him when a person knows he is burdened with an unforgiven mortal sin.

1304. May a person who has a mortal sin on his soul receive Holy Communion?

A person who has mortal sin on his soul may not receive Holy Communion. He is bound by divine and ecclesiastical law to receive sacramental absolution in the sacrament of penance. As the Church teaches, "No one who is conscious of being guilty of mortal sin, however repentant he may feel, may receive Holy Communion until he has received sacramental absolution."

1305. Must we confess venial sins before receiving Holy Communion?

We need not confess venial sins before receiving Holy Communion although it is useful to do so. By purifying the soul, the sacrament of penance removes many obstacles that prevent the soul from receiving precious benefits from Holy Communion.

1306. What are some helpful ways to profit more from Holy Communion?

Some helpful ways to profit more from Holy Communion are: Make spiritual communions frequently through the day by telling our Lord we desire to receive him in the Holy Eucharist; recollect ourselves in the evening before receiving Holy Communion; during Mass participate as intently as possible and unite ourselves with the priest at the altar; receive our Lord with sentiments of humility, love, and confidence; and after Communion spend some time in thanksgiving and asking Jesus in the Blessed Sacrament for whatever graces we need.

1307. How should we appear and act as we approach Christ in the Holy Eucharist?

When we approach Christ in the Eucharist we should be neatly and modestly dressed. We should avoid undue haste, and should go with hands folded. Holy Communion may be received either kneeling or standing. When received standing, the faithful should approach Communion in procession and make a sign of reverence before the Blessed Sacrament.

1308. What does the Eucharistic fast require?

The Eucharistic fast requires abstaining from eating and drinking, except water, for one hour before actual Communion time. Those who are ill, although not confined to bed, may take medicine up to the time for Communion. The sick and elderly, with those who care for them and their relatives, may reduce the time to fifteen minutes "whenever it would be difficult for them to observe the fast for one hour." The Eucharistic fast is a grave obligation.

1309. What is meant by frequent Communion?

Frequent Communion means receiving the Blessed Sacrament not only on Sunday but during the week. According to Pope St. Pius X, the first meaning of "daily bread" in the Lord's Prayer is daily Holy Communion.

1310. What are the benefits of frequent Holy Communion?

Frequent Holy Communion increases our union with Christ, nourishes the spiritual life of the soul, strengthens our practice of virtue, and gives us a sure pledge of eternal happiness.

1311. When should children receive their first Communion?

Children should receive Holy Communion as soon as they have attained the use of reason, and after having made their first confession.

1312. Who is to see that the sick receive the Eucharist?

Pastors have the first duty to see that the sick receive Holy Communion without delay. They are to make sure that the faithful are nourished by the Eucharist while in full possession of their faculties. Relatives or friends of the sick are obliged to notify a priest so that he can carry out his priestly duties.

1313. What is Holy Communion as viaticum?

Holy Communion as viaticum is the reception of the Holy Eucharist by one who is in probable danger of death.

1314. Is it obligatory to receive viaticum?

Yes, the faithful who are in danger of death from any cause whatsoever are obliged to receive Holy Communion as viaticum.

1315. How is the Holy Eucharist a sacred banquet?

The Holy Eucharist is a sacred banquet because Christ's body and blood is the principal source of nourishment for the spirit through the infusion of divine love.

1316. May the faithful receive Holy Communion under both kinds.

Yes, according to the norms set down by the Church, the faithful may receive Holy Communion under both kinds. Receiving from the chalice clearly expresses Christ's intention that the new and eternal Covenant should be ratified in his blood. However,

Christ is received whole and entire in a complete sacrament under one kind only. And the people are not thereby deprived of any grace necessary for salvation.

1317. What is spiritual communion?

Spiritual communion is the fervent desire to receive Jesus in the Blessed Sacrament when it is impossible, for whatever reason, to receive the Eucharist sacramentally. The purpose of spiritual communion is to keep the soul united with Jesus throughout the day. It merits special graces from God and better prepares a person for sacramental Communion.

Penance

1. Institution, Necessity, and Forms

1318. What is penance?

Penance means repentance or satisfaction for sin. It is also a virtue, and one of the sacraments instituted by Christ.

1319. What is the virtue of penance?

Penance is the supernatural virtue that inclines a person to detest his sins because they have offended a loving God and deserved his just punishment, to firmly resolve not to commit these sins again, and to make satisfaction for one's offenses against God.

1320. Why is the virtue of penance necessary?

The virtue of penance is necessary for a sinner to be reconciled with God. If we expect his forgiveness, we must repent. Penance is also necessary because we must expiate and make reparation for the punishment which is due for our sins. That is why Christ tells us, "Unless you repent you will all perish" (Luke 13:5).

1321. What is the sacrament of penance?

Penance is the sacrament instituted by Christ in which sinners are reconciled with God through the absolution of the priest.

1322. Why did Christ institute the sacrament of penance?

Christ instituted this sacrament to give us a ready and assured means of obtaining remission for the sins committed after baptism.

1323. When did Christ institute the sacrament of penance?

Christ instituted the sacrament of penance as his first gift to the Church on Easter Sunday night. He said to the apostles, " 'Peace be with you,' and showed them his hands and his side. The disciples were filled with joy when they saw the Lord, and he said to them again, 'Peace be with you. As the Father sent me, so am I sending you.' After saying this he breathed on them and said, 'Receive the Holy Spirit. For those whose sins you forgive, they are forgiven; for those whose sins you retain, they are retained' " (John 20:19–23).

1324. What did Christ mean by this?

When Christ spoke these words, he meant that the apostles and their successors should not only declare that a person's sins are forgiven, but actually have the power to forgive in his name. By these words, he also gave them the right to withhold absolution.

1325. Is the sacrament of penance necessary?

Yes, the sacrament of penance is necessary for all who have fallen into mortal sin after baptism. If the sacrament cannot actually be received, the desire for its reception suffices. But then a person must make an act of perfect contrition.

1326. What is the matter and form of the sacrament of penance?

The form of the sacrament is the words of absolution, which are said orally by an authorized priest. Essential for absolution are the words "I absolve you from your sins." The matter of the sacrament is the required acts of the penitent, namely, contrition, confession, and satisfaction.

1327. Do all bishops and priests have the power to forgive sins?

All bishops and priests have the power to forgive sins or absolve sins. Christ conferred this power on the apostles, and on the bishops and priests who would succeed them. However, the Church reserves the right to determine when a priest may use the power to forgive sins. Without this authorization his absolution would be invalid.

1328. What is meant by an authorized priest?

An authorized priest is one whom the bishop of the diocese gives the right to hear confessions and give absolution. Every validly ordained priest is authorized by the Church to absolve anyone in danger of death.

1329. Why may a priest refuse to give absolution?

A priest may refuse to give absolution when the penitent shows that he has no sorrow for the grave sins he has committed or no intention of avoiding what he knows will lead him into some grave sins in the future.

1330. How is the sacrament of penance communal and ecclesial?

The sacrament of penance is communal in reconciling the sinner first and mainly with God but also with others who are offended by sin. It is ecclesial because the sacrament restores (or increases) our friendship not only with God, but also with the Church. This sacrament heals the soul of the sinner by restoring or increasing the virtue of infused charity, which enables us to love God above all things and our neighbor as Christ has loved us.

1331. How may the sacrament of penance be administered?

The sacrament of penance may be administered in three ways: individual confession, common celebration with individual confession with absolution, and entirely communal including collective absolution.

1332. What is the reason for this variety?

The reason for this variety is to emphasize the twofold aspect of penance as personal and social, and to meet the special needs of the faithful.

1333. What is the ritual followed in individual confession?

The ritual followed in individual confession is: the priest greets the penitent, a scriptural passage may be read, the penitent confesses his sins, the priest offers encouragement and advice, imposes a penance, the penitent expresses sorrow and absolution is given.

1334. When does the Church require children to receive the sacrament of penance?

The Church has for centuries, in accordance with the teaching of the Fourth Council of Lateran (1215), decreed that children receive the sacraments of penance and the Eucharist as soon as they had attained the use of reason. That prescription was applied throughout the Church and has borne and still bears abundant fruit in Christian life and spiritual perfection (Declaration *Sanctus Pontifex,* May 24, 1973).

1335. What is the age of reason or discretion?

The age of reason or discretion is the time when a person can distinguish right from wrong, that is, has sufficient intelligence to make any kind of free choice. It is the age of moral responsibility. In Church law, this is normally about seven years of age.

1336. Should children receive the sacrament of penance before first Communion?

Yes, children should receive the sacrament of penance before their first Communion, although it is assumed they have not committed any mortal sins. This is the firm teaching of the Church. Through the sacrament of penance, children grow in sanctifying grace, are enlightened in the practice of virtue, strengthened to resist temptation, and introduced to a sacrament that should be habitual in their lives as Catholics.

1337. What is the ritual for the communal celebration of penance with individual absolution?

This form of the sacrament of penance comes in three parts. There is first a communal penitential service, led by the priest and shared by the faithful in a liturgical celebration. Then each penitent goes individually to one of a number of priests to receive personal absolution. And finally the whole assembly comes together again for a communal act of thanksgiving for God's mercy.

1338. When may general absolution be given?

General or collective absolution may be given only in most exceptional cases because individual confession and absolution is, by divine law, the ordinary way the faithful are to be reconciled with God and the Church. Exceptions to this practice are allowed only when private confession and individual absolution are physically or morally impossible. The local bishop, after conferring with other members of the national episcopal conference, is to decide when general absolution may be permitted.

1339. What dispositions are necessary for those who receive general absolution?

Those who receive general absolution must be sincerely sorry for their sins, make a firm purpose of amendment, and resolve to individually confess their mortal sins to a priest in due time. Without these dispositions, the absolution is invalid.

2. Requirements of the Penitent: Sorrow, Confession, and Satisfaction

1340. What should a person do immediately after falling into mortal sin?

Immediately after falling into mortal sin a person should make an act of perfect contrition and have the intention of confessing the sin as soon as possible.

1341. Can venial sin be forgiven even though mortal sins are not forgiven?

Venial sins cannot be forgiven if the mortal sins have not been remitted. A person must be in the state of grace to merit divine mercy for his venial sins.

1342. If only venial sins are confessed must a person repent of all of them?

For valid absolution a person must be sorry for at least one venial sin. In the absence of this sorrow, in good faith, the sacrament is merely invalid. In bad faith, it is also sacrilegious.

1343. How should we repent of venial sins?

We should repent of venial sins by reflecting on the holiness of the all-perfect God whom we have offended; on the ingratitude for his loving kindness, and the selfishness that every deliberate sin manifests against our loving Creator and merciful Savior.

1344. How can we obtain sufficient knowledge of our sins for confession?

To obtain sufficient knowledge of our sins for confession we should ask for light from the Holy Spirit and examine our conscience carefully.

1345. What is an examination of conscience?

An examination of conscience is a review of our past actions to find out how well or badly we have behaved during a certain period of time. It is the ordinary means of obtaining self-knowledge.

1346. Should we examine our conscience only before going to confession?

We should examine our conscience not only before going to confession, but every day. Frequent examination of conscience is necessary to make progress in the spiritual life.

1347. What are the two principal forms of daily examination of conscience?

The two principal forms of daily examination of conscience are the particular and general.

1348. What is the particular examen?

The particular examen is a method of reflecting on one's past conduct by concentrating, for a period of time, on one fault to be overcome or one virtue to cultivate.

1349. What is the special value of the particular examen?

The special value of the particular examen is the practical one of concentration. By stressing one dominant failing or one contrary virtue we focus attention on one course of action and center our willpower on one moral object—with marvelous results that have been proved by centuries of spiritual experience.

1350. How should the particular examen be made?

There is no single prescribed method. But one strong recommendation is to keep some written record of each examen. This helps to concentrate one's moral energy, keeps the mind alert during the day and, afterward, offers a means of following one's spiritual progress from day to day.

1351. What is the general examen?

The general examen is a method of reflecting on the main features of our moral conduct over a certain period of time, usually the past day or half day.

1352. What is the special value of the general examen?

The special value of the general examen is the useful one of periodic self-awareness. Unless we regularly look back over the recent past, to see how we have behaved, we tend to overlook even glaring defects and lose golden opportunities for the practice of virtue. Most people are too preoccupied with external things to pay much attention to their interior motives or the presence of God within their souls. The general examen has the power of making people conscious of the divine indwelling and the need for purity of intention in their moral conduct.

1353. What is contrition?

Contrition is an interior sorrow of the soul and aversion for past sins, with the firm determination of not sinning again.

1354. What is perfect contrition?

Perfect contrition is sorrow for sin whose motive is the love of God. It remits mortal sins even before actually receiving the sacrament of penance, provided there is a real desire to receive the sacrament. "I," says God, "love those who love me" (Proverbs 8:17). God loves those who are sorry for having offended him by now loving God to make up for the failure in love when they sinned. An example of such contrition is the Good Thief on Calvary, who, while being crucified with Christ, freely admitted his guilt and asked Christ's mercy: " 'We are paying for what we did. But this man has done nothing wrong. Jesus,' he said, 'remember me when you come into your kingdom' " (Luke 23:41–42).

1355. Why is the willingness to confess one's sins necessary for an act of perfect contrition?

The willingness to confess one's sins is necessary for an act of perfect contrition because the sacrament of penance is the ordinary, divinely established means of becoming reconciled with God in the New Law. A sinner cannot truly be sorry without sincerely wanting to avail himself of this means of reconciliation at an opportune time.

1356. Is perfect contrition necessary?

Perfect contrition is necessary for salvation for all sinners who cannot receive the sacraments of baptism, penance, or anointing.

1357. Is it easy to make an act of perfect contrition?

It is impossible without supernatural help to make an act of perfect contrition that will remit sin. But with divine grace we can readily make an act of perfect love of God, who is all good and deserving of all our love.

1358. When should we make acts of perfect contrition?

We should make an act of perfect contrition when we had the misfortune of offending God seriously, when in danger of death, and anytime through the day when the thought occurs to us. We should also help the dying make acts of perfect contrition by reminding them of God's mercy and assuring them of his forgiveness, especially if no priest is available to give them absolution.

1359. What is imperfect contrition?

Imperfect contrition is an act of sorrow for sin from a supernatural motive other than the pure love of God. It is sorrow for having offended God indeed, but because we now fear his just punishment whether in this life or after death; or because, by offending God, we have acted foolishly or ungratefully or contrary to right reason enlightened by faith.

1360. Why is this contrition called imperfect?

This contrition is called imperfect because it is inspired by a motive less perfect than the selfless love of God. It is also called attrition.

1361. What are the effects of imperfect contrition?

Imperfect contrition is a true sorrow that prepares a person for the reception of grace. When motivated by faith, it is pleasing to God. "To fear the Lord," we are told, "is the beginning of wisdom" (Ecclesiasticus 1:14).

1362. What kind of contrition is necessary for valid absolution?

Valid absolution requires at least imperfect contrition. However, we should always strive to make an act of perfect sorrow when receiving the sacrament of penance.

1363. Why is contrition necessary in the sacrament of penance?

Contrition is necessary in the sacrament of penance because without it there can be no remission of sin. God is willing to forgive only those who are sincerely sorry. As we read in the book of Joel, " 'Come back to me with all your heart, fasting, weeping, mourning.' Let your hearts be broken, not your garments torn, turn to Yahweh your God again, for he is all tenderness and compassion, slow to anger, rich in graciousness, and ready to relent" (Joel 2:12–13).

1364. What else is necessary to obtain forgiveness of sins?

Besides sorrow, a firm purpose of amendment is also necessary for sins to be forgiven. This means that the penitent must sincerely will not to sin again. Our contrition is genuine only if it excludes all affection for past sins committed and all deliberate desire to commit these sins in the future. As the prophet Isaiah wrote, "Let the wicked man abandon his way, the evil man his thoughts" (Isaiah 55:7).

1365. Does relapse into sin show that there was no firm purpose of amendment?

Relapse into sin does not, of itself, show there was no firm purpose of amendment, but rather that a person had changed his will. One should, however, doubt his firm purpose if, immediately after confession, he relapses into the same sins or makes no effort to avoid what he foresees will lead to sin.

1366. Why is confession an act of self-accusation?

Confession is an act of self-accusation because it is the actual telling of what we have done wrong. It is not a simple admission of guilt nor a mere act of confidence in God's mercy.

1367. How must the accusation be made?

The accusation of one's sins to the priest must be made vocally or orally, that is, by spoken word. If vocal confession is impossible, it is permissible and encouraged to write out one's sins, but this is not strictly necessary.

1368. Why is personal, specific confession necessary?

Personal, specific confession (called auricular confession) is necessary because this was taught by Christ. He gave his apostles and their successors the power to forgive sins, but also to not forgive them, implying that the faithful had to tell their sins in order for the priest to judge whether they should be absolved. Auricular confession has been taught and practiced by the Church from the earliest times. It was defined by the Council of Trent, and has been defended by the Church as a divine precept that no earthly authority may change. Moreover, "in faithfully observing the centuries-old practice of the sacrament of penance—the practice of individual confession with a personal act of sorrow and the intention to amend and make satisfaction—the Church is therefore defending the human soul's individual right: man's right to a more personal encounter with the crucified forgiving Christ, with Christ saying, through the minister of the sacrament of reconciliation, 'Your sins are forgiven': 'Go, and do not sin again.' As is evident, this is also a right on Christ's part with regard to every human being redeemed by him: his right to meet each one of us in that key moment in the soul's life constituted by the moment of conversion and forgiveness. By guarding the sacrament of penance, the Church expressly affirms her faith in the mystery of the Redemption as a living and life-giving reality that fits in with man's inward truth, with human guilt, and also with the desires of the human conscience" (John Paul II, *Redemptor Hominis,* 20).

1369. What are the qualities of a good confession?

A good confession must be sincere, that is, the penitent must accuse himself honestly, without consciously lessening his sins, excusing them, or even magnifying the wrong he has done. It must be entire, which means one must confess all the mortal sins that can be recalled after a serious examination of conscience, with their number and circumstances that affect their seriousness. Venial sins ought also to be confessed, to make the confession complete. A good confession should also be simple, that is, one should accuse himself without ambiguity or needless detail. Finally, it should be prudent, which means the penitent should avoid saying anything, unless really necessary, that would blame others or reveal their sins.

1370. Is it necessary to confess the exact number of our sins?

It is necessary to confess the exact number of mortal sins. If the exact number cannot be recalled we must tell the number as nearly as possible. Regarding venial sins it is good to confess for how long they were committed.

1371. Should we confess the circumstances surrounding our sins?

Yes, we should confess the circumstances surrounding our mortal sins and such details as substantially affect the nature of the sins.

1372. Must doubtful sins be confessed?

Doubtful sins need not be confessed, although it is advisable to do so. People with a lax conscience should confess their doubtful sins; the scrupulous should never do so.

1373. Must we confess grievous sins forgotten in a preceding confession?

We must confess grave sins forgotten in a previous confession because, according to divine law, every known mortal sin committed after baptism must be "submitted to the keys," that is personally acknowledged in the sacrament of penance.

1374. What further sin does one commit who willfully conceals a mortal sin in confession?

One who willfully conceals a mortal sin does not receive valid absolution and commits the grave sin of sacrilege.

1375. What reasons may excuse a person from confessing his sins?

The confession of sins is legitimately excused by involuntary forgetfulness, invincible ignorance, danger of violating the seal of confession, and physical or moral impossibility.

1376. What is frequent confession?

Frequent confession means the reception of the sacrament of penance at least twice a month. This is useful because by it "genuine self-knowledge is increased, Christian humility grows, bad habits are corrected, spiritual neglect and tepidity are resisted, the conscience is purified, the will is strengthened, a salutary self-control is attained, and grace is increased in virtue of the sacrament itself" (Pius XII, *Mystici Corporis Christi,* 88).

1377. Should a person go to Holy Communion often if he has no mortal sin on his soul?

Yes, every Catholic is encouraged to receive Holy Communion frequently, even daily. In this way, grace is received to keep out of mortal sin and to grow in the supernatural life.

1378. Are we obliged to answer the questions asked by the priest in confession?

We are obliged to answer the questions asked us by the priest if they concern confession. He has the duty to find out the state of our soul, not only to judge our dispositions, but to help us cope with moral failings and improve our service of God.

1379. When do we recite the act of contrition?

We recite the act of contrition after the priest has assigned our penance and given us counsel or direction. Normally he will indicate when the act of contrition should be said and remains silent while we recite it.

1380. What does the priest do after we recite the act of contrition?

After we recite the act of contrition, the priest pronounces the words of absolution, as follows: "God, the Father of mercies, through the death and resurrection of his Son has reconciled the world to himself and sent the Holy Spirit among us for the forgiveness of sins; through the ministry of his Church may God give you pardon and peace, and *I absolve you from your sins* in the name of the Father and of the Son and of the Holy Spirit." To which we are to answer, "Amen." Only the italicized words are essential for absolution, during which the priest makes a sign of the cross over the penitent.

1381. What does the priest say after he gives absolution?

After giving absolution, he says, "Give thanks to the Lord, for he is good." The penitent concludes, "His mercy endures forever." Before dismissing the penitent, the priest recites one of several prayers, of which the best known is a plea for divine mercy, "May the Passion of our Lord Jesus Christ, the merits of the blessed Virgin Mary and of all the saints, and also whatever good you do and evil you endure, be cause for the remission of your sins, the increase of grace, and the reward of everlasting life. Amen."

1382. Why does the priest assign a special penance to be said or done after confession?

The priest assigns this penance as partial satisfaction for the sins that were confessed and remitted.

1383. What is the seal of confession?

The seal of confession is the strict obligation to remain silent concerning everything that is disclosed in sacramental confession.

1384. Who is bound by the seal of confession?

Those bound by the seal of confession are the confessor and all who in any way either directly or indirectly obtain knowledge from a person's confession. The penitent is not obliged by the seal.

1385. May a priest in the court of justice make known what he learned in the confessional?

A priest in the court of justice may not make known what he learned in the confessional. If he is questioned, he must declare that he knows nothing of the subject in question. What the priest learns through confession he knows not as man but only as a representative of Christ and therefore is not subject to any earthly authority.

1386. Why must satisfaction be made for sins already forgiven?

Satisfaction must be made for sins already forgiven because normally some—and even considerable—temporal punishment is still due, although the guilt has been removed.

1387. How do we know that temporal punishment may still be due after sins have been forgiven?

It has been the Church's constant teaching that guilt of sins can be removed and yet temporal punishment may still be due. The doctrine is based on divine revelation and underlies the Church's whole penitential discipline, including the practice of granting partial or plenary indulgences.

1388. What is the purpose of satisfaction for sins?

Satisfaction for sins is expiatory, remedial, and spiritually beneficial to the sinner.

1389. How is satisfaction expiatory?

Satisfaction is expiatory by making up for the failure in love of God which is the root cause of sin, by voluntarily suffering to make up for self-indulgence, and by enduring pain in reparation for the harm or disorder caused by the commission of sin.

1390. How is satisfaction remedial?

Satisfaction is remedial by meriting grace from God to enlighten and strengthen a person against committing the same sins in the future.

1391. How is satisfaction spiritually beneficial?

Satisfaction is spiritually beneficial by inspiring the sinner to strive after greater holiness. Except for the humiliation and reliance on God brought on by past sins, a person might not have attained the sanctity that was occasioned by the remembrance of God's mercy.

1392. How can we make satisfaction for our sins?

We make satisfaction for our sins by every good act we perform in the state of grace, but especially by prayer, penance, and the practice of charity. While all prayer merits satisfaction for sin, it is most effective when we ask God to have mercy on us, and unite our prayers with voluntary self-denial. Penance for sin is not only bodily, like fast and abstinence, but also spiritual, like restraining curiosity or conversation and avoiding otherwise legitimate recreation. Moreover, the patient acceptance of trials or humiliations sent by God is expiatory. Finally, the practice of charity toward others is a powerful satisfaction for our lack of charity toward God. "Above all," we are told, "never let your love for each other grow insincere, since love covers over many a sin" (1 Peter 4:8).

1393. How can we make reparation to our neighbor?

We make reparation to our neighbor by becoming reconciled to a person from whom we may have been estranged, by making restitution for what had been unjustly taken away, by trying to restore his good name if we have injured a person's reputation, by apologizing for any unjust offense that was given, and by praying for those whom we have in any way harmed.

1394. What is sacramental satisfaction?

Sacramental satisfaction is the penitential work imposed by a confessor in the confessional in order to make up for the injury done to God and atone for the temporal punishment due to sin already forgiven. The penitent is obliged to perform the penance imposed by the priest, and deliberate failure to perform a penance imposed for mortal sin is gravely sinful. We should perform the penance exactly, fervently, and promptly. If one forgets the penance, he ought to ask the priest again, if convenient. Otherwise, it is enough to perform what was most likely the penance imposed.

1395. What is extra-sacramental satisfaction?

Extra-sacramental satisfaction is every form of expiation offered to God outside the sacrament of penance. Our works of satisfaction are meritorious if they are done while in the state of grace and in a spirit of penance.

1396. What kind of punishment is due to venial sins?

Venial sins carry only temporal punishment either in this life or in purgatory. In this life, the punishment can be bodily or spiritual. As spiritual punishment it is mainly the deprivation of grace.

1397. What kind of punishment is due to mortal sin?

Mortal sin always carries the penalty of eternal punishment, which is always taken away with the remission of guilt, even when unexpiated temporal punishment may still be due.

1398. How do we know that sins deserve punishment from God?

It is a revealed truth that sins deserve punishment for the offense against God's justice and the disorder they cause in the world. As St. Paul tells us, "Where a man sows, there he reaps: if he sows in the field of self-indulgence he will get a harvest of corruption out of it" (Galatians 6:7–8).

1399. Why does God impose punishment for sin?

God in his mercy and justice imposes punishment for the reconciliation of sinners, the purification of souls, the defense of the sanctity of the moral order, and the restoration of the injury done to his divine majesty.

1400. How can we make up for sin?

We can make up for sin through the sorrows and trials of life, including the pain of death, or through the purifying penalties in the life beyond. Sin can also be expiated through indulgences.

3. Indulgences: Meaning, Kinds, Conditions for Gaining

1401. What is an indulgence?

An indulgence is the remission through the merits of Christ and his Church of the temporal punishment still due to forgiven sins.

1402. How do indulgences remove temporal punishment?

Indulgences remove temporal punishment through the Church's right to dispose the merits of Christ to her members. The Savior won the graces of expiation for sinners by his Passion and Death. The Church administers these benefits in consideration of the prayers and other good works performed by the faithful.

1403. Who can gain indulgences?

Indulgences can be gained by Christians who are rightly disposed and who fulfill the requirements set down by the Church as the dispenser of Christ's merits of redemption.

1404. How many kinds of indulgences are there?

There are two kinds of indulgences: plenary and partial. A plenary indulgence removes all the temporal punishment due to sin; a partial indulgence removes some or part of the temporal penalties still owed to God after he forgives our sins.

1405. What does it mean to apply an indulgence?

An indulgence is said to be applied when the person who performs the prescribed work asks God to transfer its expiatory value to someone else. It cannot be transferred to other living persons but may be applied to the souls in purgatory, either in general or to anyone in particular.

1406. Can a person gain a plenary indulgence for himself during his lifetime?

Yes, a person can gain a plenary indulgence in his lifetime. However, only God knows for certain when a plenary indulgence is actually gained because only he knows whether a person's dispositions are adequate.

1407. On what does the value of an indulgence depend?

The value of an indulgence depends on two things: the supernatural charity, love of God and neighbor, with which the indulgenced task is performed, and the dignity of the indulgenced task itself. In other words, the value of an indulgence depends on what we do and how well we do it.

1408. What dispositions are necessary to gain a plenary indulgence?

To gain a plenary indulgence, one must be free from all attachment to any sin at all, even venial sin. He must also receive the sacraments of penance and Holy Communion, and pray for the intentions of the Holy Father.

1409. Must these conditions be fulfilled on the same day?

No, these conditions may be fulfilled several days (to about a week) before or after the prescribed indulgenced work. But Holy Communion should be received and prayers for the pope's intention ought to be said on the same day the work is performed.

1410. What prayers are to be said for the intention of the Holy Father?

At least one Our Father and one Hail Mary are required. These fully satisfy the condition unless a person wishes to substitute some other prayer according to his own piety and devotion toward the Holy Father.

1411. How often can a plenary indulgence be gained?

A plenary indulgence can be gained only once a day except by those who are on the point of death.

1412. How often can a partial indulgence be gained?

Unless there are explicit provisions to the contrary, a partial indulgence can be gained more than once a day.

1413. What prayers are required for a plenary indulgence connected with visiting a Church?

To gain a plenary indulgence while visiting a Church, a person must say at least an Our Father and the Apostles' or Nicene Creed.

1414. What is necessary to gain a plenary indulgence at the point of death?

To gain a plenary indulgence at the point of death, even when a priest is not available, three conditions are required. The person must be in the state of grace, at least through an act of perfect contrition; should have been in the habit of reciting some prayers during his lifetime; and have at least the implicit intention to gain final remission of all temporal punishment due to sin. It is a laudable practice to use the crucifix to dispose oneself for gaining this plenary indulgence.

1415. Can a plenary indulgence purify a soul for immediate entrance into heaven?

Yes, depending on the person's disposition, a plenary indulgence can purify a soul for immediate entrance into heaven without suffering the pains of purgatory.

1416. When is a partial indulgence generally granted to the faithful?

A partial indulgence is granted to any of Christ's faithful who, in the performance of their duties and bearing the trials of life, raise their minds to God in humble confidence and add, even mentally, some pious invocation; who in the spirit of penance, freely abstain from something that is permissible and pleasing to them; and who, led by the spirit of faith, with a kindly heart expend themselves or some of their possessions in the service of others who are in need.

Marriage

1. Contract, Covenant, and Sacrament

1417. What is Christian marriage?

Christian marriage is a sacrament instituted by Jesus Christ, who raised the natural contract of wedlock to a supernatural covenant between God and the marrying spouses.

1418. How is marriage a contract?

Marriage is a contract because it is the voluntary agreement of a man and woman to live together as husband and wife for the rest of their lives. The essence of the contract consists in the mutual consent.

1419. Why is marriage a covenant?

Marriage is a covenant because it is a sacred contract. God himself established marriage as the natural means of procreating and educating his choicest earthly creatures. It is also sacred because it is the means of mutual help for husband and wife, not only for their temporal well-being, but also to lead them to their eternal destiny in heaven with God. It is finally sacred because Christian marriage mystically represents the union of the divine and human natures in the Incarnation of the Son of God, and symbolizes the abiding love of Christ for the Church, his spouse and second Eve.

1420. How is marriage an institution?

Marriage is an institution in that the marrying partners agree not only to take each other as husband and wife but also to continue taking each other until death. At marriage they begin to live with one another in the most intimate union possible between two people and to share their respective lives with each other by forming a family.

1421. What kind of institution is marriage?

Marriage is the basic institution of human society on which all other corporate establishments somehow depend.

1422. When is marriage a sacrament?

Marriage is a sacrament when contracted between two baptized persons.

1423. Who is the minister of the sacrament of matrimony?

The ministers of the sacrament of matrimony are the contracting parties. The priest, however, is an indispensable witness and gives the nuptial blessing.

1424. Is the sacrament of marriage received when two baptized persons marry outside in a civil ceremony?

The sacrament of marriage is received when two baptized persons who are not Catholic marry, either before a minister or in a civil ceremony. Every valid marriage between two baptized persons is a sacrament. Unless dispensed by the bishop, a Catholic must marry before a duly authorized priest and two witnesses.

1425. How is Christian marriage a sacrament?

Christian marriage is the sacrament in which two people of different sexes, who are free to marry, associate in an undivided life communion by mutual agreement for the generation and education of offspring, and the fostering of their mutual love, and in which they receive grace from God for the fulfillment of all the duties of their state of life.

1426. Why was the rite of the sacrament of marriage revised?

The rite of the sacrament of marriage was revised and also enriched in such a way that the grace of the sacrament is more clearly signified and the duties of the spouses are taught. It also reemphasized the fact that marriage is normally to be celebrated with the offering of the Eucharistic Sacrifice (Second Vatican Council, Constitution on the Sacred Liturgy, 77).

1427. When did Christ institute the sacrament of marriage?

Christ raised marriage to a sacrament of the New Law during his visible stay on earth. The Fathers of the Church commonly recognize that by his participation in the feast at Cana, the Savior sanctified Christian marriage among the faithful.

1428. Why did Christ raise marriage to the dignity of a sacrament?

Christ raised marriage to the dignity of a sacrament because he elevated human society to a new and higher level of existence. Christ gave the world a new commandment of love, "as I have loved you" (John 15:12). He restored monogamy, and redefined adultery to include attempted remarriage after divorce (cf. Matthew 19:9). Given these sublime demands on human nature, Christ instituted the sacrament of matrimony. He did so in order to give Christian spouses the lifelong assistance of his supernatural grace, to meet the beyond natural requirements of the New Law.

1429. What does the sacrament of marriage signify?

The sacrament of marriage signifies the mystery of unity and faithful love between Christ and the Church (cf. Ephesians 5:32). In this comparison are divinely revealed the two principal attributes of Christian marriage.

1430. What are the two revealed attributes of Christian marriage?

The two revealed attributes of Christian marriage are unity and indissolubility.

1431. In what does unity in marriage consist?

Unity in marriage consists in the union of one man with one woman, which excludes all forms of polygamy.

1432. Why is unity of marriage prescribed by the law of God?

Unity of marriage is prescribed by the law of God in order to secure the physical and moral education of the children, the protection of marital fidelity, the imitation of Christ in union with the Church, and peace and harmony within the family.

1433. Is it lawful to marry after the death of one's spouse?

It has always been lawful to marry after the death of one's spouse. But the Church, following the lead of St. Paul, teaches that widowhood is, by itself, more perfect (cf. I Corinthians 7:40). Widowhood is a special call from God and is honored by the Church, if it is accepted courageously, as a continuation of the call to the married state.

1434. What is the indissolubility of marriage?

This means that the marital bond of a sacramental marriage cannot be broken except by the death of either party. "Everyone who divorces his wife and marries another is guilty of adultery, and the man who marries a woman divorced by her husband commits adultery" (Luke 16:18).

1435. Are all marriages equally indissoluble?

No, not all marriages are equally indissoluble. An absolutely indissoluble marriage is a sacramental union, between two baptized persons, who enter a valid marital contract, and then "seal" the marriage by legitimate (not contraceptive) conjugal intercourse.

2. Disposition, Effects, and Obligations

1436. What are the proper dispositions for the sacrament of marriage?

The proper dispositions for the sacrament of marriage are adequate preparation by a virtuous Christian life; great prudence in the choice of one's marriage partner; purity of intention in desiring to do God's will; sufficient knowledge of one's faith and of the responsibilities of marriage; the state of grace and earnest prayer for a happy married life.

1437. Why is the state of grace necessary to receive the sacrament fruitfully?

The state of grace is necessary to receive matrimony fruitfully because it is a sacrament of the living. To merit the graces of the sacrament, the marrying partners must be in God's friendship. Whoever receives the sacrament in the state of mortal sin commits a sacrilege and deprives himself, until he becomes reconciled with God, of the special graces of this sacrament. Although contracted in the state of sin, in one or both partners, the marriage is valid and sacramental. The graces due to the sacrament are conferred when either or both parties are reconciled with God.

1438. What are the matter and form of the sacrament of marriage?

The matter of this sacrament is the mutual consent of the contracting parties to give themselves to each other. The form consists in their expression of mutual consent to take each other.

1439. What is the purpose of marriage and married love?

By its very nature the institution of marriage and married love is intended for the procreation and education of the offspring. It is in the children that marriage finds its crowning glory. "Thus the man and woman, who 'are no longer two but one' (Matthew 19:6), help and serve each other by their married partnership; they become conscious of their unity and experience it more deeply from day to day. The intimate union of marriage, as a mutual giving of two persons, and the good of the children demand total fidelity from the spouses and require an unbreakable unity between them" (Second Vatican Council, The Church in the Modern World, 48).

1440. What is absolutely necessary for a Catholic to be validly married?

For a Catholic to be validly married, it is necessary that there exist no invalidating impediments, that (unless legitimately dispensed) the marriage is contracted before an authorized bishop or priest and before two witnesses, and that both parties want to marry each other and express their free consent to the marriage.

1441. What are the effects of the sacrament of marriage?

The sacrament of marriage increases sanctifying grace in those who receive it worthily; confers on them sacramental grace at the time of marriage and the title to a lifetime of actual graces necessary to properly fulfill their duties as man and wife, and as Christian parents; and confirms the unity and indissolubility of the matrimonial contract. For the children, it makes them legitimate, and subjects them to parental authority.

1442. What are the obligations imposed by the sacrament of marriage?

The obligations imposed by the sacrament of marriage are of three kinds: those common to both parties; those proper to each of them; and obligations to their children.

1443. What are the obligations of the married couple?

The mutual obligations of the married couple are that they love each other with a fruitful, chaste, patient, devoted, and supernatural love until death.

1444. What are the special duties of the husband?

The special duties of the husband are that he exercise the authority he has received from God, treat his wife with gentleness, love, and respect, and provide for all her legitimate needs. As prescribed by St. Paul, "Husbands should love their wives just as Christ loved the Church and sacrificed himself for her to make her holy . . . In the same way, husbands must love their wives as they love their own bodies; for a man to love his wife is for him to love himself" (Ephesians 5:25, 28).

1445. What are the special duties of the wife?

The special duties of the wife are that she ought to be submissive to her husband, devoted, watchful, zealous, and industrious in the discharge of her domestic duties. Again, as directed by St. Paul, "Wives should regard their husbands as they regard the Lord, since as Christ is head of the Church and saves the whole body, so is a husband the head of his wife; and as the Church submits to Christ, so should wives to their husbands, in everything . . . Let every wife respect her husband" (Ephesians 5:22–24, 33).

1446. What are the duties of the married couple to their children?

The duties of a married couple to their children are to teach them in the Catholic faith and train them in the practice of virtue; to provide for their physical, intellectual, and spiritual needs; to show them loving care and give them the example of a truly Christian home. In the words of St. Paul, "Parents, never drive your children to resentment but in bringing them up correct them and guide them as the Lord does" (Ephesians 6:4).

1447. Can a natural, nonsacramental marriage ever be dissolved?

Yes, a natural marriage between nonbaptized persons can be dissolved by what is known as the Pauline privilege.

1448. What is the Pauline privilege?

The Pauline privilege, so called from the teaching of St. Paul (cf. 1 Corinthians 7:12–16), permits the dissolution of a legitimate marriage, even if consummated by intercourse, provided two conditions are fulfilled. One of the parties (not both) is validly baptized; this presupposes that since contracting a legitimate and valid marriage one of the partners has become a Christian. Moreover, the unbaptized party 1) departs or refuses to live peacefully with the baptized party, or 2) refuses to live with the other without offense against God.

1449. What is divorce?

As commonly understood, divorce means the dissolution of a marriage bond. In civil law it is the judicial declaration that a valid marriage is dissolved, and the former partners have a legal right to remarry.

1450. Has the civil law the right to dissolve a marriage between Christians?

Civil law does not have the right to dissolve a marriage between baptized people. Legal divorce does not, of itself, give a baptized couple the right to remarry. By divine law, authority over Christian marriage belongs to the Church. At most, the State may determine certain civil conditions of such divorced persons, for example, alimony and custody of the children.

1451. May the Church permit married couples to separate?

The Church may permit couples to separate for grave reasons, either for a time or (on occasion) permanently. Although separated, and dispensed either from living together or also from possessing their goods in common, their bond of marriage still remains. As St. Paul writes: "A wife must not leave her husband —or if she does leave him, she must either remain unmarried or else make it up with her husband—nor must a husband send his wife away" (1 Corinthians 7:10–11).

1452. What reasons make such a separation lawful?

Reasons that would make such a separation lawful are mutual consent which originates from a just cause, serious danger to soul or body, and certainty that one of the parties has committed adultery.

3. Mixed Marriages, Banns, and Impediments

1453. What is the Church's position on mixed marriages?

The Church is aware that mixed marriages, precisely because they admit differences of religion, do not generally help to foster unity among Christians. There are many problems in a mixed marriage because from the wedding day on a certain division is introduced into the living cell of the Church, as the Christian family is rightly called. Moreover, the fulfillment of the Gospel teachings becomes more difficult because of conflicts in matters of religion, especially with regard to divine worship and the education of children. However, the Church is also conscious that people have a natural right to marry and beget children. She tries to make such arrangements that, while respecting these rights, the principles of divine law are carefully observed.

1454. Whose permission is necessary for a mixed marriage?

The local bishop must give permission for any mixed marriage. This permission is necessary because mixed marriages are by their nature an obstacle to the full spiritual communion of the married parties. The bishop must decide whether to grant permission or not.

1455. What must the Catholic partner in a mixed marriage promise to do?

The Catholic partner in a mixed marriage must be ready to remove all dangers of falling away from the faith. He or she is gravely bound to make a sincere promise to do everything possible to have all the children baptized and brought up in the Catholic Church.

1456. What instruction must precede a mixed marriage?

Instruction on the purpose and essential properties of marriage must be given to both parties. Also, the non-Catholic party must be informed of the promises that the Catholic party has to make, and agree to marry the Catholic party on these conditions.

1457. Who may be the official witness at a mixed marriage?

Without a very special dispensation from the bishop, the official witness at a mixed marriage must be a duly authorized priest. Two witnesses are to be present also for validity.

1458. Are there exceptions to this requirement of a priest witnessing a mixed marriage?

For exceptional reasons, the local bishop may allow a Catholic to marry before a non-Catholic minister of religion. But without such dispensation, the marriage would be invalid.

1459. Is it permitted to have another religious ceremony after the Catholic ceremony?

It is not permitted to have another religious ceremony before or after the Catholic ceremony for the purpose of giving or renewing matrimonial consent.

1460. What are the banns of marriage?

The banns of marriage are public proclamations informing the faithful that a marriage is to be contracted by a certain couple. They are published to find out whether there are any impediments to the marriage. The faithful are gravely bound in justice and charity to make known any major impediments to a projected marriage.

1461. What impediments would nullify a marriage?

Impediments that would nullify a marriage are: lack of age (under sixteen for the boy, under fourteen for the girl) or of liberty; error concerning the purpose of marriage or the person of the contracting party; a bond resulting from an existing marriage or from a solemn vow of chastity or sacred order; natural relationship within certain degrees; spiritual relationships which sponsors contract with the person baptized; affinity or relationship that husband and wife each contract with brothers, sisters, uncles, and aunts of the other; difference of religion between the two parties; and clandestinity, when parties do not get married in the presence of their own priest or his delegate and two witnesses.

1462. What impediments make marriage unlawful?

Impediments that make a marriage unlawful are: failure to have the banns published, marriage with a baptized non-Catholic, marriage to a person with a simple vow of chastity or virginity, and, in some countries, legal relationship.

1463. Who has the power of dispensing from impediments?

The pope has the power of dispensing from all ecclesiastical impediments of the natural law, and of such divine laws as are based on free human acts. Bishops can dispense from certain impediments in their diocese in cases determined by canon law. Moreover, some impediments to marriage may cease through lapse of time, as when a spouse dies. Others cease through legitimate consent of both parties, as impediment of error, violence, or fear.

Holy Orders

1. Institution, Reception, and Effects

1464. What is the sacrament of orders?

Orders is a sacrament of the New Law by which a share in the spiritual powers of Christ's ministry is conferred together with the grace to perform worthily the duties of one's office in the Church.

1465. What is the basis for the sacrament?

The basis for the sacrament of orders is Christ's own priestly ministry on earth, and the revealed fact that he associated others with him to learn his teachings, acquire his spirit, receive his powers, and thus continue his work of salvation until the end of time.

1466. When did Christ institute the sacrament of orders?

Christ actually instituted the sacrament of orders at the Last Supper. After he had consecrated the bread and wine, and changed them into his own body and blood, he told the apostles to "do this as a memorial of me" (Luke 22:19). By this he was conferring on the apostles and their successors the principal power of this sacrament, namely to consecrate and offer his body and blood in the Sacrifice of the Mass.

1467. Did Christ confer the fullness of the sacrament of orders all at once?

Christ did not confer the fullness of the sacrament of orders all at once. He advanced the apostles only gradually to their priestly orders. First he placed them above his other followers. Then on Holy Thursday he gave them the Eucharistic power of transubstantiation. On Easter Sunday night he conferred on them the power to take away sins: "Receive the Holy Spirit. For those whose sins you forgive, they are forgiven; for those whose sins you retain, they are retained" (John 20:22–23). Finally, before his Ascension, he ordered them to preach and to baptize, "Go, therefore, make disciples of all the nations; baptize them in the name of the Father and of the Son and of the Holy Spirit, and teach them to observe all the commands I gave you" (Matthew 28:19–20).

1468. What are the effects of the sacrament of orders?

The sacrament of orders imprints an indelible character on the soul; confers the power corresponding, separately, to the diaconate, the priesthood, and the episcopate; increases sanctifying grace; and imparts sacramental grace as a title to the actual graces necessary for fulfilling the ecclesiastical responsibilities that belong to each of the three stages of this sacrament.

1469. When is the sacramental character imprinted on the soul by ordination?

The sacramental character is imprinted by ordination on the soul when the bishop pronounces the words "receive the Holy Spirit." There is also at this moment a special conferral of divine gifts.

1470. What are the necessary conditions for receiving the sacrament of orders validly?

To receive the sacrament of orders validly, a person must be a male, baptized with water, and have the intention of receiving ordination.

1471. From what bishop may a candidate receive the sacrament of orders?

A candidate may receive ordination from his own bishop, unless he has written permission from his bishop to be ordained by another.

1472. Can a priest ever become a layman?

A priest can never become a layman because of the character which is imprinted by ordination.

1473. Why is a priest once ordained always a priest?

A priest once ordained is always a priest because the Catholic Church believes that the priestly character is indelible and therefore unchangeable. "You are a priest of the order of Melchizedek, and for ever" (Psalms 110:4), is applied by the Church to all who are ordained to the priesthood.

1474. What is the process of laicization?

Laicization is the process whereby a priest is dispensed from priestly duties. If he had been celibate, he may even be allowed to marry. This does not mean, however, that he is literally reduced to the lay state.

2. Deacons, Priests, and Bishops

1475. How many different sacred orders are there?

There are three different sacred orders: deacons, priests, and bishops.

1476. What is the sacramental matter in the ordination of deacons, priests, and bishops?

The sacramental matter in the ordination of deacons, priests, and bishops is the imposition of the bishop's hand upon each individual candidate.

1477. What is the form in the ordination of deacons, priests, and bishops?

The form in the ordination of deacons, priests, and bishops consists of the words of the consecrating prayer.

1478. Who are deacons?

Deacons are at the lowest level of the hierarchy. They received the imposition of hands not for the priesthood but for the ministry. They are dedicated to the people of God, in cooperation with the bishops and their body of priests, in the service of the liturgy, of the Gospel, and of works of Christian charity. St. Paul said of them, "Those of them who carry out their duties well as deacons will earn a high standing for themselves and be rewarded with great assurance in their work for the faith in Christ Jesus" (1 Timothy 3:13).

1479. What is the consecrating prayer in the ordination of deacons?

In the ordination of deacons the essential consecrating prayer, said by the bishop, is: "Lord, we pray, send forth upon them the Holy Spirit so that by the grace of your seven gifts, they may be strengthened by him to carry out faithfully the work of the ministry."

1480. What are the main functions of a deacon?

The main functions of a deacon are: to administer baptism solemnly; to be a custodian and distributor of the Eucharist; in the name of the Church, to assist at and to bless Christian marriage; to bring Viaticum to the dying; to read the Sacred Scripture to the faithful; to instruct and exhort the people; under the priest, to preside over the worship and prayer of the faithful; to administer sacramentals; and to officiate at funeral and burial services.

1481. What are the two forms of the diaconate?

The diaconate in the Roman Rite of the Catholic Church now has two forms: a permanent diaconate that remains for life, and a transitional one which precedes ordination to the priesthood.

1482. Before a deacon is ordained what decision must he make?

Before a deacon is ordained he must make out a formal statement indicating which form of the diaconate he wishes to enter. He must also testify to the fact that he is doing so freely and of his own accord. At the same time he makes his choice between a celibate and married diaconate. Married men can be ordained deacons, but celibate deacons may not marry, without forfeiting their right to exercise their diaconal ministry. Also, a married deacon who has lost his wife cannot enter a new marriage. In her official legislation the Church favors a celibate, permanent diaconate (cf. Paul VI Sacrum Diaconatus Ordinem, 1967; Ad Pascendum, 1972).

1483. What are the principal ceremonies in the ordination of a priest?

The principal ceremonies in the ordination of a priest are the consecration with holy oil made on the palm of each hand of the candidate, and the bishop's imposition of hands on the individual candidates, done in silence, which is followed by the words of the consecratory prayer.

1484. What is the form of the sacrament in the ordination of priests?

The form of ordination of priests is the following prayer: "We ask you, all-powerful Father, give these servants of yours the dignity of the presbyterate. Renew the Spirit of holiness within them. By your divine gift, may they attain the second order in the hierarchy and exemplify right conduct in their lives."

1485. What is the main emphasis in the ordination of priests?

The main emphasis in the ordination of priests is the holiness expected of them. They are to be holy in order to be an example of sanctity for the faithful to imitate; to witness to the truth of what they say so their teaching may be acceptable to the people they serve; and to merit grace for others by their lives of virtue. Their self-immolation in the following of Christ should testify to what every priest should be, namely a person who offers sacrifice.

1486. What are the obligations imposed on priests by the sacrament of orders?

The general obligation imposed by the sacrament is to lead a holy life. Priests are further obliged to recite the Divine Office daily; and, in the Latin Rite, priests are to observe the law of celibacy.

1487. What is the basis for clerical celibacy?

The basis for clerical celibacy is the example of Christ and his apostles. In the words of the Second Vatican Council: "By means of celibacy, priests profess before men their willingness to be dedicated with undivided loyalty to the task entrusted to them, namely, that of espousing the faithful to one husband and presenting them as a chaste virgin to Christ" (Decree on the Ministry and Life of Priests, 16).

1488. What is the primary ministry of a priest?

The primary ministry of a priest is to consecrate and offer the Holy Eucharist, and to forgive sins. In this, priests differ from deacons who do not receive the power to consecrate the Eucharist, offer Mass, or forgive sins by sacramental absolution.

1489. What are the pastoral duties of a priest?

The pastoral duties are to teach, lead, and sanctify.

1490. What are the duties of the priest in teaching the Catholic faith?

The duties of a priest in teaching the Catholic faith are mainly three. He is to have a strong, enlightened faith himself, nourished by prayer and study. He is to communicate this faith to others. Indeed, "priests owe it to everybody to share with them the truth of the Gospel" (Vatican Council II, Decree on the Ministry and Life of Priests, 4). Priests must live the faith they profess because "Their very ministry makes a special claim on them not to conform themselves to this world" (Ibid., 3).

1491. What are the duties of a priest as leader?

The duties of a priest as leader arise from his assimilation to Christ the King. A priest is to direct others on the way of salvation by his words and example but also by the exercise of such authority as he shares, through delegation, with the bishop.

1492. What are the main duties of a priest to sanctify others?

The main duties of a priest to sanctify others are his faithful offering of the Sacrifice of the Mass, administration of the sacraments, and preaching the Word of God.

1493. What are the duties of the faithful toward the priesthood?

The duties of the faithful toward the priesthood are to hold priests in great esteem, to pray for them and offer sacrifice for their sanctity and perseverance, to foster worthy vocations to the priesthood, to help priests live up to the high demands of their calling, and to cooperate in every reasonable way with priests for the preservation and extension of the Kingdom of Christ on earth.

1494. What is the consecrating prayer in the ordination of bishops?

The form of ordination of bishops is this prayer: "Now pour out upon this chosen one that power which flows from you, the perfect Spirit whom you gave to the apostles, who established the Church in every place as the sanctuary where your name would always be praised and glorified."

1495. What is the main power received by episcopal ordination?

The main power that a bishop receives at his ordination is to confer the sacrament of orders. Only bishops can ordain deacons, priests, and other bishops.

1496. What is the role of bishops in the Catholic Church?

Bishops have been designated by the Holy Spirit to take the place of the apostles as pastors of the faithful and, together with the bishop of Rome and subject to his authority, they are commissioned to perpetuate the word of Christ, the eternal Shepherd of souls (cf. Vatican Council II, Decree on the Pastoral Office of Bishops, 2).

1497. What is the extent of the bishops' pastoral responsibility?

The pastoral responsibility of bishops first includes the people under their immediate care as in a diocese. But it extends to all the people of God. They form an episcopal community that succeeds the college of the apostles, and is therefore called episcopal collegiality.

1498. Does the pope possess a power of order superior to that of the bishop?

The pope does not possess a power of order superior to that of the bishop because the pontificate is not a special order. Upon election, however, the pope has, by divine right, as successor of St. Peter, the primacy of jurisdiction over the universal Church. This entitles him to the exercise of supreme authority over the whole hierarchy.

1499. Does a bishop or priest who does not recognize the pope have the right to exercise his office?

A bishop or priest who does not recognize the pope does not have the right to exercise his office.

1500. Are the faithful subject to such bishops or priests?

The faithful are not subject to bishops or priests who do not recognize the pope as visible head of the universal Church. Bishops and priests have the right to teach and govern only insofar as they are themselves subject to the teaching and authority of the Roman pontiff.

3. Order of Ministries

1501. What is the order of ministries?

The order of ministries, preserved in the Latin Church and adapted to present-day needs, is that of reader and acolyte. They may be laymen. Their functions formerly belonged to the subdeacon. Consequently the major order of subdiaconate no longer exists in the Latin Church.

1502. What are the duties of the reader?

The duties of the reader are to read the Word of God in the liturgical assembly, except for the Gospel in the Mass and other sacred celebrations. He may recite the psalms between readings; present the intentions for general intercessions, direct singing, and the participation of the faithful; and instruct the faithful for worthy reception of the sacraments.

1503. What is the function of an acolyte?

The function of an acolyte is to aid the deacon and minister to the priest, especially in the celebration of Mass. He may distribute Holy Communion as an auxiliary minister at the Eucharistic liturgy and to the sick. In extraordinary circumstances he may be entrusted with publicly exposing the Blessed Sacrament for adoration by the faithful and afterward replacing it.

1504. Who may confer the order of ministries?

The order of ministries is conferred by the bishop of the diocese and, in clerical religious institutes, by the major superior, according to the liturgical rites for this purpose by the Church. The order of ministries is reserved to men.

Anointing of the Sick

Meaning, Recipients, Effects, and Ritual Changes

1505. What is the sacrament of anointing?

The sacrament of anointing is a sacrament of the New Law instituted by Christ to give the sick spiritual assistance, strengthen their supernatural life, and, if need be, forgive their sins. Moreover, if God wills it, anointing restores physical health to the body of the Christian who is seriously ill.

1506. Why did Christ institute the sacrament of the sick?

Christ instituted the sacrament of the sick in order to give spiritual aid to the Church's suffering members to enable them to bear their pain for love of him, to heal them if it is the will of God, and to prepare them for death when the time comes to enter eternity.

1507. When did Christ institute this sacrament?

The Church says that the holy anointing of the sick as a true and proper sacrament is implied in Mark's Gospel, when Christ said to the apostles, "If any place does not welcome you and people refuse to listen to you, as you walk away shake off the dust from under your feet," and leave the place. "So they set off to preach repentance; and they cast out many devils, and anointed many sick people with oil and cured them" (Mark 6:11–13). However, the main biblical text cited in favor of anointing occurs in the letter of James. As declared by the Council of Trent, the sacrament of holy anointing "is commended to the faithful and promulgated by the apostle James, the brother of the Lord: 'If one of you is ill, he should send for the elders of the church, and they must anoint him with oil in the name of the Lord and pray over him. The prayer of faith will save the sick man and the Lord will raise him up again; and if he has committed any sins, he will be forgiven'" (James 5:14–15).

1508. In what does the sacrament consist?

The sacrament consists in the anointing by a priest of the body of the sick person, accompanied by a suitable form of words. The matter of the sacrament is blessed olive oil and the form is the prescribed words.

1509. What does anointing with oil represent?

The anointing with oil represents the action of the Holy Spirit who strengthens the soul of the sick person by his invisible grace.

1510. Who may bless the oil used in anointing?

The oil used in the anointing of the sick must be blessed for this purpose by the bishop, or by a priest who, either by law, or by a special grant of the apostolic see, has the faculty to do this. Besides the bishop, the law provides that the oil necessary for the anointing of the sick can be blessed by the person whose authority is equivalent to the bishop of the diocese, and in case of real necessity by any priest (Paul VI, *Sacram Unctionem Infirmorum*, 1974).

1511. Who may receive the sacrament of anointing?

The sacrament of anointing may be received by any baptized person who has reached the use of reason and is either seriously ill or advanced in age.

1512. May the sacrament, then, be conferred on the aged?

The sacrament of anointing may be conferred on the aged who are notably weakened in physical strength, even when there are no signs of dangerous illness. Therefore, old age of itself is enough to allow the valid reception of holy anointing provided there is notable debility of one's native powers.

1513. Are children permitted to receive this sacrament?

Children may receive the sacrament from the time they reach the use of reason in order to obtain the strength to bear their sufferings patiently, overcome tendencies to discouragement, or, if it is God's will, be restored to health.

1514. Can the sacrament be conferred on unconscious people?

The sacrament can be conferred on the sick, even though they have lost the use of their senses or reason, if as believers they would likely have asked for the holy anointing while they were in possession of their faculties. This may be applied to those baptized persons who would even probably have wanted to be anointed before they lapsed into unconsciousness.

1515. Should a priest anoint a person who is apparently dead?

When a priest is called to a person who is certainly dead, he should ask God to assist him to be delivered from his sins and mercifully receive him into his kingdom. If the priest is in any doubt whether the person is really dead, he can give him the sacrament conditionally.

1516. May the sacrament be received before surgery?

The sacrament may be received before surgery if a dangerous illness is the cause of this surgery.

1517. Who can administer the anointing of the sick?

Bishops and priests are the only valid ministers of the anointing of the sick. Relying on the words of St. James, the Church declares that the presbyters mentioned by the apostles, "Does not refer to the older men nor to the more influential men in the community, but to the bishops or priests properly ordained by them through the laying on of hands of the presbyterate" (Denziger, 1597).

1518. What are the spiritual effects of anointing?

The spiritual effects of anointing are: forgiveness of the guilt of unremitted sin, even grave sin for which the person had at least imperfect sorrow; remission of the temporal punishment still due for remitted sin, to such a degree that the expiation can be complete; supernatural patience to bear with the sufferings of one's illness; extraordinary confidence in God's mercy, which a person certainly needs when he faces eternity; and special infusion of moral courage to resist temptations of the devil.

1519. What are the bodily effects of anointing?

The bodily effects of anointing are restoration of bodily health, if, as God foresees it, the cure would be good for the person's spiritual welfare.

1520. How long do the effects of this sacrament continue?

The effects of this sacrament continue as long as the one who receives it remains in the same physical condition that occasioned the reception of the sacrament. In other words, the effects of the sacrament continue until the need for its sacramental efficacy has passed. The remission of sins and the temporal punishment due to forgiven sin continues indefinitely, even after an anointed person recovers from a grave illness.

1521. What is the formula for conferring the sacrament?

The formula of the sacrament of the anointing of the sick is: "Through this holy anointing may the Lord in his love and mercy help you with the grace of the Holy Spirit."

The sick person responds: "Amen."

The priest continues: "May the Lord who frees you from sin save you and raise you up."

The sick person again responds: "Amen."

1522. Why was the ritual for anointing revised?

The ritual for anointing was revised to accommodate the administration of this sacrament to the changed situation in modern times. There has been a remarkable development in medical care in all countries and a corresponding increase in life expectancy everywhere. The Church wants her liturgy of anointing to reflect these changes in the care of the sick.

1523. How was the name of the sacrament changed?

The sacrament that was formerly known as extreme unction, or final anointing, is now more fittingly called anointing of the sick. The new term is preferred because this sacrament is intended for all who are gravely ill or advanced in age and not only for persons at the point of death.

1524. Which parts of the body are to be anointed?

The forehead and hands are to be anointed. In case of necessity, one anointing is sufficient and even this may be of some other part of the body. But in every case, the whole formula must be pronounced.

1525. May the sacrament of anointing be received during the Eucharistic Sacrifice?

The sacrament of anointing may be received during the Eucharistic Sacrifice, depending on the physical condition of the sick or the aged. And if a person was gravely injured or became mortally ill during Mass, the Eucharistic Sacrifice could be interrupted to administer the sacrament of anointing.

1526. Does the Church favor a solemn liturgy of anointing?

The Church favors a more solemn liturgy of anointing when it can be prudently done. This anointing should take place in the presence of relatives and friends who can participate in the ceremony and in so doing represent the whole Church of God.

1527. May a person be anointed more than once?

Yes, a person may be anointed more than once if there is physical recovery after a previous reception of the sacrament. It may and should also be conferred again even during the same illness, whenever the sick person's condition becomes more serious.

1528. Is the sacrament of anointing necessary for salvation?

The sacrament of anointing is not strictly necessary for salvation because a person can be saved by the sacrament of penance. But for a person who is physically unable to confess his sins, or even give some sign of sorrow, anointing may be the only way he can be saved. This assumes he has unconfessed grave sins on his soul which the sacrament of anointing certainly removes provided at some time the person had, in faith, been sorry for his sins at least out of fear of God's punishments. Like the sacrament of penance, anointing remits the guilt and eternal penalty of mortal sin with only sincere imperfect contrition. But whereas anointing does not require external manifestation of one's sins, it is commonly believed that for valid absolution in the sacrament of penance the penitent must give some sensibly perceptible sign of his sins (when this is possible) or at least of sorrow for the sins committed.

1529. Are sick people obliged to receive the sacrament of anointing?

It is seriously sinful for sick people to refuse the sacrament of anointing out of contempt or in a way that gives scandal, and when in the state of mortal sin if a person cannot receive the sacrament of penance.

1530. What does the Church expect of her sick and suffering members?

The Church expects the faithful who are sick and suffering to contribute to the welfare of the Mystical Body by the graces they obtain for all the people of God. These graces are merited by the loving invitation of Christ in his Passion and Death. St. John tells us: "This has taught us love—that he gave up his life for us; and we, too, ought to give up our lives for our brothers" (1 John 3:16).

1531. How should one assist persons in their last moments?

One should assist persons in their last moments by being present at their side and comfort them by whispering aspirations with or at least to them, helping them recite acts of faith, hope, love, and sorrow, offering them the crucifix to hold and venerate and encouraging them to offer their suffering in union with Christ, for particular persons, living or dead, or for the whole Church of God.

1532. What are the obligations of the sick person's relatives?

The sick person's relatives are bound to see that the person receives the sacrament in due time so that he can draw all the merits of the sacrament. It is seriously wrong to withhold the sacrament under the pretext of sparing the feelings of the patient.

1533. *What is the apostolate of suffering?*

The apostolate of suffering is the patient endurance of bodily pain or spiritual trial, in union with Christ, as a form of prayer for some living person, or all the faithful on earth, or the souls in purgatory.

IV.

SACRAMENTALS

1. Meaning, Conditions, and Kinds

1534. What are the sacramentals?

Sacramentals are objects or actions the Church uses in order to confer blessings on the faithful through the merits of the Mystical Body of Christ.

1535. Why are these called sacramentals?

They are called sacramentals because they resemble the sacraments as external signs by which spiritual blessings are received. Moreover, many of them are used in the administration of the sacraments whose beauty they enhance and whose meaning they help to explain to the faithful.

1536. Why did the Church institute sacramentals?

The Church instituted sacramentals in order to give greater dignity to the ritual of the sacraments, to encourage the piety of the faithful for a more fruitful reception of the sacraments, to emphasize the doctrine of the Communion of Saints, and to help our daily lives by constant association with the things of God.

1537. What is the main condition for receiving grace through sacramentals?

The main condition for receiving grace through sacramentals is an active faith in Christ and his Church.

1538. How do sacramentals differ from sacraments?

Sacramentals differ from sacraments in three ways: in institution, cause, and effectiveness. Unlike the sacraments, sacramentals were not directly instituted by Christ but by the Church. Unlike the sacraments in which Christ confers grace through the sacrament itself, they are forms of prayer that obtain grace through the merits of the Church and depend on the dispositions of the person who uses sacramentals. And, unlike the sacraments, they do not really produce the extraordinary and distinctive grace they signify but are the occasion for receiving some blessing from God through the Church because a person uses sacramentals with faith.

1539. How are sacramentals classified?

Sacramentals are classified according to sacred time and sacred place; they are also sacred actions, words, or objects.

2. Sacred Actions, Words, and Objects

1540. What does the Church attach to sacred actions, words, and objects?

The Church attaches a ritual blessing to sacred actions, words, and objects. As a result, they become sacramentals.

1541. What are sacramental actions?

Sacramental actions are the heart of Catholic devotional practice. They are principally the gestures, postures, and bodily movements that the Church officially associates with the Eucharist and administration of the sacraments.

1542. Name some sacramental actions that are standard Catholic practice.

Among sacramental actions are genuflecting and kneeling, folding one's hands in prayer, making the sign of the cross over one's self or another person or some object, bowing the head, and sprinkling with holy water.

1543. When do words become sacramentals?

Words become sacramentals when what is said or sung, or the

time it is done, or the manner of doing it has been "sacramentalized," that is prescribed or officially approved by the Church. Indulgenced prayers belong to this category.

1544. How is the sign of the cross the sign of a Catholic Christian?

The sign of the cross is the sign of a Catholic Christian because it testifies to a person's faith and, on the Church's authority, carries the promise of God's help, always in spirit and often also temporally and in body.

1545. What is the power of the sign of the cross?

The sign of the cross has the power to put the devil to flight, to banish or weaken temptation, and to draw down God's blessing on those who make it with devotion.

1546. How should we make the sign of the cross?

We should make the sign of the cross with lively sentiments of faith and loving confidence in the Holy Trinity.

1547. When should we make the sign of the cross?

The sign of the cross should be made at the beginning and end of all our prayers, and actions, and especially in times of danger and temptation.

1548. Describe the proper way of making the sign of the cross.

The proper way of making the sign of the cross is to place the fingers of the right hand to the forehead while saying, "In the name of the Father," then to the chest, saying, "and of the Son," then to the left and the right shoulders, saying, "and of the Holy Spirit. Amen."

1549. What objects are considered sacramentals?

Any material object becomes a sacramental when it is blessed by a qualified person and according to a ritual approved by the Church.

1550. What does the expression "blessed object" mean?

A blessed object is any place or thing that has been ritually blessed by a priest or bishop. It may be a building like a church, cemetery, or shrine; it may be a statue, medal, or sacred picture; it may be altar vessels used at Mass or vestments for divine service; or the distinctive habits of men and women religious; or the rings exchanged by a couple at marriage; it may be water used for blessing oneself or others, or in the home, or in the ritual blessing of religious objects; it may be oil to be applied in case of sickness or some physical disability. The only limit to the number and variety of blessed objects is the Church's ritual legislation.

1551. How are objects blessed?

Objects are blessed by a sign of the cross, by the recitation of the words prescribed for each blessing, by sprinkling with holy water, and by whatever ritual forms are required by the Church. Moreover, the one who gives the blessing must be authorized to do so by either special privilege or the Church's general law.

1552. What does the blessing of the priest or bishop confer on the object blessed?

The blessing of the priest or bishop confers on the object blessed a special title to God's protection and assistance, or to its being set aside for the exercise of divine worship.

1553. What are reserved blessings?

Reserved blessings are those that only certain priests, with special faculties, can confer, or, in some cases, only the bishop. Thus only Franciscan priests can normally set up the Stations of the Cross, and only bishops may consecrate a Church.

3. Liturgical Year, Feasts and Fasts

1554. What is sacred time?

Sacred time refers to the liturgical year and its seasons, the feasts and fasts of the Catholic Church. It is a periodic reminder to keep alive and deepen our realization of the truths of the faith.

1555. How does sacred time qualify as a sacramental?

Sacred time qualifies as a sacramental because it has been established by the Church to stimulate the faith of the people by disposing them to a regular and more generous service of God.

1556. What are the five liturgical seasons of the Church?

The five liturgical seasons of the Church are: Advent, Christmas, Lent, Easter, and Pentecost.

1557. What is Advent?

Advent is the time during which the Church prepares for the coming of Christ in three ways. We look back historically to the age of prophecy foretelling the birth of the Messiah. We look at the immediate present to anticipate liturgically the celebration of the Lord's birth on Christmas Day. We finally look forward prophetically to his coming at the dawn of our own eternity, and to his majestic coming at the end of the present world on the last day.

1558. How long does the Advent season last?

The Advent season seldom completes a four-week cycle. Advent begins on the Sunday nearest the feast of St. Andrew, which is on November 30, and includes four Sundays. These four Sundays or weeks symbolize the traditional four thousand years that the people waited for the Savior.

1559. What is the spirit of the Church during the Advent season?

The spirit of the Church during the Advent season is one of hopeful waiting and preparation. We wait in confidence for the coming of Christ, and we prepare ourselves by coming to Christ with hearts purified of sin.

1560. What is the Christmas season?

The Christmas season commemorates the mysteries of Christ's birth, infancy, and hidden life.

1561. How long is the Christmas season?

The Christmas season begins on Christmas Day and extends to the Feast of Christ's Presentation in the Temple.

1562. What is the spirit of this season?

The spirit of the Christmas season is one of joy that Christ was born of the Virgin Mary at Bethlehem, of peace that he came to reconcile a sinful world, and of love in response to God's great love for us in becoming man.

1563. What is the special privilege that a priest enjoys on Christmas Day?

On Christmas Day, a priest may celebrate three Masses. The first is for the intentions of the Holy Father, the second is to be said for his diocese or parish (if he is bishop or pastor), and the third may be offered for the priest's own intention.

1564. Why do priests have the privilege of saying three Masses on Christmas Day?

The three Masses on Christmas Day symbolize the three generations of Christ: his generation within the Trinity as the eternal Son of the Father, his coming in Bethlehem when he was born of the Virgin Mary, and his coming into our souls at baptism by his grace and in the Eucharist by his Real Presence.

1565. What is the Lenten season?

Lent is the season that commemorates the forty days that Christ spent fasting and praying in the desert before he began his public life. It reminds the faithful of Christ's last days before and during his Passion and Death and it anticipates the holy season of Easter.

1566. How long does the season of Lent last?

The season of Lent lasts from Ash Wednesday through Holy Saturday.

1567. Why has the Church instituted the Lenten season?

The Church instituted the Lenten season originally to imitate Christ's forty days' fast in the desert. But in modern times the emphasis is on commemorating the Lord's Passion and Death, as an annual preparation for our own death and final resurrection.

1568. How is Lent a liturgical season of penance?

Lent is a liturgical season of penance during which the faithful are to give themselves to a more than ordinary life of mortification.

1569. What are the prescribed forms of mortification during Lent?

During Lent the faithful are gravely obliged to fast on Ash Wednesday and Good Friday, which means only one full meal, and abstain from meat and meat products on Ash Wednesday and all the Fridays of Lent.

1570. What are the main practices to be observed during Lent?

The main Lenten practices are prayer, self-denial, and almsgiving or charity.

1571. What forms of prayer should be specially practiced during Lent?

During Lent we should attend Mass more frequently, even daily, and receive Holy Communion. We should read the Scriptures and recite the Rosary.

1572. What are some forms of self-denial to be practiced during Lent?

During Lent we are obliged to observe fast and abstinence on the days prescribed by the Church; and we are to practice other forms of mortification, e.g., giving up certain legitimate recreations, sweets and delicacies, and in general living a more austere way of life.

1573. What kind of almsgiving or charity should be practiced during Lent?

By almsgiving the Church understands every form of practical generosity to others, by feeding the hungry, providing food and shelter for the poor, visiting and care for the sick, handicapped and elderly, giving voluntary service to the Church and, in general, meeting whatever spiritual or bodily needs of others that should be filled.

1574. What are the most important days of Lent?

The most important days of Lent are Ash Wednesday, Passion or Palm Sunday, Holy Thursday, Good Friday, and Holy Saturday.

1575. What is Ash Wednesday?

Ash Wednesday is the beginning of Lent. It is called Ash Wednesday because on that day the priest places ashes in the form of a cross on the foreheads of the faithful. While doing so, he says, "Remember, man, that you are dust and unto dust you shall return," or "Turn away from sin and be faithful to the Gospel."

1576. With what sentiments should we receive the ashes?

We should receive the ashes with sentiments of humility and contrition: humility because we acknowledge that, of ourselves, we are only dust, and contrition because we have offended God by our sins.

1577. What is Passion (Palm) Sunday?

Passion or Palm Sunday is the last Sunday of Lent. It is so called because on this day the faithful receive branches of palm which they carry in liturgical procession. It is a commemoration of the triumphal entrance of Jesus into Jerusalem.

1578. What begins on Palm Sunday?

Holy Week begins on Palm Sunday. During Holy Week the Church honors the Passion and Death of our Lord Jesus Christ with special solemnity.

1579. What mysteries of faith does the Church commemorate on Holy Thursday?

On Holy Thursday the Church especially commemorates five mysteries of the faith: 1) Christ's washing the feet of the apostles to teach us the humility we need to be his followers, 2) the new commandment of mutual charity after the example of Christ's love for us, 3) the Holy Eucharist as sacrifice, communion, and Real Presence, 4) the sacrament of the priesthood, and 5) Christ's bloody agony in the Garden of Olives.

1580. What are the principal ceremonies of the liturgy on Holy Thursday?

The principal ceremonies on Holy Thursday are: Holy Mass, which is to be held in the evening in commemoration of the Last Supper; the Gloria is sung and bells rung as a sign of joy, but they are then silenced until Holy Saturday; the Washing of the Feet; Procession of the Blessed Sacrament to the repository in commemoration of Jesus going into the Garden of Olives to pray to his Father before his arrest; the stripping of the altar as a reminder that Jesus was stripped of everything, even his garments, during the Passion.

1581. What mysteries are commemorated on Good Friday?

On Good Friday the Church commemorates the Passion and

Death of Jesus Christ. There is no Mass on Good Friday. The liturgy of the Word is read, prayers are said, and the crucifix is venerated but there is no consecration. Communion is distributed from the hosts reserved from the preceding day.

1582. How should the faithful sanctify Good Friday?

The faithful should sanctify Good Friday by participating in the liturgy and making the Way of the Cross, by fast and abstinence and a sense of deep sorrow for sin.

1583. What are the principal ceremonies of the liturgy on Holy Saturday?

The principal liturgical ceremonies on Holy Saturday are four blessings: of the fire which represents Jesus as light of the world; of the incense grains to honor the five wounds; of the paschal candle which is to be lit during services until after the reading of the Gospel on Ascension Thursday; and of the Easter water which is used in the conferral of baptism; then follows the offering of Mass during which the Gloria is sung, the bells rung, altars decorated, candles lighted, and the Alleluia intoned.

1584. What is the Paschal season?

The Paschal season is the period of time between the Easter Vigil Mass when the Alleluia is sung until Trinity Sunday. The season relives the Resurrection and Ascension of Christ and closes with the Sunday after Pentecost.

1585. Why is Easter the greatest feast of the Church?

Easter is the greatest feast of the Church because it commemorates the Resurrection of the Savior, which completed our Redemption and confirmed our faith in Jesus Christ as truly God.

1586. What is Ascension Day?

Ascension Day is the feast which celebrates Christ's Ascension to his heavenly Father. The event occurred forty days after his Resurrection in the presence of his Mother Mary and the disciples.

1587. What is the feast of Pentecost?

Pentecost honors the coming of the Holy Spirit upon the apostles. It is the birthday of the Church. On this day St. Peter, head of the Church, preached a sermon, after which three thousand persons were converted and received baptism.

1588. What is the season of Pentecost?

The season of Pentecost, now called Ordinary Time, is the period from Pentecost Sunday to the first Sunday of Advent.

1589. What is the basic theme of the weeks between Pentecost and Advent?

The basic theme of this season is salvation history. It brings out God's continued providence toward his chosen people from Abraham to Jesus Christ. The stress is on the covenant between the Savior who calls and the faithful who are to give themselves generously in his loving service.

1590. What is Trinity Sunday?

Trinity Sunday is the annual feast on which the Church honors the mystery of one God in three divine Persons. It is the last day of the Easter season.

1591. What is meant by sacred place?

The most important sacred place is a church or chapel where Mass is offered and the Blessed Sacrament is reserved. It is also the normal place for the celebration of other sacraments. Other sacred places are shrines where it is believed that God bestows special favors on those who come to pray there.

4. Liturgy of the Hours, Fast and Abstinence

1592. Which sacramentals are in a class by themselves?

Sacramentals that are in a class by themselves are the liturgy of the hours and fast and abstinence.

1593. Why are these sacramentals special?

The Divine Office and fast and abstinence are special because of their antiquity, going back to the early Church, and their universality, being practiced throughout the Catholic world.

1594. What is the liturgy of the hours?

The liturgy of the hours is the public prayer of the Church for sanctifying the day by praising God. It is also known as the Divine Office.

1595. What is the origin and basis for the liturgy of the hours?

The origin and basis for the liturgy of the hours is the tradition of the Catholic Church. Already in the first century the faithful devoted themselves to prayer at certain hours. Therefore, in keeping with ancient Christian tradition the liturgy of the hours is so devised that the whole course of the day and night is made holy by the praise of God.

1596. What is the form of the Divine Office since the Second Vatican Council?

The Divine Office in the Roman Rite now consists of the following: Lauds and Vespers, the Morning and Evening Prayers, called "the hinges" of the office; Matins, to be said at any time of the day, which retains the form of a nocturnal vigil service and is called the Office of Readings; Terce, Sext, and None, any one of which may be chosen for prayer at an appropriate time of the day, approximately midmorning, noon, or midafternoon; and Compline, which is the Night Prayer.

1597. Who is obliged to recite the liturgy of the hours?

The recitation of the office is a sacred duty of men in holy orders and of men and women religious according to their rule of life.

1598. Does the Church recommend the liturgy of the hours for lay people?

The Church strongly encourages the laity to recite the Divine Office, either with the priest, or among themselves, or even individually.

1599. Why is the practice of fast and abstinence a unique sacramental?

Fast and abstinence is a unique sacramental because it partakes of sacred time and place and because its foundation lies deep in Christian revelation. Moreover, throughout the Church's history it was assumed that doing penance was a necessary condition for salvation.

1600. How many kinds of fast and abstinence are there?

There are two kinds of fast and abstinence: the Eucharistic fast before Holy Communion and the penitential fast and abstinence prescribed by the Church at stated times during the liturgical year.

1601. What are the prescribed norms for Fridays as days of penance?

All Fridays of the year are prescribed days of penance. This is a grave obligation. They also remain days of abstinence from meat and meat products. But the faithful have the choice of substituting some other external form of penance, instead of abstinence, on the Fridays outside of Lent. The substituted penance should be at least as penitential as abstinence.

V.
PRAYER

1. Motives, Vocal and Mental

1602. Why do we pray?

We pray because God wants us to praise him, thank him, and ask him for what we need.

1603. How do we praise God?

We praise God by recognizing his infinite majesty and acknowledging our total dependence on him.

1604. How do we thank God?

We thank God by showing our appreciation for all that he has done for us by bringing us out of nothing through creation, redeeming us by his Incarnation, and promising to give us himself in heaven for all eternity.

1605. What is the prayer of asking?

The prayer of asking is of two kinds, either back to the past or forward to the future. Looking to the past, we plead for God's mercy for our sins. Looking to the future we beg for the many things in this life that we cannot give ourselves or obtain from other people but depend on God to provide. In both forms of petition, we declare that we are totally helpless to do anything on the road to heaven without the grace of God, which only he can supply.

1606. What are the principal kinds of prayer?

The principal kinds of prayer are vocal, which can be either private or public, and mental, which can be either meditation or contemplation.

1607. What is meant by vocal prayer?

In vocal prayer, the words used are determined beforehand. They are the words of someone else, with which those who pray identify themselves in spirit.

1608. What is private vocal prayer?

Private vocal prayer is recited either out loud or silently by a single individual praying alone.

1609. What is public vocal prayer?

Public vocal prayer is recited or sung out loud by several people praying together. When this prayer is prescribed by the Church for public service by the faithful, it is liturgical prayer.

1610. Why is liturgical prayer the most excellent prayer?

Liturgical prayer is the most excellent prayer because it is offered in the name of the Church and draws on the special merits of the communion of saints.

1611. What is mental prayer?

In mental prayer, the words used are not determined or prescribed. Those who pray mentally express themselves spontaneously, according to the sentiments of their own mind and heart.

1612. What is meditation?

Meditation is that form of mental prayer in which the mind is specially occupied with reflecting on divine things. These prayerful reflections become the means of stimulating the will to make acts of confidence and sorrow, of gratitude and petition, and of adoring love of God.

1613. Is mental prayer for everyone?

Yes, everyone in every state of life needs mental prayer in order to fulfill the divine precept of praying always, to obtain the graces needed daily and throughout the day, to remain in God's presence in the midst of secular activity, and to attain the measure of sanctity intended by God for every human being.

1614. What is contemplation?

Contemplation is that form of mental prayer in which the mind is not so much reasoning about God as looking at God in simple faith and adoration. It may be called the end or purpose of meditation. We reflect on God and divine things (meditation) in order to remain intent and enjoy what we had been meditating (contemplation). To contemplate is to see God with the eyes of faith.

2. The Lord's Prayer

1615. What is the most excellent of all prayers?

The most excellent of all prayers is the Our Father, or the Lord's Prayer.

1616. Why is the Our Father called the Lord's Prayer?

It is called the Lord's Prayer because it was given to us by Christ our Lord, who commanded us to say it (Matthew 6:9–13; Luke 11:1–4).

1617. What does the Lord's Prayer contain?

It contains a short introduction and seven petitions made to God.

1618. What is the introduction of the Lord's Prayer?

The introduction is the words: "Our Father, who art in heaven."

1619. To whom do we address the Lord's Prayer?

We address the Lord's Prayer to God as our Father for many reasons: 1) God is the first Parent of the human family because he created us; 2) he is the source of the supernatural life which he shares with us as his children; 3) he cares and provides for us by his constant fatherly love; 4) like a good father he has prepared for us a heavenly inheritance.

1620. Why do we say "our" and not "my" Father?

We say "our Father" because, unlike the Savior, we cannot say "my Father" since there is only one natural Son of God who became man in the person of Christ. Moreover, in this way we affirm that God is the Father of the whole human race, that we are all his children and should therefore love one another as brothers and sisters in God.

1621. What do we mean by the words "who art in heaven"?

These words tells us that, although God is everywhere, he is especially in heaven as the eternal joy of the angels and saints and in our souls as the indwelling Trinity. These words remind us that we are only pilgrims on earth and that our true home is in the heaven that awaits us.

1622. What do we ask for in the first petition, "hallowed be thy name"?

In the first petition we pray that God may be known, loved, and served by all mankind, and that his name may never be profaned by blasphemy, cursing, or irreverent use in speech or writing.

1623. What do we ask for in the second petition, "Thy kingdom come"?

In this petition we ask that God's kingdom on earth, the Catholic Church, may be extended in numbers and intensified in the faith and holiness of her members. We also pray that the kingdom of divine grace, already present in the hearts of believers, may grow to God's glory. And we pray that after this life, we may all be admitted into the heavenly kingdom which God has prepared for those who love him.

1624. What do we mean by the third petition, "Thy will be done on earth as it is in heaven"?

In this petition we ask that all the people on earth may do the will of God as faithfully and joyfully as the angels and saints do it in heaven. We also ask for the grace to submit ourselves always and in all things to the holy will of God.

1625. What do we ask for in the fourth petition, "give us this day our daily bread"?

In this petition we ask for ourselves and for all of mankind the nourishment we need for our daily sustenance, in body but mainly in soul. In this petition we pray that more and more people will have the faith and devotion to receive Holy Communion every day as the necessary food for their supernatural life. In terms of our bodily needs, we do not ask for riches but only for what we need to live a decent physical life. "As long as we have food and clothing," St. Paul tells us, "let us be content with that" (1 Timothy 6:8).

1626. What do we ask for in the fifth petition, "forgive us our trespasses as we forgive those who trespass against us"?

In this petition we ask God to forgive us in the way that we forgive others. This means that our practice of mercy toward others is both the condition and measure of God's mercy to us. Christ has told us, "The amount you measure out is the amount you will be given back" (Luke 6:38).

1627. For what do we ask in the sixth petition, "lead us not into temptation"?

In this petition we ask to have the light to recognize temptations when they come and the strength to resist them. We do not ask to be delivered from all temptation, since it is part of God's providence to test our loyalty in his service. We pray to be protected from all manner of temptations: those of the flesh or concupiscence, of the world or the bad example of other people, and of the devil who was permitted to tempt even Christ the Lord.

1628. For what do we pray in the seventh petition, "deliver us from evil"?

In this petition we ask God to preserve us from all evil of soul, or sin, and especially from eternal damnation. We ask to be preserved from all other evil which God foresees would not be beneficial for our spiritual life, either because we lack the strength to endure the evil or the generosity to profit from whatever suffering God may send us.

1629. Why do we add "Amen"?

We add "Amen" to express our sincere desire to obtain what we ask for in the Lord's Prayer and our confidence that God will hear our petitions.

3. The Hail Mary

1630. What prayer do Catholics usually say after the Our Father?

They usually say the Hail Mary after the Lord's Prayer.

1631. What is the Hail Mary?

The Hail Mary is a combination of two prayers: a prayer of praise of our Lady and a prayer of petition for her help.

1632. What is the prayer of praise in the Hail Mary?

This prayer repeats the words of the Angel Gabriel when he addressed the blessed Virgin, saying, "Hail [Mary] full of grace the Lord is with thee; blessed art thou among women"; followed by the words addressed to her by St. Elizabeth, "and blessed is the fruit of thy womb," to which the Church adds the name "Jesus."

1633. What is the prayer of petition in the Hail Mary?

The prayer of petition was added by the Church, asking our Lady, "Holy Mary, Mother of God, pray for us sinners, now and at the hour of our death. Amen."

1634. Why do we address Mary with the words "full of grace"?

We address her in this way because, conceived without sin, she was, already at the Annunciation, the holiest of human persons; she was chosen to become the mother of the Author of all grace; and she was destined to become the Queen of the angels and saints in heavenly glory.

1635. Why do we say "the Lord is with thee"?

We use these words to declare that the Blessed Virgin is, of all creatures, the closest to the Holy Trinity. She is venerated as the daughter of God the Father, the true Mother of God the Son, and the immaculate spouse of the Holy Spirit.

1636. Why do we address her as "blessed art thou among women"?

We address her in these words because she, of all women, was chosen to be the Mother of God; she alone is a mother while remaining a virgin; and, as the second Eve, she brought us salvation through her Son, the second Adam, even as the first Eve brought sin into the world by her tempting the first Adam.

1637. Why do we add the words "blessed is the fruit of thy womb, Jesus"?

We add these words to show that giving honor to Mary is never separated from the honor that is due to Christ. We praise the mother, for the sake of the Son, and our veneration for him is increased by the honor we give his mother.

1638. For what do we ask in the prayer of petition of the Hail Mary?

In this petition we ask our Lady to intercede with her Son for us sinners, by obtaining the remission of our guilt and the removal of the punishment we have deserved for our sins. We especially pray for the gift of final perseverance, asking that our death may be like that of our Lord; that like him, in Mary's company, our final words may be, "into your hands, O Lord, I commend my spirit."

4. Glory Be to the Father

1639. What is the best-known prayer to the Holy Trinity?

The best-known prayer to the Holy Trinity says: "Glory be to the Father, and to the Son, and to the Holy Spirit. As it was in the beginning, is now, and ever shall be, world without end. Amen."

1640. What kind of prayer is this?

This is a prayer of adoration by which we declare our faith in God who has one nature in three divine Persons.

1641. What else do we say in this prayer?

We ask that God may be further glorified by all the people on earth through their loving recognition of his goodness and obedience to his divine will.

5. Favorite Prayers: Morning and Evening, Angelus, Grace at Meals, Rosary, Sacred Heart, Way of the Cross, Novenas

1642. What are some favorite prayers that Catholics recite every day?

Among the favorite daily prayers are the morning and evening prayers, the Angelus, grace before and after meals, and the Rosary.

1643. What are the morning prayers?

The morning prayers may include acts of faith, hope, and charity, and the morning offering to the Sacred Heart of Jesus. The Angelus is a prayer in honor of the Incarnation to be said morning, noon, and night.

1644. What is the prayer of the Angelus?

In the prayer of the Angelus, which may be said with one person leading and others responding, we say:

The Angel of the Lord declared unto Mary.

And she conceived by the power of the Holy Spirit. (Hail Mary)

Behold the handmaid of the Lord.

Be it done to me according to your word. (Hail Mary)

And the Word was made flesh.

And dwelled among us. (Hail Mary)

Pray for us, O Holy Mother of God.

That we may be made worthy of the promises of Christ.

Let us Pray.

Pour forth, we beseech you, O Lord, your grace into our

hearts; that we, to whom the Incarnation of Christ your
Son was made known by the message of an angel, may, by
his passion and cross, be brought to the glory of his
Resurrection; through the same Christ our Lord. Amen.

1645. What is the evening prayer?

The evening prayer may be whatever a person's devotion sug-
gests, but it should include at least a brief examination of conscience and an act of contrition, like the following:

O my God, I am heartily sorry for having offended you, and I
detest all my sins, because I dread the loss of heaven and the
pains of hell, but most of all because they offend you, my God,
who are all good and deserving of all my love. I firmly resolve,
with the help of your grace, to confess my sins, to do penance,
and to amend my life. Amen.

1646. What is the grace before and after meals?

This is an act of thanksgiving to be said before and after each
meal. The familiar prayer before meals says:

Bless us, O Lord, and these your gifts which we are about to
receive from your bounty; through Christ our Lord. Amen.

After meals, we may say:

We give you thanks, Almighty God, for these and all the gifts
we have received from your bounty; through Christ our Lord.
Amen.

Like the Angelus, the grace at meals may be recited by one person while the others simply answer, "Amen."

1647. What is the Rosary?

The Rosary is a mental and vocal prayer honoring the Blessed
Virgin by recalling fifteen mysteries in her life and that of her
Son, beginning with the Incarnation of her Son on earth and clos-
ing with her glorification by him in heaven.

1648. What are the fifteen mysteries of the Rosary?

The mysteries of the Rosary are divided into three groups of
five mysteries each. The joyful mysteries are the Annunciation,
the Visitation, the Birth of Jesus, the Presentation in the temple,
and the Finding of Christ in the temple. The sorrowful mysteries
are the Agony in the Garden, the Scourging, the Crowning with
thorns, the Way of the Cross, and the Crucifixion. The glorious

mysteries are the Resurrection of Christ, his Ascension, the Descent of the Holy Spirit on Pentecost, the Assumption of our Lady into heaven, and her Crowning as Queen of the universe.

1649. What are some other popular forms of Catholic piety?

Other forms of Catholic piety include devotion to the Sacred Heart, the Way of the Cross, devotion to the angels and saints, novenas, and various litanies.

1650. What is devotion to the Sacred Heart?

Devotion to the Sacred Heart is devotion to the bodily Heart of Christ as the chief sign and symbol of that love "with which the Divine Redeemer unceasingly loves his eternal Father and all mankind." This love of Christ draws a responsive love from us, shown by our consuming desire to do his will. The Church teaches that "devotion to the most Sacred Heart of Jesus is so important that it may be considered, so far as practice is concerned, the perfect expression of the Christian religion" (Pius XII, *Haurietis Aquas,* 143).

1651. What is the Way of the Cross?

The Way of the Cross is fourteen short meditations on the Passion and Death of Christ, in memory of his painful journey to Calvary. They are made by moving from one station to another in church or elsewhere, while prayerfully reflecting either on the particular station or in general on the sufferings of the Savior. A plenary indulgence may be gained for making the Stations of the Cross, as they are sometimes called.

1652. What is devotion to the angels and saints?

Devotion to the angels and saints is commonly expressed in the numerous forms of prayer addressed to them as the special friends of God.

1653. What is a novena?

A novena is nine days of public or private prayer for some special occasion or intention. The first novena was the nine days that Mary and the disciples spent in Jerusalem between Christ's Ascension and the descent of the Holy Spirit on Pentecost Sunday.

1654. What is a litany?

A litany is a series of prayerful aspirations or invocations, addressed to God, to Jesus Christ, our Lady, the angels, or the saints. Many litanies are approved by the Church but only the following are also indulgenced: the Holy Name, the Sacred Heart, the Precious Blood, the Blessed Virgin, St. Joseph, and the Saints.

VI.
LITURGY

1. Public Worship, Necessity, Principal Forms, Church Authority

1655. What is the liturgy?

The liturgy is the public worship given to God by the whole Mystical Body, that is, by Christ the Head and the faithful who are his members. It is the exercise of Christ's priestly office now on earth, as a continuation of the priesthood which he instituted during his visible stay in Palestine in the first century.

1656. What is the priestly work of Christ?

The priestly work of Christ is the worship of God and the sanctification of the human race.

1657. What does worship mean?

Worship means giving due honor to God as the Supreme Being, who is Creator and therefore Lord of the universe. It is the practice of justice toward God, who is most deserving of our reverence and praise.

1658. How are liturgy and worship related?

Liturgy is the highest form of worship, because it glorifies God publicly as the origin and destiny, not only of man individually but of mankind as a society, and the worship is given officially, by the Church and under her divinely established authority.

1659. How is worship a form of sanctification?

Worship is itself a form of holiness, because when we worship we are united with God, not only in words or gestures but in spirit, communicating with the Author of our being and the Hope of all our desires.

1660. How does worship lead to holiness?

Worship leads to holiness because it is the principal source of divine grace, without which no one can even be saved and much less sanctified. If the first purpose of worship is to glorify God, its second purpose is to sanctify man.

1661. What is public worship?

Public worship is another name for the liturgy. It is called public because it is given by the Church and in her name, and not only by individuals on their own, private initiative.

1662. Is private worship also pleasing to God?

Yes, private worship is very pleasing to God, as Christ more than once showed by his prayer in solitude with his Father. Moreover, he told us, "when you pray, go to your private room and, when you have shut your door, pray to your Father who is in that secret place, and your Father who sees all that is done in secret will reward you" (Matthew 6:6).

1663. Is public worship necessary?

Public worship is necessary because God wants us to honor him as social beings.

1664. What are the principal forms of public worship?

The main forms of public worship are the sacrifice of the Mass and the sacraments, the liturgy of the hours or the Divine Office, and the sacramentals authorized by the Church.

1665. When did Christian liturgical practice begin?

Christian liturgical practice began with the foundations of the Church. The first Christians, we are told, "remained faithful to the teaching of the apostles, to the brotherhood, to the breaking of bread and to the prayers" (Acts 2:42).

1666. What was the form of the liturgy under the Mosaic Law?

The liturgy under the Mosaic Law passed through a series of early stages until it took on a definite form which lasted until the coming of the Redeemer. It consisted mainly in the sacrifice of animals, like cattle and sheep, which were slain by priests descended from the family of Aaron and assisted by Levites, descended from the tribe of Levi.

1667. Who brought the Mosaic Law to perfection?

The Mosaic Law was brought to perfection by Jesus Christ. After fulfilling all the prescriptions of the Old Law, on the eve of his death he instituted the Holy Eucharist and made the Eucharistic sacrifice the center of the liturgy of the New Law.

1668. When did Christian public worship begin?

Christian public worship began with Christ, who personally instituted the Mass and the seven sacraments, and authorized the Church he founded to glorify the Father, in union with the Holy Spirit, in his name.

1669. How did public worship develop?

Public worship developed under the Church's authority, according to the circumstances and the needs of the faithful. Hence public worship was organized, and enriched by new rites, ceremonies, and regulations.

1670. What is meant by rites and ceremonies?

Ceremonies are the actions of the liturgy. Rites are the authorized ways of performing liturgical acts.

1671. What is the origin of the liturgical rites in the Church?

Liturgical rites go back to the time of the apostles. We know this from the New Testament, notably the Acts of the Apostles and the letters of St. Paul; from the first-century liturgical manual, the *Didache* or *Teaching of the Apostles;* and from the testimony of ancient writers.

1672. How are liturgical rites preserved in the Church?

Liturgical rites are preserved in the Church by tradition, based on divine revelation as interpreted and adapted by ecclesiastical authority under the bishop of Rome.

1673. Why are there regulations in the liturgy?

Regulations in the liturgy preserve the integrity of Catholic doctrine; they help to maintain unity of faith; they foster a community of worship; and thus promote the bond of charity that unites the faithful as members of the Christian family.

1674. Who has the right to regulate the liturgy?

Only the pope and the organs of the holy see approved by him and, as the laws may determine, the bishops under the guidance of Rome have the right to regulate the liturgy in the Catholic Church. Therefore not even a priest, on his own authority, may add, change, remove, or touch anything pertaining to the sacred liturgy. The only exceptions are those clearly defined choices that are provided in the liturgy.

1675. What is the role of the bishop in the sacred liturgy?

It is mainly in the celebration and administration of the liturgy in his diocese that the bishop exercises his role as shepherd of the flock entrusted to his pastoral care.

1676. Why should the pope be the final authority in regulating the liturgy?

The pope must be the final authority in regulating the liturgy in order to protect the soundness of doctrine expressed by the liturgy and to insure uniformity of ritual practice as a sign of the Church's unity.

1677. Why is the liturgy so pleasing to God?

The liturgy is so pleasing to God because it fulfills the main purpose of our existence, to glorify God, as preserved in the first commandment of the Decalogue; and expressed in the first petition of the Lord's Prayer taught by our divine Savior.

1678. How does the liturgy instruct the faithful?

The liturgy instructs the faithful by reminding them of the principal doctrines of the faith throughout the year. Moreover, God speaks to us through the priest who presides over the assembly and we respond by either song or prayer. Thus when the Church sings or prays together the faith of those participating is nourished.

1679. Why is the liturgy so important as the Church's public worship?

The liturgy as the Church's public worship is the principal means by which the people glorify God and give witness to their faith in Jesus Christ. In this way they manifest the social nature of the Church as the Mystical Body of Christ, and the Communion of Saints composed of the Church triumphant in heaven, the Church suffering in purgatory, and the Church militant on earth.

1680. What are the benefits of the liturgy?

Through the liturgy, grace is received by those who participate, the Church is sanctified, and divine blessings are conferred on the living and the dead.

1681. How can the liturgy produce its full effects?

The liturgy can produce its full effects when we come to it with the proper disposition, that is with heart and soul ready to cooperate with the grace of God, for he says, "At the favorable time, I have listened to you; on the day of salvation I came to your help" (2 Corinthians 6:2).

2. Exterior and Interior Worship

1682. What are the two essential parts of the Christian liturgy?

The Christian liturgy is composed of interior and exterior worship.

1683. What is exterior worship?

Exterior worship is that part of the liturgy which is sensibly perceptible. It consists in those acts which belong to the body.

1684. Is exterior worship necessary?

Exterior worship is necessary because, without it, we would not honor God with our bodies and could not give him praise as social beings. Exterior worship reveals and emphasizes the unity of the Mystical Body, nourishes its holy zeal, and intensifies its action day by day.

1685. What are some practices of exterior worship?

For the participants some practices of exterior worship are: kneeling, genuflecting, standing, sitting, and bowing; reciting prayers aloud in unison, singing praises to God, and observing periods of silence; folding the hands and marching in procession. All the words and gestures of celebrant and ministers of the liturgy are part of exterior worship, as are all the objects used, like vestments, altar, sacred vessels, liturgical books, incense, flowers, and holy water.

1686. Do the faithful perform a true ministry in the celebration of the liturgy?

The faithful perform a true ministry in the celebration of the liturgy as servers, readers, commentators, and members of the choir. They should be carefully trained to exercise these functions with sincere piety, reverent decorum, and with spiritual profit to the faithful who participate.

1687. Who are the extraordinary ministers of the Eucharistic liturgy?

Extraordinary ministers of the Eucharistic liturgy are the faithful, whether religious or lay, who are duly authorized by the bishop. They may distribute Holy Communion only when there is no priest, deacon, or acolyte; when the priest is impeded by illness or advanced age; or when the number of the faithful is so large as to make the celebration of Mass excessively long.

1688. What is expected of those who have a liturgical duty to perform?

Those who have a liturgical duty to perform, whether ordained or appointed, should carry out only those parts which pertain to their office by the nature of the rite and the rules of the liturgy.

1689. How important is Sacred Scripture in the liturgy?

Sacred Scripture is very important in the liturgy. It provides the lessons to be read and explained in the homily, and psalms to be sung or recited. It inspires the prayers that are said and gives meaning to the actions and signs by which God is glorified and the faithful are sanctified by his grace.

1690. May other readings be substituted for Sacred Scripture in the Eucharistic liturgy?

No, other readings may not be substituted in the Eucharistic liturgy because in the Scriptures it is God himself speaking to his people, and Christ, present in his word, who is proclaiming his Gospel.

1691. What is communal celebration?

Communal celebration means that those who worship are physically present in one place, and that they actively participate in the liturgy for which they assemble.

1692. What is active participation in the liturgy?

Active participation means that those who worship together are mentally aware of what is taking place, that their hearts are united with the sacred ceremony, and that they join their voices and actions with those of the celebrant and the other worshippers in the liturgy.

1693. Is communal celebration of the liturgy preferred to individual?

In general, communal is preferred to the individual. This is especially true of Mass and the administration of the sacraments. "For where two or three meet in my name, I shall be there with them" (Matthew 18:20).

1694. Why is the homily such an important part of the Mass?

The homily at Mass is so important because instruction in the faith is an essential part of the liturgy. Through the homily, based on divine revelation, Christ himself is teaching the people the way to salvation.

1695. Has the Church forbidden that Mass be said in Latin?

No, far from forbidding the practice, the modern popes have encouraged the saying of Mass in Latin in two ways: urging that Latin Mass, following the new ritual, be made regularly available to the faithful; and declaring that the faithful chant or recite those parts of the Mass which pertain to the congregation, such as the Gloria, Credo, Sanctus, Pater Noster, and the Agnus Dei.

1696. Who determines when Mass is to be said entirely or partially in Latin?

The bishop determines for each diocese, according to the people's legitimate desires, when Masses are to be said entirely in Latin; and the pastor determines for each parish regarding the people's participation at Mass in Latin.

1697. Why is the vernacular used in the liturgy?

The vernacular is used because it contributes to a greater understanding of the liturgy.

1698. What is interior worship?

Interior worship is the chief element of divine worship. It consists of those acts that take place in the soul.

1699. What are the principal acts of interior worship?

The principal acts of interior worship are faith, hope, and love; adoration, praise, and petition; humility, sorrow for sin, and resignation to the will of God.

1700. Is interior worship necessary?

Interior worship is absolutely necessary, and without it there would be no liturgy. Christ made this plain when the Pharisees complained about the disciples eating with unclean hands. He said, "This people honors me only with lip-service, while their hearts are far from me. The worship they offer me is worthless, the doctrines they teach are only human regulations" (Mark 7:7).

1701. Are nonliturgical devotions recommended by the Church?

Nonliturgical devotions are recommended provided they conform to the laws and norms of the Church, and harmonize with the liturgical seasons. Properly performed they deepen the faith of the people and obtain many graces needed for oneself and others. They are an essential part of the spiritual life of a devoted Catholic.

JOHN A. HARDON, S.J., is a highly regarded Jesuit scholar whose *Catholic Catechism* has been widely used. He holds a master's degree from Loyola University in Chicago and a doctorate in theology from the Gregorian University in Rome. He has taught at the Jesuit School of Theology in Chicago and is a professor in the Institute for Advanced Studies in Catholic Doctrine at St. John's University in New York. He is the author of many books, the latest of which is *Modern Catholic Dictionary*.